Seven Votes

Seven Votes

How WWII changed South Africa forever

Richard Steyn

Jonathan Ball Publishers
Johannesburg • Cape Town • London

All rights reserved.
No part of this publication may be reproduced or transmitted,
in any form or by any means, without prior permission
from the publisher or copyright holder.

© Text Richard Steyn 2020
© Photographs, as credited individually
© Published edition 2020 Jonathan Ball Publishers

Published in South Africa in 2020 by
JONATHAN BALL PUBLISHERS
A division of Media24 (Pty) Ltd
PO Box 33977
Jeppestown
2043

ISBN 978-1-77619-035-5
EBOOK ISBN 978-1-77619-036-2

*Every effort has been made to trace the copyright holders and to obtain their
permission for the use of copyright material. The publishers apologise for any errors
or omissions and would be grateful to be notified of any corrections that should be
incorporated in future editions of this book.*

www.jonathanball.co.za
Twitter: www.twitter.com/JonathanBallPub
Facebook: www.facebook.com/JonathanBallPublishers

Cover by publicide
Design and typesetting by Triple M Design
Set in 11,75/16 pt Bembo Std

In memory of my father, Stephen, who served in the Second World War, and my mother, Anthea, who lived through it.

'History attains coherence and drama only in hindsight.'
– Michael Wolff

'History has to be rewritten every generation because although the past does not change, the present does.'
– Christopher Hill

'The function of history is to put wisdom and experience at the disposal of each generation.'
– CW de Kiewiet

Contents

PREFACE ix

PART ONE: SEVEN VOTES
1 The Principals 3
2 Overture 13
3 Friday and Saturday 23
4 Sunday 31
5 Monday 38
6 Tuesday and Wednesday 48

PART TWO: A DIVIDED NATION
7 Two Streams 59
8 'By Their Fruits ...' 72
9 Fights and Strikes 83
10 The ANC Awakens 95
11 Seismic Shifts 107
12 Opposed to Racism 116
13 Year of Tumult 126
14 Indian Winter 136
15 In the Middle 144
16 Smuts Wins 154

17 Congress Youth League 162
18 Victory 174

PART THREE: POST WAR
19 Taking Stock 187
20 Miners' Strike 198
21 Prejudices Rearranged 209
22 Pandit Attacks 218
23 Out of Step 230
24 The Doctors' Pact 239
25 Movers and Shakers 248
26 Smuts Defeated 260

PART FOUR: AFTERMATH
27 The Screws Tighten 271

EPILOGUE 283
ACKNOWLEDGEMENTS 293
NOTES 295
SOURCES 308
INDEX 313

Preface

In the end, it hinged on a mere seven votes. If seven more MPs had voted in favour of neutrality, the destiny of South Africa might have been different. At the conclusion of a tense debate in the all-white House of Assembly on Monday 4 September 1939, the faction within the ruling Fusion government led by General JC Smuts had unexpectedly defeated the supporters of the prime minister, General JBM Hertzog, by 80 votes to 67, a majority of 13. The decision by seven MPs to abandon Hertzog was to change the course of the country's history.

That the debate in Cape Town took place one day after Great Britain had declared war on Adolf Hitler's Germany was itself a quirk of fortune. The German poet Friedrich Schiller was one who believed there is no such thing as chance: 'What seems to us mere accident springs from the deepest source of destiny,' he proclaimed. Yet it was accident rather than fate that brought South Africa's parliamentarians hastening back from their homes and farms to the Cape, compelling them to make a choice of historic consequence for their constituents, and for us, the generations that followed after them.

When South Africa's Parliament was prorogued in early June 1939, the threat of war hung heavily over Europe, causing those who were aware of the rapidly deteriorating international climate to speculate fearfully over what the country's immediate future might hold. Hertzog's Fusion government, an uneasy marriage of convenience between Afrikaner and English-speaking interests, held together largely through the determination and capacity for compromise of its deputy leader, Smuts. He, like the prime minister, had been tiptoeing carefully around the war issue for some time. Whenever the question was asked what South Africa might do if Britain were to go to war with Germany, Hertzog would carefully sidestep it and answer that the choice would be left to Parliament.

In World War One (WWI, 1914–1918), the country's constitutional status had been different. As an imperial Dominion, neutrality was not an option for the Union of South Africa, which had been formed in 1910. In 1931, that was changed by the passage of the Statute of Westminster, which established the legislative independence of Britain's self-governing Dominions (at the time consisting of Canada, Australia, New Zealand, South Africa, the Irish Free State and Newfoundland). South Africa could henceforth decide its own fate.

In September 1938, as an increasingly aggressive Hitler threatened neighbouring Czechoslovakia with invasion, Hertzog kept insisting that South Africa's existing relationships with other nations would remain unaffected by any outbreak of hostilities in Europe. He also browbeat a quiescent cabinet into agreeing in principle with his neutral stance. Yet, in order to preserve the uneasy peace within his government, Hertzog never made the cabinet's decision public, and Smuts never had cause to repudiate it. Both men concurred, however, that if war came, it would be up to Parliament to decide.

Whenever Parliament was not in session, members of the House and Senate were scattered far and wide. Their dispersion had given rise to fears among MPs supportive of Empire that if war in Europe were to break out while they were away from Cape Town in 1939, Hertzog might deliberately dilly-dally about recalling Parliament until neutrality had become a fait accompli. And that might well have happened had it not been realised, in mid-August, that the five-year term of South Africa's Senate would run out on 5 September. Under the constitution, without the assent of the upper house, any subsequent decision by Parliament would be ultra vires.

Made aware of the looming impasse, Smuts hastened to alert Hertzog, who was rusticating peacefully on his Orange Free State farm. Both men knew instinctively that, given the highly charged emotions on either side of the war issue, civil conflict between whites was always a real possibility. And so Parliament was hastily reconvened for a single purpose – to prolong the life of the Senate for a further 12 months.

On Saturday 2 September, as MPs assembled in the Mother City for an exercise in legislative rubber-stamping, the news broke of Hitler's invasion of Poland the previous day. There was now only one question on everyone's mind: was South Africa, as a Dominion within the Commonwealth, constitutionally and honour-bound to support Britain and plunge into another far-off foreign war, or could the country stay out of the conflict? In these fraught circumstances, the assembled parliamentarians found themselves faced with the momentous choice: was it to be neutrality or war?

The eventual outcome of the slim, 13-vote margin in the House of Assembly in favour of war accurately reflected the narrow division of opinion between English- and Afrikaans-speakers, the only tribes directly represented in the South African Parliament. Given the country's turbulent past, both sides were aware that entering the war on Britain's side for the second time in a quarter century was likely to have unforeseen and wide-ranging internal consequences. And so it proved. The outcome of the war vote not only put an abrupt end to Fusion, the decade-and-a-half-long attempt by Hertzog and Smuts to repair the long-standing breach at the heart of white politics, but it caused ruptures within Afrikanerdom itself that were never properly to heal. It also galvanised South Africa's black African, coloured and Indian communities, who had been given no direct say in the war debate. And it provoked the African majority, during the early 1940s, to stand up meaningfully for the first time in the history of black nationalist politics and begin taking matters into its own hands.

It was in the economic and social spheres, however, that the most profound impact of South Africa's involvement in World War Two (WWII) was felt. Although mining remained the bedrock of the economy, manufacturing grew exponentially to meet wartime demands. South Africa became a leading supplier of strategic minerals to Britain and the US, and the Cape sea route became a significant supply line for munitions, clothing, food and other essentials for the Allied forces in North Africa and Asia.

Industrial expansion drew ever more people of colour into the economy, and into the cities and towns. By 1946, there were more blacks than whites in urban South Africa.[1] Many of these incomers settled in squatter communities on urban fringes, making nonsense of separatist theories that blacks could be confined to their own rural backwaters and prevented from becoming a permanent presence in towns. But as the informal economy in and around the shanty settlements flourished, so too did violence and crime, providing plenty of encouragement to segregationist planners. As racial divisions within the country's labour force grew sharper, African workers formed themselves into trade unions, and embarked on frequent boycotts and strikes.

During the early war years, Dr AB Xuma began to revive and reorganise the almost moribund African National Congress (ANC), formed to assert the equal rights of all individuals to a common citizenship, irrespective of colour. In 1944, the ANC formed a Youth League, in which young firebrands such as Anton Lembede, Nelson Mandela and Jordan Ngubane called for the eradication of all racial discrimination. At the United Nations (UN) in New York in 1946, Xuma skilfully exploited international concern over the Smuts government's colour policies to oppose the incorporation of the former German South West Africa into the Union. Together with a soon-to-be-independent India, he was able to thwart Smuts and negate much of the goodwill generated by South Africa's contribution to the Allied victory in the war.

WWII further deepened the divisions between South Africa's two million whites. As in WWI, the country's war leader this time, Smuts, found himself having to fight on two fronts. The most radical of dissident Afrikaners formed themselves into paramilitary groups such as the Ossewabrandwag, whose membership at its peak in 1941 comfortably exceeded the number of Union Defence Force (UDF) soldiers in uniform, and whose aim was to hamper the war effort.

To reduce the shortage of skilled labour, the government relaxed the pass laws and eased the rigidity of the job colour bar, rendering the dividing lines between white and black communities more porous.[2] Fears of interracial violence drew cries from Nationalist politicians that race relations were building up to a crisis that only stricter segregation could avert. While Smuts lamented, in 1942, that segregation had 'fallen on evil days' (perhaps meaning that it hadn't worked in practice), National Party (NP) leader DF Malan and social engineers such as HF Verwoerd countered that *apartheid* (apartness or separation) along racial lines was a panacea for social peace and the preservation of white 'civilisation'.

As Saul Dubow has observed, 'it was the war that shook up established certainties and lent the 1940s its remarkable sense of fluidity and flux'. Parliament's narrow decision brought to the surface an 'explosive cocktail of political poisons', but it also gave a powerful stimulus to fresh thought and competing visions of a better future for all races. These ideas were widely aired in a politically charged atmosphere in which new plans germinated and took root, yet often only shallowly and temporarily.[3]

Seven Votes aims to recount, for a modern readership, this seminal time in South Africa's history, which began with the fateful war vote and ended with the fall of the Smuts government and the tightening of racial segregation in 1948. It was a period alive with hope, offering the tantalising prospect of a transition towards a fairer, common society, but destined to end in despair by the advent of apartheid in 1948.

The book describes the impact of WWII on South Africa's people, recounts some of the passions it unleashed, and assesses its effects on politics and race relations. In so doing, it revives memories of some of the larger-than-life characters who bestrode those tumultuous times. And, in considering the impetus the war gave to the two powerful nationalisms – Afrikaner and African – that fought for supremacy in the second half of the 20th century, it reminds us how the absence of a mere seven votes changed South Africa forever.

Note on terminology: The terms 'native' and 'coloured' did not have the pejorative meaning during the years covered in this book that they have today. I have used, therefore, the racial terms that were in use at the time.

PART ONE

Seven Votes

CHAPTER I

The Principals

In the spring of 1939, war came to South Africa with a disconcerting suddenness. Though storm clouds had been gathering over Europe since Hitler came to power in Germany six years earlier, the Munich Agreement of September 1938 had brought fresh hope that hostilities might somehow be averted. 'Peace in our time,' as British prime minister Neville Chamberlain described the agreement, might spare South Africa from having to decide – for the second time in only 25 years – whether or not to take up arms on the British side.

Three exceptionally tough-minded and resilient politicians were at the forefront of the parliamentary drama that played itself out in Cape Town during the war vote in early September 1939. They were the prime minister of the Union, JBM Hertzog, his deputy, Jan Smuts, and the leader of the Purified National Party, DF Malan. A fourth key member of the cast was the governor-general of South Africa, Sir Patrick Duncan, who enters our story later.

Hertzog

By late 1939, James Barry Munnik Hertzog had been prime minister of South Africa for a decade and a half. Four years older than his former arch-foe Smuts, Hertzog was born in 1866 in Wellington, near Cape Town, in the Boland region of the Cape Colony. Although unaware of it until after becoming premier, he was named after a woman – the famous Dr James Barry (1795–1865), attached to British forces at the Cape, who had passed for a man throughout her medical career. A Mrs Munnik who had married into the Hertzog family was so grateful for her treatment by Dr Barry that she christened her son James Barry Munnik, in honour of the doctor who had saved her life. The name Barry Munnik had passed down from one generation of Hertzogs to another.[1]

Barry Hertzog was a farmer's son, the fifth of twelve children. During the agricultural depression of the 1860s, his penurious father was forced to move his large family to Kimberley, where he established a butchery and bakery and made enough money to give his children a decent education. As a pupil in Kimberley, the young Barry formed a dislike of the children of immigrant diggers, especially those from Britain. After school, he was sent to Victoria College, Stellenbosch, to study law, at which he proved to be a good student. In 1892, he was able to further his studies in Holland, gaining a doctorate in law from the University of Amsterdam.[2] Returning to the Cape after brief diversions to the Sorbonne and Bonn,[3] he married and immediately took his new wife to Johannesburg, where he practised as a lawyer until appointed to the bench of the Orange Free State in 1895, at the tender age of 29.

Smuts

Jan Christiaan Smuts was born on a Swartland farm, at Riebeek West, near Wellington, in 1870. As a boy, he was only sent to school at the age of 12, after the sudden death of his elder brother. Quickly catching up and surpassing his fellow pupils, the young Smuts went to Stellenbosch in 1886 to matriculate and thereafter to further his studies at Victoria College. A brilliant student with a wide range of intellectual interests, he won a scholarship to Cambridge University, where his distinguished law tutor described him as the brightest student he had ever taught.

Turning his back on a legal career in Britain, Smuts opened a practice in Cape Town and became an enthusiastic supporter of Cape premier

Cecil John Rhodes. Deeply disillusioned by Rhodes's duplicity over the Jameson Raid (1895–1896), however, the ambitious would-be politician decided he no longer had a future in the Cape. He resolved to move to the Transvaal republic, despite his misgivings about its elderly president, Paul Kruger. It was not long before Kruger became aware of the bright young Afrikaner's abilities and, bending the rules, appointed him as state attorney of the Transvaal at the age of only 28. Smuts was at Kruger's right hand during the president's negotiations with Britain's arch-imperialist envoy, Sir Alfred Milner, the failure of which led to the Anglo-Boer War of 1899–1902.

Paths diverge

The career paths of Hertzog and Smuts ran in close parallel during the Anglo-Boer War, with both becoming generals in the Boer forces and leading commando raids into the Cape Colony, during which they frequently collaborated on tactics.[4] At the peace talks in Vereeniging, they were both legal advisers to the Assembly of the People and helped to draft the treaty that ended the almost-three-year-long conflict.[5]

Shortly after Vereeniging, however, the pair began to differ over how best to bring South Africa's two white tribes together into one united nation. During the war, Smuts had grown close to the easy-going and conciliatory Boer leader, Louis Botha, while Hertzog venerated the Free State president, MT Steyn, the ageing and ailing *bittereinder* (bitter-ender) widely regarded as the uncompromising guardian of Afrikaner integrity.[6] Botha and Smuts were of a mind that, having lost the war, Afrikaners had to 'forgive and forget' and forge a new future together with their fellow English-speakers within the protective embrace of the British Empire.

For the single-minded Hertzog, on the other hand, the defeat of the Boers by the British 'was a scar that would never heal'.[7] He resented the encroachment of English customs and culture on his people's way of life, the denigration of Afrikaners by the newspapers, and the high-handed attitude of British officials, from Milner downwards, who often treated

Afrikaners as if they were foreigners in their own country. Although he realised that Afrikaner independence could not be regained by force, he never lost his determination to regain it by other means.

Language

For Hertzog, the key issue was language – the Afrikaners' most precious heritage and badge of identity. In 1907, while minister of education in the self-governing Orange River Colony, he introduced compulsory mother-tongue education for schoolchildren in the first four grades, followed by bilingual instruction in English and Dutch thereafter. His policy caused resentment among the few English-speaking teachers in the colony, and an outcry in the neighbouring Transvaal, where parents were able to choose their children's language of instruction. Botha and Smuts viewed Hertzog's policy with concern, believing it was impractical and would endanger the good relations they were seeking to build with the British. In the Cape and Natal, the Free Stater was accused – unreasonably – of 'racialism'.[8]

At the National Convention of 1908–1909, Hertzog succeeded in having the principle of bilingualism entrenched in clause 137 of the proposed new Union constitution. This meant, as Hermann Giliomee points out, that Afrikaans had to be heard in Parliament, the civil service, schools and universities, and in business.[9] But 'Hertzogism' quickly became a bogey for English-speakers, which was not fair on Hertzog, because he was not seeking a position of dominance for Afrikaans but rather a partnership of the two language groups based on full equality.[10]

Not friends

After the coming of Union in 1910, Hertzog was offered the post of minister of justice in Louis Botha's 'catch-all' South African Party (SAP) government – an uneasy coalition of Afrikaner nationalists and English imperialists.[11] Neither man had much time for the other. Botha regarded the better-educated Free Stater as narrow-minded and inward-looking, while Hertzog, for his part, had been suspicious of Botha's British leanings ever since Vereeniging and looked down on him as being weak and unprincipled.[12] As the Union's new prime minister, Botha would have much preferred to exclude Hertzog from the cabinet, but felt unable to do so in the interests of reconciliation and nation-building.

Botha tried to buy off Hertzog with a judgeship, but the obdurate Bloemfontein lawyer wasn't having it: instead, he reluctantly accepted a post in the cabinet. With Afrikaans beginning to replace Dutch, the language question frequently gave rise to tensions within the new government. Another divisive issue was South Africa's relationship with Britain. Not long after Union, Hertzog gave a speech to his constituents at Smithfield in the Orange Free State in which he insisted that, while constitutionally bound to Britain, South Africa should put her own interests first and be free to determine her own destiny.[13] This contradicted the view of Botha and Smuts, who were concerned that Hertzog's policy of 'South Africa First' might become a case of 'South Africa Alone'. At Germiston in 1911, Hertzog went even further, declaring that (white) South Africa comprised two 'streams' rather than one, a stance that further alienated English-speakers.

Strangely for so controlled and generally courteous an individual, Hertzog could be excitable and often let his tongue run away with him on public platforms.[14] In another speech at Smithfield he declared that the government should seek to make the Afrikaner (by which he meant every white whose primary loyalty was to South Africa) the *baas* (boss) in his own country. At De Wildt, a small town near Rustenburg, he declared in late 1912 that he was not one of those who talked of conciliation and loyalty: 'They are idle words which deceive no one. I have always said, I do not know what this conciliation means.'[15] This was grist to the mill of those who derided the Free Stater as a hater of all things English.

Botha resigns

The die had now been cast. After De Wildt, it was obvious that Botha, Smuts and Hertzog could no longer soldier on in the same cabinet.

Matters came to a head when Sir George Leuchars, Natal's representative in the cabinet, resigned in protest at Hertzog's remarks, whereupon Botha handed in his own resignation to the governor-general, who promptly invited him to form a new government. Leuchars and Hertzog were notable exclusions from the cabinet.

Hertzog's supporters in the colony rallied behind him, however, as did Afrikaners in the Cape and the Transvaal. At the SAP's national conference in Cape Town, the Free State leader proposed a vote of no confidence in Botha and was able to muster 90 supporters out of 221 Members of Parliament (MPs). In January 1914, the dissidents came together in Bloemfontein to found the National Party (NP), with Hertzog as leader.[16] The new party immediately set about distancing itself as far as possible from the SAP of Botha and Smuts.

The Nationalists' manifesto stipulated that the British and Dutch in South Africa should form one united nation, but that 'history, religion and morals' were to be kept separate. The interests of South Africa would come before those of any other country, and there was to be no racial mixing: black people should be confined to areas already laid down in the Natives Land Act of 1913.

Unfortunate timing

The outbreak of war in August 1914 could not have come at a more awkward time for Botha and Smuts. The wounds of the Anglo-Boer War were still raw when the new Union was called on to fight on Britain's side in the war against the Kaiser's Germany. White South Africa was a house divided: to English-speakers, there was no argument but that the country had to do its duty and respond positively to the King's call. Boer-Afrikaners, on the other hand, had no desire and felt no obligation to take up arms on behalf of a hated enemy who had left their republics in ruins. Having no doubts himself about where the country's duty – and honour – lay, Botha offered to free up the imperial troops still helping to preserve peace and security in South Africa and replace them with soldiers of the new UDF. Shortly thereafter, he was asked by Britain to seize the strategic harbours of Lüderitzbucht and Swakopmund in neighbouring German South West Africa, and to dismantle radio communications and overcome the German forces defending the territory.

Without putting the matter before Parliament, which was not in session at the time, Botha and his defence minister, Smuts, committed the tiny UDF and the volunteers of the Active Citizen Force (ACF) to South Africa's first military foray beyond its borders. Many Afrikaners, some of whom had emigrated to or had extended family in South West Africa, were outraged and flatly refused to fight on Britain's side. Their antipathy was shared by none other than the commander-in-chief of the UDF, General CF Beyers.

A bitter debate

With emotions running high, the National Party held its first congress in Pretoria and passed a motion condemning any invasion of South West Africa. When Parliament met a week later to authorise the necessary expenditure, Hertzog opposed the government with the argument that while South Africa should be ready to defend its own borders, any attack on German territory was 'against the interests of the Union and of the Empire'.[17] After a debate that, in FS Crafford's words, manifested 'an almost unbelievable recrudescence of race hatred … and a complete fading out of the convention spirit', his motion was defeated by 91 votes to 12.[18]

In the two former Boer republics, a rebellion led by former Boer officers gathered strength. Instead of leading the UDF into battle in South West Africa, Botha and Smuts found themselves first having to put down an armed and violent insurrection at home. Some 124 rebels and 19 loyalist soldiers lost their lives in the short-lived 'Boer rebellion' of 1914–1915.

After a brilliantly successful campaign in South West Africa, in which the German forces were driven out, Botha and Smuts returned to South Africa to fight the general election of 1915 – heralded by one side but taunted as 'sell-outs' and 'traitors' by the other. The outcome of the poll was deeply significant. Hertzog's Nationalists won as many as 77 000 votes against the SAP's 95 000,[19] gaining every seat in the Free State and forcing three cabinet ministers out of office. Botha's SAP lost its outright majority in the House and could only govern with the help of the Unionists – the praise-singers of Empire and opponents of Nationalist Afrikanerdom.

Malan

The third key participant in the war vote of September 1939 was Hertzog's eventual successor as Nationalist leader, the owlish Dr Daniel Francois (DF) Malan. If DF Malan had a lighter side to him, he did his best to conceal it. Black-suited, dour of visage and ponderous of manner, he epitomised the severe, unsmiling Calvinist dominee. His role model was said to be the prophet Elijah, a man of unbending principle, interested not in earthly rewards but in eternal values and the preservation of his tribe.

Born four years earlier than Jan Smuts in the same Swartland town of Riebeek West, Malan was at first a close friend but later an ideological opponent of Smuts, whose holistic philosophy was so far removed from his own. After theological studies at Victoria College, he became a doctor of divinity at the University of Utrecht in Holland in 1905. Returning to South Africa, he was ordained as a minister of the Dutch Reformed Church, serving briefly in the Transvaal parish of Heidelberg, as well as parishes in Montagu and Graaff-Reinet.

According to his recent biographer, Lindie Koorts, Malan and his student friends at Stellenbosch had been deeply influenced by the works of the Canadian-born pro-Boer historian George McCall Theal. Black people, wrote Theal, were 'fickle barbarians, prone to robbery and unscrupulous in shedding blood'.[20] Theal also accused proselytising British missionaries and philanthropists of being the enemies of Afrikaners engaged in the noble task of opening up the interior of South Africa to civilisation and Calvinist Christianity. This polarising depiction of the past, says Koorts, was to influence Malan's understanding of South Africa's history for the rest of his life.[21]

Convinced that Afrikanerdom faced extinction in the face of British cultural imperialism, the idealistic young Malan decided to devote his life to the service of his people. This would mean combining religion and politics, a prospect hitherto regarded as a choice between opposites.

Malan's opportunity to become politically active presented itself after the formation of the National Party in 1914, when a group of NP-supporting Afrikaners in the Cape banded together to launch *De Burger*, later *Die Burger*, as a mouthpiece for their views. They persuaded the highly regarded but reluctant dominee to leave the church and become the newspaper's founding editor. Editorship, they indicated, would be a means to a greater end – the establishment of a Cape provincial branch of the NP, of which Malan was to be the leader.

Appalled by the schism in Afrikanerdom following the Botha government's decision to take Britain's side in WWI, Malan went through a brief period of soul-searching before choosing finally to leave the church and join the ranks of those 'who had immersed themselves in the political arena with the Bible under their arms'.[22] In 1918, he was elected to Parliament as Nationalist MP for Calvinia, a seat he was to hold for the next 20 years.

Within parliamentary limits

Though supportive of the Afrikaner rebels' cause, and stridently critical of the SAP government, Hertzog was careful not to involve himself or the National Party in unlawful extra-parliamentary activities during the war. He signalled his hatred of 'jingoes', however, by opposing a motion in Parliament calling on the Almighty to grant success to the Allies, and refusing to sing 'God Save the King' on official occasions.[23] He also made great play of Smuts's membership of the Imperial War Cabinet, which, he claimed, served to strengthen South Africa's ties with Britain, even though the Imperial War Conference of 1917 explicitly acknowledged the growing independence of the self-governing Dominions within the British Empire.

American president Woodrow Wilson's declaration, in 1916, that all civilised people should enjoy the right to self-determination stiffened Afrikaner republican resistance and prompted Hertzog (and Malan) to lead a deputation to the peace conference at Versailles in 1919 to plead for independence. The deputation could not see Wilson and was politely stonewalled by Lloyd George, who pointed out that Botha and Smuts were South Africa's recognised representatives in France. Nonetheless, as a propaganda ploy, the NP's initiative was effective: it enabled Hertzog to portray the prime minister and defence minister as being more concerned with the affairs of other countries than with those of South Africa.

Botha dies

Botha's death at the age of only 56, shortly after his return from Paris in 1919, thrust Jan Smuts – a more steely and resolute politician – into the premiership of South Africa, and into a head-on confrontation with his former comrade and fellow jurist, Hertzog. By this time, the two former Boer leaders, so similar in background and upbringing yet so different in outlook, had begun to react to each other politically – if not personally – as oil does to water.

It is timely, at this stage, to consider why.

CHAPTER 2

Overture

South Africa's new prime minister and his Nationalist opponent were both clever and well-educated, though Hertzog's intellect did not quite match that of the cerebral Smuts. Each man was single-minded, strong-willed, apt to take decisions without consultation and did not like being contradicted. Leslie Blackwell, a front-bench opponent of Hertzog's in Parliament, described the NP leader as a courteous, cultured man whose manners were most attractive to visitors from abroad. 'He was in many ways a remarkable character,' wrote Blackwell in his memoirs, 'narrow yet intense, and autocratic to an extreme degree, loyal to the point of fanaticism to his friends and supporters, and astonishingly vindictive against his opponents or erstwhile friends with whom he had parted company … He was devoted, with all the intensity of his deep but narrow nature, to the Afrikaans language and culture, and his political career … was one long fight for what he considered to be the rights and true interests of Afrikanerdom.'[1]

Smuts's Cambridge education had given him a much broader conception of the Afrikaner's place in the world, derived to some extent from his self-formulated philosophy of 'Holism', in which the individual parts of an organism strive naturally to form a greater 'whole'. No less determined than Hertzog to safeguard the future of his people, Smuts believed that Afrikaners had to accept that the past was over and look towards a better tomorrow, grounded on white unity and nationhood. 'Let us forgive and forget,' was his credo, a high-minded approach that even his wife, Isie, had found hard to accept for many years after the end of the Anglo-Boer War.[2]

In politics, Smuts's outreach to English-speakers was born not only of idealism but also for pragmatic reasons. In the cosmopolitan Transvaal, and in the new Union, he and Botha had to draw repeatedly on the support of English-speakers in order to be elected. In the Free State, where the English population numbered less than ten per cent, it was much easier for Hertzog to disregard English opinion and champion the Afrikaner cause. However, as so often happens in politics, differences become exaggerated and stereotypes develop in the popular mind: 'Smuts was the statesman, Hertzog the fanatic: or – from a different viewpoint – Smuts was the compromiser and Hertzog the unfaltering champion of Afrikaner rights.'[3] Neither view, it should be said, was entirely true.

Out of touch

Not nearly as popular as the much-admired Botha, Smuts made up for a lack of human empathy with a dedication to public service and capacity for hard work that was truly exceptional. Having been out of touch with domestic politics since 1916, he had returned from wartime service in East Africa and Britain to find South African politics much changed. Afrikaner nationalism was on the rise, its leaders eager to exploit for political purposes the economic hardships that war invariably brings. After succeeding Botha as prime minister, Smuts continued to proclaim South Africa's loyalty to the British Empire, intensely irritating his Afrikaner opponents and adding further impetus to their republican cause.

Simmering discontent with Smuts and the SAP government was reflected in the (white) election of 1920, in which Hertzog's Nationalists won 44 seats, the SAP 41, the Unionists 25 and Labour 21. Without a majority in Parliament, Smuts was obliged to go cap in hand to the Unionist leader, Sir Thomas Smartt, to enable the SAP to continue to govern. Realising their own limitations as a separate party, the Unionists agreed to a merger with Smuts. Smartt and two others, JW Jagger and Patrick Duncan, were rewarded with cabinet posts.

Bolstered by these new supporters, Smuts called another general election in early 1921. No longer having to fight in three-cornered contests, the SAP increased its parliamentary seats to 79; Hertzog's NP held steady by winning 45 seats, but the Labour Party lost heavily, giving Smuts's party a majority of 24 over the combined opposition. It turned out to be a pyrrhic victory.

Economic depression

Since the end of WWI, the global economy had been in the doldrums, and the early 1920s found South Africa also mired in depression and plagued by drought. Farmers were struggling to survive and mineral prices were falling, while unemployment among whites and blacks was rife. Amid an atmosphere of restlessness and resentment, Smuts departed for the Imperial Conference in London in 1921, leaving Hertzog to complain once again that South Africa had become too small for the prime minister, who was far more interested in world affairs.

The perfect storm building up around the Smuts government burst with force in 1922, the flashpoint being the Witwatersrand, where white miners, many of them immigrants from Britain, had closed ranks against competition from other races. To the many desperate Afrikaners who had flocked from rural areas to the mines in search of work, the protection of semi-skilled jobs was vital. The Chamber of Mines, on the other hand, faced with declining mineral prices worldwide, was intent on lowering production costs by cutting white wages and employing cheaper black workers. By placing blacks in jobs previously reserved for whites, the Chamber was effectively bypassing the industrial colour bar, putting it at odds with the mainly English-speaking Labour Party as well as the Communist Party of South Africa (CPSA), protective primarily of the interests of its white members.

The miners' revolt

When mediation between the Chamber and the unions failed, the miners went on a strike that turned rapidly into an armed revolt against the forces of law and order. Smuts was forced to act and did so decisively, declaring martial law and bringing in the police, army and air force to put down an uprising in which no fewer than 153 people died and more than 650 were injured.[4] Special courts were set up to try the 853 people alleged to have fomented the violence, and 18 of the strike's instigators were sentenced to death. After a public outcry, only four were hanged.

The Rand Revolt and its aftermath cemented a growing alliance between English-speaking Labourites and Afrikaner Nationalists, which became formal in 1923. Not for the first time, Smuts found that 'a few dead men could do more damage to his reputation than all his living opponents put together'.[5] Hertzog made great play of the prime minister's 'ruthlessness', while the Labourites depicted him as 'pitiless'. Stung by these taunts, and by the unexpected loss of a rural by-election, Smuts decided on impulse to resign and test the mood of the electorate once more. In an election notable for the bitterness of the personal attacks on him, his Nationalist opponents won 63 seats to the SAP's 53. With the help of Frederic Cresswell's Labour Party, Hertzog was now able to form a new 'Pact' government. At the age of 58, he had defeated his nemesis to become South Africa's third prime minister, destined – against all expectations – to dictate the country's fortunes for the next 15 years.

Twin aims

As the new premier, Hertzog had two primary aims: to uphold the safety and economic interests of whites, and to enhance South Africa's constitutional independence from Britain. He was aided by the country's remarkable economic recovery, which took place from 1924 and resulted from the combination of good rains, an improvement in world trade, rich new platinum finds – and some effective policy-making. The inexperienced Pact government felt confident enough to do away with the preferential tariff on British goods, abolish British titles for South Africans, and persuade the electorate (after heated controversy) to adopt a new national flag. The achievement that pleased Hertzog most, however, was managing to persuade the British to acknowledge – in the Balfour Declaration of 1926 – that the Dominions were 'autonomous communities' within the British Empire, 'equal in status, in no way subordinate one to another in any aspect of their domestic or external affairs'. In 1931, these principles became enshrined in law in the Statute of Westminster and later in the Status of Union Act of 1934.

Hertzog was equally determined to entrench segregation as the foundation of his administration's racial policies. In 1926, he brought race to the fore by tabling four bills in Parliament, three of which made provision for blacks to develop 'along their own lines' in reserves. The legislation led to a protracted argument with Smuts, who proposed – knowing that Hertzog would reject it out of hand – an extension of the Cape franchise throughout South Africa. Race dominated the bitter *swart gevaar* (black peril) election of 1929, which the Pact government won comfortably.

Depression

Not long after the election, however, South Africa's economic fortunes began to wane once more. In October 1929, the US stock market collapsed, plunging the leading global economies into depression and endangering financial stability worldwide. Wool and diamond prices fell sharply, shrinking South Africa's export trade, and the country suffered its worst drought in living memory. In 1931, a desperate Britain was forced off the gold standard, but Hertzog – determined to demonstrate South Africa's independence – stubbornly refused to follow suit.

With financial hardship in the rural areas becoming worse by the day, and public opinion – led by the maverick Nationalist Tielman Roos – clamouring for MPs to put country before party, Smuts held out an olive branch to Hertzog by suggesting that the gold standard be abandoned and a unity government formed – a proposal to which the prime minister reluctantly agreed. In late 1932, South Africa went off gold and, after three days of talks, Hertzog and Smuts hammered out a coalition agreement between their two parties. The agreement, dubbed 'Fusion', was supported by most English-speaking whites but only half of Afrikanerdom.

The Fusion agreement set out a seven-point basis for bipartisan cooperation in a national government. It recognised South Africa's sovereign status under the Statute of Westminster, with a national flag and equal language rights for English- and Afrikaans-speakers. The parties also agreed to maintain the existing 'civilised' (ie pro-white) labour policies and promised to make an 'earnest effort' to solve the colour question by protecting 'white civilisation' without depriving 'natives' of their right to develop separately.[6]

DF Malan and the secessionist rump of the National Party walked out of Parliament in protest at Fusion, for which Hertzog publicly gave the Afrikaner Broederbond the blame. Denouncing the Bond for having forced Malan's hand, Hertzog declared that after becoming a member, Malan had changed from being a supporter of unity between Afrikaans- and English-speakers to becoming a proponent of Afrikaner domination.[7]

In May 1933, the new Fusion coalition led by Hertzog (as prime minister) and Smuts (as his deputy) romped home in a general election, winning 144 out of 150 seats in the House of Assembly. Twelve months later, during which there were many acrimonious exchanges between Hertzog and Smuts, the NP and SAP formally came together in the United South African National Party (generally United Party, UP), aimed at 'developing a strong sense of South African national unity'.

Malan's followers, largely from the Cape, formed themselves into the Gesuiwerde Nasionale Party (Purified National Party, GNP), while in Natal, dissidents from the former SAP broke away to form the Dominion Party, vowing to maintain links with Britain. Both of these parties opposed Fusion – but for completely different reasons. However, most middle-of-the-road voters hoped, by a substantial majority, that Fusion might lead to the unity that white South Africans had so far been unable to consummate.

Constitutional changes

The Hertzog-Smuts coalition held together for the ensuing six years, helped on one hand by much improved economic circumstances – especially in the gold-mining industry – but hindered by deteriorating race relations on the other, as blacks left the poor and overcrowded reserves and sought work in urban areas. Two pieces of legislation were especially far-reaching.

The Status of Union Act had amended the South African constitution to bring it into line with the Statute of Westminster. Along with the other Dominions, South Africa now had full autonomy over its internal and external affairs, enabling Hertzog and Smuts each to claim – using different arguments – that their aim of bringing the two white groups together had been successfully achieved. Hertzog believed that since the country's independence within the Commonwealth had finally been recognised, there was no further need for an Afrikaner-led republic; Smuts hoped that English-speakers might be reassured by the retention of links with Britain, and that Afrikaner republicans would now abandon their demands for secession.

In 1936, the far-from-united UP faced its severest test when, after ten years of discussion, Hertzog brought two segregationist bills before Parliament, confident that he would win the two-thirds majority required to change the Union's constitution. In return for being deprived of the qualified franchise (at the time there were around 11 000 African voters on the Cape's common roll[8]), Cape Africans would be given three white representatives in Parliament, elected on a separate roll, and all other Africans would be represented by four white senators, chosen by an electoral college. To sugar the pill, additional land would be set aside in the African tribal reserves.

Hertzog's so-called Native Bills sparked off an angry resistance (see Chapter 10). Smuts personally was opposed in principle to the legislation but went along with Hertzog in the interests of party unity – unlike his right-hand man, JH Hofmeyr, who resigned in protest. A joint sitting of both houses of Parliament duly approved the Bills by 168 votes to 11.[9]

While most of Smuts's own supporters were strongly in favour of the legislation, the SAP's right-wing fringe thought it far too 'liberal'.

Second-class citizens

If the sharp spike in the gold price in the years after Fusion helped alleviate the economic plight of so-called poor white Afrikaners in the rural areas and on the mines, it was not enough to raise their self-image and collective sense of inferiority vis-à-vis the English-speakers. In his recent book on the Ossewabrandwag (see Chapter 8), Albert Blake recounts how many Afrikaners still felt, in the 1930s, like second-class citizens in the land of their birth. Though more numerous, at 56 per cent of the white population in 1935, their collective share of income was only 60 per cent of what English-speakers earned.[10]

Although as many as half a million Afrikaners were members of organised trade unions, only ten per cent occupied leadership positions, which were dominated by people of British or Jewish descent. Despite the majority of white mineworkers being Afrikaans, they were handed 90 per cent of the most dangerous underground jobs, for which lower wages were paid.[11] In commerce and industry, and in the civil service, English-speakers predominated. As a Dutch Reformed Church study of the time reflected:

> A very great disadvantage of the South African capitalist system is that those who represent it, and wield power in it, do not belong to the people and feel nothing for our ideals, language and religion. In their mighty press and other sources of influence, there is discrimination specifically against the Afrikaner. In all possible ways, the Afrikaner is held in an inferior, subordinate position. He is welcome as a worker, but not allowed to occupy any position of power.[12]

The steady relocation of Afrikaners from farms to cities in the 1930s was accelerated by new discoveries of gold, and by the rapid growth of secondary industry around the mines. Many thousands of Africans from the impoverished reserves also migrated to urban areas, particularly along the Witwatersrand, in search of work. This seismic shift in population patterns made South Africa more multiracial, and more volatile, than ever before.[13]

Afrikaner restlessness

Despite the tensions in white politics, voters in the mid-1930s went along with a political merger in which compromises had to be made on every contentious issue. In the general election of 1938, the UP won 111 seats of 153, despite uncertainty over where the country would stand if war were to break out in Europe. Thanks to a fiercely xenophobic campaign and the anti-Semitic urgings of newspapers such as HF Verwoerd's *Die Transvaler*, Malan's NP increased its number of seats from 20 to 27. The size of the UP's majority masked a growing restiveness within Afrikanerdom, driven by pro-German sentiment on the one hand and a resurgence of nationalist fervour on the other.

The latter was inspired by the centenary of the Great Trek in 1938. The proposal to stage a symbolic repetition of the Trek emanated from a founder member of the Afrikaner Broederbond and future speaker of Parliament, Henning Klopper, then the port superintendent at Mossel Bay. In early August, two ox-wagons, carrying men and women clad in traditional dress, and spurred on by a cheering throng of some 100 000, set off from Cape Town on a 1 500-kilometre journey to the site of a new memorial to the trekkers on a ridge outside Pretoria. They were joined by other wagons en route. As the 'pilgrims' made their way slowly and steadily towards their destination, they were met with wild enthusiasm, stirring sermons and much shedding of tears.[14] Bearded men and women wearing traditional *kappies* (bonnets) held aloft burning torches as a sign of their support for republican nationhood.

According to the feisty campaigner for women's rights, Bertha Solomon, 'from August to December [1938] Afrikaans-speaking South Africa seemed able to think of nothing else'.[15] On 16 December, then known as Dingaan's Day, at a ceremony at which pro-Afrikaner English-speakers such as Alan

Paton were made to feel most unwelcome, the foundation stone of the Voortrekker Monument was laid by three female descendants of the original trekkers. Such was the Nationalist fervour aroused by the occasion, and so fierce the resentment of Hertzog for his earlier coalition-making with English-speakers (whose taxes had also contributed to the celebrations), not to mention his withering criticisms of exclusively Afrikaner organisations like the Broederbond, that the prime minister felt it wiser to stay away.

The second factor laying bare the fault lines in the Fusion government and threatening 'to bring the tottering edifice to a fall'[16] was the pull of Nazi Germany. Many of Hertzog's followers felt, as did he (and Smuts, for that matter), that Germany had been harshly punished at Versailles, and that therefore the victors were primarily responsible for the trouble that now lay at hand.

Smuts's supporters, on the other hand, were much more disturbed by Hitler's belligerent behaviour, and by his threat to reclaim South West Africa. It was fast becoming evident that the choice of neutrality or war was not merely hypothetical – as UP leaders had been asserting. Before long, a difficult choice might have to be made.

Preserving unity

Set on preserving the unity of their troubled coalition, neither Hertzog nor Smuts was keen to bring such a fundamentally divisive issue to a head. Instead, the prime minister repeated time and again that South Africa, now a sovereign state, would only go to war in Europe if its own interests were directly at stake. Ultimately, it would be up to Parliament to decide.

In September 1938, as Hitler threatened to invade Czechoslovakia, the Fusion cabinet – with Smuts present – assented without a vote to a tortuously worded proposal put before it by Hertzog. The declaration stated, in effect, that South Africa's existing relations with the 'various belligerent parties' would remain as they were – except if the country's own borders were directly threatened.[17] Put more plainly, in the event of another European war, this time South Africa would remain neutral.

CHAPTER 3

Friday and Saturday

Friday, 1 September 1939, the first day of spring, was like most others in Cape Town at this time of year – warm and windy. In normal times, the people of the Mother City would be looking forward to spending the weekend having fun outdoors. But this day was different: the news from Europe was deeply worrying and the Cape air crackled with tension. Those who listened to the wireless (radio) were aware that Hitler's invasion of Poland earlier that morning meant that war in Europe was now almost certain. As a member of the British Commonwealth, South Africa would not be unaffected.

In the city centre, last-minute preparations were under way for the reopening of Parliament. Civil servants who had barely finished unpacking after their northward migration to Pretoria at the end of the parliamentary session in mid-June had been hurriedly recalled to the Cape. For, sometime in August, it had dawned on Leslie Blackwell, a UP frontbencher in the House of Assembly, that the five-year term of the Senate, the upper house of Parliament, was due to expire in less than a fortnight. Quite why no senator had tumbled to this before has never been properly explained.

As he recounted in his memoirs,[1] Blackwell hurried to Doornkloof, Smuts's farm outside Pretoria, to inform the deputy prime minister of his discovery. An alarmed Smuts immediately contacted the prime minister, Hertzog, who ordered Parliament to reconvene in early September for the sole purpose of extending the life of the Senate for another year. During those 12 months – the two men hoped – both the House and the Senate would have the opportunity of debating the pros and cons of going to war. In a country where many citizens were deeply conflicted over links with the British Empire, civil conflict was an ever-present possibility.

White public opinion was sharply divided between those who thought South Africa was duty-bound to support Britain, and those firmly against becoming involved in another foreign conflict. There was less concern among the unrepresented majority, who were mostly unaware of or indifferent to how they might be affected by their involvement in another war not of their own making.

Feverish speculation

On the special trains from upcountry bringing parliamentarians, diplomats and political correspondents down to Cape Town for what promised to be far more than an exercise in legislative box-ticking, news of the Polish crisis provoked long and earnest discussions – and the feverish counting of heads. If matters came to a crunch, would MPs choose to take the side of Britain and break off diplomatic relations with Germany, vote to remain neutral, or abstain? Louis Esselen, canny chief whip of the United Party and close confidant of Smuts, had been listening carefully to the opinions of MPs and doing his sums. Hertzog's lieutenants – Oswald Pirow, Tom Naude and Paul Sauer – were also counting heads. No one had any doubt that the vote would be close – either way.

On the streets of Cape Town, special editions of the *Cape Times* and *Die Burger* splashed the news of German troops massing on the Polish border, only a week after the signing of the Molotov-Ribbentrop non-aggression pact between Germany and Soviet Russia. Frightened housewives began stocking up on foodstuffs and basic essentials. Throngs of worried Capetonians streamed from the suburbs to the city centre, milling around Parliament to await developments. Elsewhere in the country, police and military leave was cancelled and measures put in place to protect key points such as mines, naval facilities, oil depots and the South African Broadcasting Corporation (SABC). The closure of the Johannesburg Stock Exchange was another indication of the gravity of the situation.[2]

Time to choose

Prime Minister Hertzog, suffering from a bad throat, arrived at Cape Town station at 10 am on Friday, having just been informed of the German invasion of Poland. He now realised the debate that he and the cabinet had put off for so many months could no longer be avoided. Curiously, but significantly, he did not immediately summon the UP caucus or his deputy, Smuts, but instead called the Nationalist leader of the opposition, DF Malan, to his official residence, Groote Schuur. Smuts had already flown in to Cape Town the previous evening and taken up residence at the Civil Service Club in Church Square, a stone's throw from Parliament.

For both of these veteran politicians, the stakes could not have been higher. If Parliament chose neutrality, it would undo all of Smuts's efforts (and those of the long-deceased Louis Botha) to reconcile and unify Afrikaners and English-speakers under the protective embrace of the British Empire. A vote for war, on the other hand, would put an immediate end to the experiment of Fusion, and probably bring Hertzog's long political career to an end too. Neither prospect appealed to the two political leaders, who had devoted a lifetime to the service of their country.

As minister of justice, Smuts, as usual, had been thinking ahead. Back in April, he had taken the precaution of sending 300 policemen to South West Africa to forestall any attempt by Hitler to make good on his threat to reclaim the mandated territory. Intelligence had revealed that preparations were afoot by forces loyal to Germany to stage a coup in the former German colony, and Smuts was taking no chances. 'Austria and other small states have been invaded on the plea that they could not keep internal order,' he declared, 'but the Union will never lay itself open to invasion on that ground.'³ His pre-emptive action had met with Hertzog's approval, but some members of the Fusion cabinet fumed about it in silence, while Malan's Nationalists expressed their outrage publicly at such 'provocation' of Germany.⁴

Soul mates

At his meeting with Malan, Hertzog rose above the animosity that had bedevilled their relationship for the preceding six years. Hoping to obtain Purified Nationalist support for extending the life of the Senate, but no doubt with the neutrality issue in mind, he greeted the GNP leader as a soul mate.⁵ Intent on embarrassing the Fusion government by leaving the country temporarily without a parliament,⁶ Malan was initially reluctant, but sensing that Hertzog was feeling him out on the much bigger issue, he agreed without consulting his caucus to give the prime minister his party's backing in the debate that lay before them.

At 2.30 pm, Hertzog called a meeting of the cabinet to discuss the impending Senate legislation. He informed those present that the Dominion and Labour parties, under the leadership of JS Marwick and Walter Madeley, respectively, had agreed to support the Senate Bill, and the meeting ended within the hour without any contentious matters being raised.

At 4 pm, the GNP caucus met to receive a report-back from Malan on his meeting with Hertzog. Despite objections from the Transvaal hardliner JG Strijdom to giving the premier his way, it was decided by those present to back the Senate Bill. Thereafter, discussion of the 'neutrality' question went on well into the night.⁷ Realising that the Fusion cabinet was deeply divided, the caucus decided to send a formal letter to Hertzog to say that if he put a motion in favour of neutrality before the House, the GNP would stand four-square behind him.

Malan drafted and signed the letter and sent his chief whip, Paul Sauer, post-haste to deliver it. Arriving at Groote Schuur around 10 pm, Sauer was given a friendly reception by Hertzog and his confidants, chief among them NC (Klasie) Havenga, minister of finance in the Fusion cabinet, and the minister of defence, Oswald Pirow. A formal response to the letter, Sauer was told, would be forthcoming in due course.

Press opinion

Saturday's morning newspapers brought further extensive coverage of events in Europe, their editorials demanding clarity from the government on where South Africa stood on the war issue. A leading article in the Nationalist mouthpiece, *Die Burger*, criticised the government for being 'blind and deaf' to the wish of *die volk* to stay out of the hostilities in Europe, and called on Hertzog to declare, once and for all, in favour of neutrality. The *Cape Times*, by contrast, repeated its belief that South Africa should take Britain's side in any confrontation with Hitler, while the *Cape Argus* pronounced loftily that South Africa's duty, 'whether judged from deepest honour or highest self-interest', was to help meet the challenge posed by the events in Eastern Europe.

In the Senate Hall of Parliament, proceedings got under way at 10 am with a brief, informal opening ceremony presided over by the gout-stricken governor-general, Sir Patrick Duncan. As soon as the formalities were over, MPs moved across to the House of Assembly and gave their unanimous support to the Senate Bill, which Smuts had piloted through its early stages because of Hertzog's sore throat. Having tipped off the prime minister in advance, Malan then enquired by way of a written question what the government intended to do if Britain went to war with Germany, because that would determine the GNP's actions in any forthcoming debate. Hertzog duly responded, proposing that the whole of Monday be devoted to a discussion of the war in Europe, promising to take members into his confidence and putting forward a proposal that he hoped would be acceptable to all.

Hertzog's confidence

With Malan's letter in his pocket, Hertzog was confident that even if the full UP caucus were not to line up behind him on Monday, the support of the Malanites would give him a majority in the House. Although Smuts had expressed his concern at Hitler's belligerence in Europe, he had not repudiated the cabinet's decision of a year earlier, leading Hertzog to believe that his deputy was still bound by it.

But the minister of defence, Oswald Pirow, was not so sure. From his sources, he had learned that Smuts no longer felt constrained by a decision taken before Hitler's expansionist intentions had become blindingly obvious. Pirow was also aware that the shrewd Louis Esselen had concluded that Smuts's supporters in the United Party, plus the Dominion and Labour MPs, as well as the three Native Representatives, would give the pro-war faction in the House a narrow majority. As soon as the House adjourned for the day, Pirow hurried to inform Hertzog accordingly. The prime minister called for Smuts to come and see him.

According to the Afrikaner journalist At van Wyk, at the meeting – attended also by Havenga and Pirow – it became clear to Smuts that Hertzog had not changed his mind and was still firmly in favour of neutrality. It also dawned on Hertzog that Smuts no longer felt bound by the cabinet decision of the previous September. An urgent meeting of the cabinet was called for 4 pm.[8]

At Groote Schuur

All 13 members of the Fusion cabinet – eight Afrikaans- and five English-speakers – were present at Groote Schuur that afternoon. To Deneys Reitz, a close colleague of Smuts's, it appeared that Hertzog – accustomed to getting his own way – had called his ministers together not to consult but rather to give them orders.[9] In Reitz's vivid recollection, Hertzog paced up and down the carpet of the ornate reception chamber, speaking for more than an hour, raking up bitter memories of the Anglo-Boer War, and recalling with great passion the humiliation Afrikaners had suffered at the hands of the British. (Reitz says that Hertzog spoke for over three hours, but his memory for detail seems suspect. It probably just felt like three hours.)

Dwelling on the aftermath of Versailles, Hertzog spoke approvingly of Hitler's 'mighty attempts' to reconstruct Germany out of the ruins of defeat. The essence of his argument was that if there were to be war in Europe, South Africa should uphold the cabinet agreement of a year before and stay out of it. 'If Hitler won the war, he would not molest us,' Hertzog asserted, 'and if the British won the war, we would be safe anyhow.'[10]

According to Harry Lawrence's account of the meeting, one or two other ministers spoke up in support of Hertzog, most notably the former Boer *bittereinder* General Jan Kemp, who declared that the United Party had been formed to put South Africa first; unless Parliament voted in favour of neutrality, he foresaw a 'bloodbath' ahead.[11] In hastening to support Hertzog, Havenga said with unconscious irony: 'We mustn't take part because of England. Of course England will go to war. The trouble about England is that she's given her word to Poland, and she always keeps her word.'[12]

From a seat on the sofa, Smuts voiced his disagreement. Speaking 'calmly and dispassionately', the decision he had come to, he said, was the most solemn of his life. A year ago he had been in favour of neutrality, but Germany's aggression since then had opened his eyes: South Africa could no longer stay neutral – in its own interests, as well as Britain's. As minister of justice, he saw no reason to believe that a declaration of war would lead to the bloodbath that Kemp had predicted.[13]

Close call

In hindsight, it is obvious that Smuts, with his more finely tuned understanding of international affairs, had fathomed Hitler's intentions more accurately than had Hertzog. But Van Wyk surmises[14] that, politicians being politicians, Smuts also sensed an opportunity to return to power himself. That was why, in more than 20 recent speeches to his English-speaking supporters, he had warned of the rising danger of Hitler and hinted that, if war came, South Africa would be bound to take Britain's side.

After Smuts had made his case, every other minister was given an opportunity to express his view. By early evening, it was apparent that seven members were in support of Smuts and war, and six were for Hertzog and neutrality. As war in Europe had not yet been declared, it was not necessary to put the matter to a formal vote, so the meeting was adjourned until the next afternoon, Sunday 30 September.

Later that evening, Pirow was summoned to Groote Schuur, into the presence of Hertzog and Havenga, to be told that a cablegram had arrived from the British premier, Neville Chamberlain, saying that South Africa could adopt one of three alternatives: 'You can declare war on Germany, break off diplomatic relations with her, or remain neutral. I beg of you not to follow the third course.' Asked by Hertzog what he should do, Pirow replied that after his (Hertzog's) many speeches, anything other than neutrality was 'unthinkable'.[15]

On the other side of the divide, uncertain whether Hertzog would continue to insist on neutrality in the face of a divided cabinet, Smuts and six colleagues, including Deneys Reitz and Harry Lawrence, came together over dinner and decided that if Hertzog did not desist, they would force the matter to a vote in the House on Monday.[16]

Elsewhere in Cape Town, quite unaware of the split in the cabinet, MPs of all parties were in earnest discussion among themselves, and their whips were counting and recounting heads. Esselen produced a detailed scorecard that showed Smuts that he would have an 85–80 majority of MPs and senators in the UP caucus, and a lead of 81–67 in the House of Assembly. Smuts was far less certain that the caucus would follow his lead over that of the prime minister. His concern was the number of MPs thought to be still sitting on the fence.[17]

CHAPTER 4

Sunday

None of the central characters in the looming parliamentary confrontation was in church in the Cape Peninsula on the morning of Sunday 3 September to hear the prayers being offered up for peace.[1] Hertzog, who was not a regular churchgoer, was huddled in conference with Havenga at Groote Schuur. Not even the prospect of war would deter Smuts from walking with his medical-student daughter, Louis, amid the flowers at Kirstenbosch. And at Malan's house in Sea Point, Nationalist MPs had gathered to make plans for the next day's debate.

In Britain, the Polish crisis had come to a head. At 9 am, Chamberlain issued a formal demand to Hitler to withdraw his forces from Poland by 11 am. At 11.15, the ultimatum ignored, Britain declared war on Germany, with France declaring war some hours later. At noon, Chamberlain addressed the House of Commons in London, and half an hour later the BBC transmitted his words to radio listeners around the world, including South Africa. Messages of support for Britain came immediately from all quarters of the Commonwealth besides South Africa, which had to remain uncommitted until its Parliament could decide. Unlike in 1914, no Dominion was constitutionally bound to do as the British government decreed.

Smuts invited Harry Lawrence, the Cape lawyer and youngest member of the UP cabinet, to breakfast with him at the Civil Service Club. Other MPs present were given no hint of what had transpired in cabinet the previous day. Once breakfast was over, Smuts took Lawrence up to his room, pulled a draft resolution out of his pocket, and invited him to read it. 'Do you think,' Smuts said, 'that after all Britain has done for this country, I would ever desert her?' Quite apart from the interests of South Africa itself, the magnanimity that Britain had shown the country meant that he (Smuts) was not going to let the British down in an emergency. 'I went away quite happily,' Lawrence recounted later.[2]

Under pressure

Now under immense pressure to respond to Britain's declaration of war, Hertzog called cabinet members away from their Sunday lunches to Groote Schuur to inform them of the latest developments in Europe. Discussion was held over for the cabinet meeting at 4 pm. In Sea Point, Malan's house was a hive of activity as Nationalist MPs discussed what might be done to keep South Africa out of the war. Eric Louw's proposal that another last-minute appeal be made to Hertzog was accepted, and a call went through to Groote Schuur asking whether a message from Malan could be submitted before the start of the cabinet meeting later that afternoon.

Shortly before 4 pm, Paul Sauer once again sped across the city bearing a letter from Malan, who warned that a decision in favour of war would drive white South Africans further apart and deepen – perhaps irretrievably – the divisions within Afrikanerdom itself. The NP leader promised the prime minister the wholehearted support of his party and suggested that standing together in opposition to war would open the way to the future cooperation so ardently desired by the Afrikaner people.

Trump card

Now armed with the GNP's promise of support, Hertzog had good reason to feel confident, still believing he could persuade the cabinet to abide by the neutrality agreement of a year before. On so many occasions in the past, Smuts had deferred to him in order to maintain the unity of the Fusion government, and was likely to do so again. Would his deputy really put English-Afrikaner relations, which they had championed together since 1933, in jeopardy in order to go to war again? And if he did, the prime minister had a trump card to play – a request to the governor-general to dissolve Parliament and call a general election, which Herzog felt quite confident of winning. Although South Africa and the other Dominions were now self-governing in terms of the Statute of Westminster, the British monarch – via his governors-general – retained certain constitutional prerogatives, including emergency powers in times of war.

Hertzog began the cabinet meeting by reading out the telegram he had been sent by Chamberlain the evening before. He then launched into a long and impassioned repetition of the case for the Union's neutrality, before announcing that he would be proposing a motion to that effect in Parliament the next day. Why the hurry, some ministers wanted to know. Would it not be better to put the matter before the party caucus first? Hertzog dismissed the suggestion out of hand. To Reitz, this came as no surprise. The PM was such an autocrat by nature, he wrote later, 'that I verily believe he had never paused to consider whether he could carry his motion through the House ... I am convinced that he thought he could walk into Parliament in the same way on Monday morning and force his neutrality motion on us by sheer domination of his personal prestige.'[3]

Smuts responds

Then it was Smuts's turn to speak. Repeating that the decision he had reached was the most difficult of his political career, he set out the reasons why South Africa should declare war on Germany. Though he was frequently interrupted by Hertzog, the gravity of the occasion ensured that the discussion remained calm and restrained throughout. When Smuts said he also wanted the issue to be put to a vote in Parliament, there was dead silence. Everyone present realised the six-year-long experiment of Fusion had finally run to its end.

After a discussion lasting less than an hour, Hertzog declared it was

SEVEN VOTES

General JC Smuts
KEYSTONE/HULTON ARCHIVE/GETTY IMAGES

General JBM Hertzog
KEYSTONE/HULTON ARCHIVE/GETTY IMAGES

Dr DF Malan
WORLD HISTORY ARCHIVE/ALAMY STOCK PHOTO

Sir Patrick Duncan
ARCHIVE PL/ALAMY STOCK PHOTO

obvious that the division among ministers could not be bridged. Reitz brought proceedings to a close by standing up and saying to the prime minister, 'Sir, it is quite evident that we have reached a parting of the ways. Those of us who are opposed to neutrality cannot remain in office with you; therefore this meeting is our last as fellow colleagues. I wish to thank you for the courtesy you have invariably shown us during the time we served under you and I hope the personal friendships we made will not be affected by what has happened.' With that, what Reitz described as 'perhaps the most critical cabinet meeting ever held in South Africa'[4] was over. As Nasson records, sherry was brought out, but to this day it is not known whether it was sweet or dry.[5]

Even at this late stage, Hertzog and his pro-neutrality cohorts in the UP had not lost hope. Governor-General Duncan could hardly refuse their call for a general election, which – with the support of Malan's Nationalists – they felt confident of winning. And such a request might not even be necessary, for, according to Pirow's calculations, a narrow victory for the prime minister was the most likely outcome of the parliamentary vote the next day.

Enter Duncan

Taking no chances nonetheless, Hertzog went to see Sir Patrick Duncan at 8 pm that evening. The two former cabinet colleagues, who regarded one another as friends, spent three-quarters of an hour discussing the governor-general's potential constitutional dilemma. Hertzog warned Duncan that he was immovable on the question of neutrality. If his motion the next day was defeated, he would demand that Parliament be dissolved and ask for a general election. To his consternation, Duncan responded by saying that if Smuts commanded a majority in the House in favour of war, he (Duncan) would regard it as his duty to accept the prime minister's resignation and invite Smuts to form a government.

In reply, Hertzog raised an even trickier question. If, as expected, he was to win his motion by a narrow majority of two or three votes, he would be unable to govern effectively and would have no option but to request the dissolution of Parliament and a general election. This gave Duncan pause for thought, and the two men parted company amicably, each having given the other much to reflect on overnight.

Malan called in

On returning to Groote Schuur, Hertzog immediately called for Dr Malan to come and see him. Arriving around 9 pm, the Nationalist leader was received in friendly fashion by the prime minister and the five other Fusion ministers in favour of neutrality – Havenga, Pirow, Fourie, Kemp and Fagan. Malan was informed of the split in the cabinet and had read out to him Hertzog's proposed 'neutrality' motion to be tabled the next day.

Would GNP cooperation with Hertzog and his supporters mean the founding of a new party? Malan enquired. That was not necessary, he was told, as the last six years could simply be wiped out and the pre-1933 National Party resurrected. And who would lead it, asked Malan. Hertzog would be leader for two years, it was suggested, until Afrikaners were reunited, at which point he would stand down and retire from politics.[6] In the meantime, Malan would become leader of the House. Satisfied with these responses, Malan promised the gathering the GNP's full support the next day. Back home in Sea Point by 11 pm, he assured caucus members who had eagerly awaited his return that, for Nationalist Afrikaners, exciting times lay ahead.[7]

Pro-war amendment

Over at the Civil Service Club, Smuts and six ministerial colleagues had assembled in the library around 8.30 pm to draft an amendment to Hertzog's neutrality motion. The nub of the amended resolution was that South Africa should refuse to adopt a neutral posture, sever relations with Germany, carry out its obligations to the Commonwealth, and take all necessary measures for the defence of the country. The amendment was approved by all ministers present.

In another room at the club, Esselen was poring over a list of MPs expected to be present in the House next day, dividing them into pro-Hertzog and pro-Smuts factions. The numbers showed that the hard core of supporters on either side was almost equally divided. A source of worry to Esselen was that four pro-Smuts supporters would not, for various reasons, be present in the House. Aware that Pirow had promised Hertzog a majority, Esselen went carefully through the names of fence-sitters and doubtfuls again, before reporting to a still sceptical and somewhat downbeat Smuts that he, not Hertzog, was more likely to come out the winner.

Of greater concern to Smuts was what might happen if a defeated Hertzog asked the governor-general to dissolve Parliament and call an election. So at 10 pm that evening, accompanied by Esselen, Smuts also went across to see Duncan, who gave him the same message he had given Hertzog. An election would be called only if neither leader was able to form a government.

Both Hertzog and Smuts went to bed that night uncertain of the outcome in the House the next day, not knowing which of them would emerge as victor. Each man realised, however, that losing the vote would probably bring a premature conclusion to his political career.

CHAPTER 5

Monday

Easily the most remarkable aspect of the parliamentary showdown that took place on Monday 4 September – and that had most of white South Africa on tenterhooks – was that not once had the prime minister and his deputy put their heads together to see if their mutual predicament could have been avoided. Such was the extent of the philosophical gulf between these two former arch-enemies, forced by economic circumstance into a marriage of convenience that had run its course and could no longer be held together. Both men felt they had reason to be aggrieved by the actions of the other: Hertzog thought that Smuts had reneged on an undertaking given in cabinet a year earlier; Smuts was nonplussed by the prime minister's high-handed disregard of the UP caucus, and was furious – when he became aware of it later – at Hertzog's secret overtures to the Nationalist opposition in Parliament.[1]

What At van Wyk regards as the most decisive moment in Hertzog's political career took place in his office shortly after 9 am, when the British High Commissioner for Southern Africa, Sir William Clark, arrived to present him with another message from Neville Chamberlain. The cable read in part:

> I ask you at this most difficult hour to consider what an immeasurable source of strength it would be to us to have your country

fighting on the side of those who are fighting against oppression and bad faith ... I feel that it would be most heartening ... to us and indeed to world opinion generally to have the knowledge that the Union Government would in this conflict stand with its partners in the British Commonwealth. Before you reach your decision as to the course you will recommend to the Union Parliament, may I make a personal appeal to you as one with whom we here have worked so long together in the fullest and friendliest cooperation to do your utmost to help us at this critical time.[2]

The elderly Hertzog, his drawn features indicating to Clark the tension of the past few days, felt the weight of the world on his shoulders. As the most senior of the Commonwealth leaders, he had enjoyed a cordial relationship with Britain, from whom he had won important concessions on self-determination for the Dominions. Giving Clark a preview of the resolution he was about to introduce in the House, Hertzog declared that his ultimate concern was not good relations with Britain but what was best for South Africa. The Union would maintain existing ties with the warring parties but also uphold its obligations to the Commonwealth and the League of Nations and ensure that its territory was not misused for offensive purposes by any country. He wished to afford Britain the most favourable treatment within the bounds of neutrality, but he could not let down the members of his party who had supported his anti-war stance.

The high commissioner was in the midst of explaining why it was in South Africa's best interests to take Britain's side when the discussion had to be terminated so that Hertzog could attend cabinet at 9.30 am.[3]

At what was a painful cabinet meeting for all present, no substantive matters were raised. Six years of cooperative government had come to an abrupt end, and any high-minded notions of Afrikaner-English reconciliation and amity lay in the dust once again. Individual ministers kept their own counsel and wondered what might lie in store for them personally. Harry Lawrence recollected: 'I was young, by far the youngest member of the cabinet, and my political world seemed to be tumbling down before me.'[4]

Parliament sovereign

In South Africa's post-1994 democracy, in which the Constitution rather than Parliament is sovereign, MPs are elected indirectly by a combination of proportional representation and party lists, a system that enables party 'bosses' – often not parliamentarians themselves – to determine and lay down party policy. It was quite different in the South Africa of 1939, where an all-white Parliament was supreme. In the House of Assembly and the Senate, the great issues of the day were thrashed out and decisions taken that bound the government of the day. MPs representing urban and rural constituencies across the country were directly elected, made up their own minds, and could be held individually accountable for the way they voted in Parliament. MPs wishing to represent a constituency had therefore to ensure that they faithfully represented the interests of the majority of their constituents. Racially unrepresentative though the system was, it meant that individual MPs were close to their voters, who felt they had someone to take account of their views.

Rumours run wild

By early morning of that fateful Monday in September, the parliamentary rumour mill was running wild.[5] From 9 am, MPs were congregating in the lobby, buttonholing ministers to ask whether it was true that the cabinet was divided, and Hertzog about to introduce a neutrality motion in the House. 'How could he do so without consulting members of his caucus?' and 'What right have we to vote on the matter without knowing where the party stands?' MPs of the governing party demanded to know.[6]

At 10.35 am, 148 out of 153 members of the House assembled for the opening prayer and formal adoption of the second and third readings of the Senate Bill. Four members were absent, and one seat was vacant. The

United Party had 104 members present (minus the Speaker, Dr EG Jansen, who by tradition did not cast a vote), the Purified Nationalists 29, the Dominion Party 9, Labour 4, and there were 3 Native Representatives. Together, the minority parties could muster around 40 votes, a substantial number against war and in favour of neutrality.

After the House had voted to extend the life of the Senate, Prime Minister Hertzog rose to his feet amid a tense silence. In the crowded public gallery and around the country, South Africa – collectively – held its breath. Speaking in Afrikaans only, he proposed that the House should endorse the cabinet's decision of a year before that, in the event of war, existing relations between the Union and the belligerents should be upheld and maintained as if no war were being waged. It was understood, Hertzog continued, that existing links between the Union and Great Britain or any other Commonwealth member arising from contractual undertakings relating to the naval base at Simon's Town, or from South Africa's membership of the League of Nations, would be unimpaired.[7]

Urging Afrikaners and English-speakers to stand together in common cause, Hertzog declared that if South Africa went to war on the side of Britain, it would mean that a section of the people cared more for British than South African interests. Such an attitude was incompatible with the country's freedom and independence.[8] South Africans had no interest in a conflict between Poland and Germany, and to become involved would damage relations between the (white) races for the next 50 or 100 years. The Union should take its own decision on the matter, just as Britain was doing.

Hertzog's was a powerful argument, put across with quiet conviction, until he made a fateful mistake, as from time to time he was inclined to do. Responding angrily to an interjection, he departed from his written notes and launched into a defence of Hitler's aggressive behaviour in Europe. 'It is urged that we should take part in the war because the German Chancellor has demonstrated he is out to obtain world domination … Where can we find proof?' the prime minister demanded, before going on to justify Hitler's seizure of the Rhineland, Austria and Czechoslovakia and rail against the unfairness of 'the monster of Versailles'.[9]

Almost a third of Hertzog's speech was taken up by his defence of the German dictator.[10] Even his most fervent supporters conceded that he had made a fateful mistake, which had reduced the effectiveness of his argument, and done little to draw doubters, fence-sitters or moderate English-speaking MPs to his side. As Van Wyk comments, instead of promoting unity, the prime minister had aroused suspicion, resentment and opposition to his motion.[11]

At the end of a lengthy oration, Hertzog proposed that South Africa should remain neutral, the wording of his motion almost identical to the resolution put before cabinet a year earlier. By this time, friend and foe alike had been disconcerted by his strident defence of Hitler. In her memoirs, Bertha Solomon, one of the few female MPs, recollected that after Hertzog's outburst, the case for neutrality was lost. 'Even the doubtfuls were not prepared to stomach a pro-Nazi South Africa,' she wrote.[12]

In the middle of the debate, news broke of the sinking of the *Athenia*, a British passenger liner on her way to Canada, by a German U-boat. It reminded MPs of the sinking of the *Lusitania* in 1915 and gave 'a sinister interpretation' to Hertzog's pro-German remarks.[13] What ought to have been the crowning moment of the prime minister's political career had become a personal disaster from which his reputation would never recover.[14]

Smuts disagrees

Smuts could hardly believe his luck. After Senator Tom Naude had seconded Hertzog's motion, the deputy prime minister rose to his feet to propose an amendment to the motion. Speaking in English, Smuts seized the opportunity to depict an aggressive Germany as a growing threat to world peace. Hertzog's proposed neutrality, he claimed, would not work; it would amount to a half neutrality, respected by no one – especially the Germans. Moreover, it would be suicidal for the Union, 'poor as it is in defence, rich as it is in resources, to dissociate itself from the Commonwealth'.[15] 'In war, you were either friend or enemy,' he declared.[16]

Disagreeing strongly with his prime minister over Hitler's true intentions — and territorial ambitions — Smuts reminded the House of Hitler's vow to recover every one of its colonies in Africa lost in 1919, one of which was neighbouring South West Africa. (The Reichskolonialbund, a propagandising organisation set up by the Nazis in 1936, agitated for the return of the overseas colonies Germany had lost under the Treaty of Versailles. Its relevance diminished with the onset of war, however, and it was dissolved in 1943.) A neutral South Africa, separated from the Commonwealth, would stand alone if the Germans demanded the return of South West Africa 'at the point of a bayonet'. If Hitler triumphed in Europe, South Africa would be powerless to resist. This was the price the country would pay for neutrality, Smuts declared.[17]

Smuts's three-part amendment proposed that South Africa should not stay neutral, but should sever relations with Germany and stand by its friends in Britain and the Commonwealth. The country should take all necessary measures to defend its territory and interests but not send troops to fight overseas, as in the last war. And, with the freedom and independence of the Union at stake, it was in South Africa's interests to oppose the German use of force as an instrument of national policy.[18] His amendment was seconded by Colonel WR Collins, the Afrikaans-speaking minister for agriculture and fisheries.

Best speech

After the two leaders had spoken, the UP frontbencher from Natal, George Heaton Nicholls, a respected and usually effective speaker, came close to undermining Smuts's position by claiming that the entire debate was unnecessary because the country, by virtue of its allegiance to Britain as a member of the Commonwealth, was already at war with Germany.

It took a timely intervention from the former editor of the *Cape Times*, BK Long, to save the day for the Smuts faction. In what was generally agreed to be the best speech of the session, Long stated bluntly that, as an English-speaker, he did not agree with Nicholls. Under the Statute of Westminster and the Status of Union Act, South Africa was a free and independent member of the Commonwealth, constitutionally entitled to decide to remain neutral. But to do so, Long argued, would be disastrously unwise 'in the interests of our own country'. 'The world was divided into two camps,' he said, then demanding, rhetorically, 'Could anyone doubt that freedom, liberty and the right to live one's life as one chose, was to be found within the camp of the British Commonwealth? ... Will anyone have the effrontery to get up in this House and tell me that in the German Reich today there is any vestige of individual liberty and freedom? Will anyone deny that in the German Reich the will of one man is dominant over the wishes of every individual ...?'[19]

Support for Hertzog

Malan followed the eloquent Long after the lunch break, adding little to what Hertzog had already said but promising him the support of the GNP.[20] His objection to Fusion in 1933 had been that it would end in the disaster that was now unfolding. Reminding Smuts of his own criticisms of the Treaty of Versailles in 1919, the GNP leader argued that Hitler was simply trying to overcome the unfair provisions of the treaty. This was not a South African but a British war, for which not a single South African bullet should be fired, nor a single drop of South African blood shed, Malan declared.[21]

As the debate went back and forth – amid the feverish lobbying of MPs behind the scenes – an atmosphere of calmness and restraint pervaded the House. Shortly before the evening adjournment, the UP's General EA Conroy made an earnest plea to Smuts not to destroy the unity between Afrikaners and Englishmen. If it was not necessary to send troops overseas, he asked, why should the Union go to war so hastily? No answer was forthcoming before the supper break intervened.

As Bertha Solomon recalled, as Cape Town offices closed in the late afternoon, the silent throng outside Parliament grew larger and the tension increased hourly.[22] In cities around the country, and on university

MONDAY

The front page of The Star, *4 September 1939.*
MUSEUM AFRICA, JOHANNESBURG

campuses, pro- and anti-war demonstrators noisily made their feelings known, and large crowds gathered outside newspaper offices to await the outcome of the parliamentary debate.

The vote

In the House after supper, it became apparent that the spark had gone out of the proceedings. By now, everyone wanted to get on with the vote. There had been 17 speeches during the day – 12 in favour of going to war and 5 in favour of neutrality. It was noticeable that several of the strongest opponents of war – Pirow and Havenga for the UP; JG Strijdom, Eric Louw and Paul Sauer for the GNP – had chosen to keep silent. Van Wyk ascribes their apathy to a wish to avoid further Afrikaner disunity, and their confidence of winning a general election if the vote were to be lost.[23]

At 9.10 pm, the Speaker finally put Smuts's amendment to Hertzog's motion to the House, and the division bells rang. In a strained, expectant atmosphere, MPs in favour of Hertzog's motion took up seats to the right of the Speaker's chair, while those against the war turned left. The minutes ticked slowly by as the tellers on either side completed their tallies and handed the result to Speaker Jansen, who solemnly intoned: 'Ayes in favour of the Hon the Prime Minister's motion – 67; Noes in favour of Gen. Smuts's amendment – 80.'

An astonished Hertzog turned in anger on his minister of defence, sitting nearby, for while Esselen had done his sums correctly, the overconfident Pirow had not.[24] By a margin of 13 votes, South Africa would be at war once again.

Hertzog ashen

Reitz had been watching Hertzog closely as the votes were counted: 'His face was ashen. And it seemed to me that only now had it dawned on him that he was staring at defeat. The other five cabinet ministers who had voted for him looked angry and perturbed and I gained the impression that they were furious at the way their leader had bungled himself into an impasse.'[25] In Reitz's view, it was possible that Hertzog might have secured a small majority had he not blundered into eulogising Hitler, and had it not been for the forceful and powerful speech by Smuts, which had brought around many waverers.[26]

Smuts's Australian biographer, Sir Keith Hancock, asserts that Smuts was the deserving winner of the debate. Hertzog's analysis of the situation in Europe had not been convincing, particularly his strictures about the Treaty of Versailles. After the Molotov-Ribbentrop Pact, the Treaty of Versailles had lost much of its relevance for practical statesmen. Hitler, moreover, had made plain his intention to demand the return of the former German South West Africa, and Hertzog had made it equally clear that the Union would never surrender the territory. If Hitler were to win the war, a conflict with neutral South Africa was inevitable.[27]

In cities and towns up and down the country, the white public was as divided over the outcome as MPs in the House had been. Crowds of excited people rejoiced at Smuts's victory and sang 'God Save the King', while opponents flew the old republican flag, the Vierkleur, and gave voice to '*Die Stem*'.

In Cape Town, as the throng outside Parliament gradually drifted away, a crestfallen Hertzog made his way across town to ask the governor-general to dissolve Parliament and call a general election. Accompanied by colleagues, a tired but victorious Smuts, for his part, adjourned to the Civil Service Club to wait patiently on Sir Patrick Duncan's invitation to form a new government.[28]

CHAPTER 6

Tuesday and Wednesday

For Hertzog and the anti-war faction inside and outside Parliament, all was not lost yet. Their hopes were pinned on Governor-General Duncan, who, they believed, could hardly decline their demand for a general election.[1] Shortly after losing the vote, the prime minister had gone to see Duncan for the second time in 24 hours. Earlier, he had believed he would return as the winner of a slim majority; now, he had to approach the de facto head of state as a losing supplicant.[2]

Hertzog formally requested Duncan to dissolve Parliament on the grounds that the outcome in the House did not accurately reflect the wishes of the electorate at large, which could only be determined by a general election. The governor-general asked for time to consider the request, indicating that although he had thought long and hard about his decision, he was still in two minds. His provisional opinion, he told Hertzog, was that he would have to decline the request, but would like to think more about it overnight and give his final decision the next day. The exchanges between the two friends were cordial, and they parted company on good terms.[3]

Duncan

The man in whose palm lay the immediate destiny of South Africa was a 56-year-old Scottish-born South African-naturalised former cabinet colleague of Hertzog's. Sir Patrick Duncan was liked and respected on both sides of the House for his competence and integrity. An outstanding law graduate of Balliol College, Oxford, he had arrived in South Africa in 1901 as the first member of 'Milner's Kindergarten', a group of bright young colonial administrators recruited by Sir Alfred Milner. Brought out as colonial treasurer of the Transvaal, and subsequently made colonial secretary and acting lieutenant-governor, Duncan served at Milner's right hand before electing to settle in South Africa after the latter's return to the UK – the only member of the Kindergarten to do so. From 1907 to 1910, Duncan practised as an attorney, serving as law adviser to the Transvaal delegation at the National Convention of 1908–1909.

In need of employment after the coming of responsible government to the Transvaal, Duncan had gone back to the Inns of Court in London to qualify as a barrister, before returning to practise at the Transvaal Bar. Typically, he refused to take the pension to which he was entitled as an ex-civil servant, because he did not think it right that a person of his age, who could earn a living, should draw money from public funds.[4]

From the outset, Duncan was a firm believer in unification as the cure for the difficulties of the four colonies, and as a means of 'obliterating the dividing lines, whether racial, geopolitical or historical which today are hampering the development of South Africa'.[5] Entering politics in the first Union Parliament as a member of the Unionist Party, in opposition to the government of Botha and Smuts, he served as an MP for 26 years, becoming a cabinet member under Smuts when the Unionists merged with the SAP in 1920. In 1933, he played a significant role in the negotiations over Fusion and was rewarded with the key portfolio of minister of mines in the Hertzog-led administration.

In 1935, Duncan accompanied the prime minister on the long 17-day sea voyage to Britain and back to attend the silver jubilee celebrations of King George V. Perhaps because of the favourable impression he made, Hertzog invited Duncan to succeed Lord Clarendon as governor-general of South Africa in 1937. Duncan thus became the first South African citizen to be appointed as the sovereign's representative, having had to be persuaded to accept the post by Hertzog, whose government had abolished British titles in 1925.[6] Reluctantly, he accepted a non-hereditary knighthood and membership of the Privy Council.

Described by the maverick journalist-politician Arthur Barlow as a 'good, humble, kindly soul with no side',[7] Sir Patrick was a shy, reserved character who – in his friend Leslie Blackwell's estimation – was 'one of the finest men whom Scotland had ever sent to this country'.[8] The right-wing Free State Nationalist, NJ van der Merwe, is reputed to have said of Duncan, who learnt Afrikaans quickly and used it in speeches in the *platteland* (countryside), that he was the only man 'on the other side' with whom he would have dinner.[9]

In his book *Farewell to Parliament*, Blackwell recounts an amusing incident during question time at a Unionist election meeting addressed by Duncan in the working-class suburb of Fordsburg, Johannesburg. An aggressive-looking miner demanded to know of the speaker whether he was a member of the Rand Club. 'Yes,' replied the mild-mannered Duncan, 'but what of it?' 'I'd rather go to Hell than the Rand Club,' yelled the miner. 'No doubt you would; you'd find it easier to get in,' was Duncan's calm response.[10]

In spite of Smuts being godfather to one of his sons, Duncan actually enjoyed a much warmer personal relationship with Hertzog. The liking and mutual regard the two had for one another made the governor-general's dilemma over the outcome of the war vote – whether to follow head or heart in considering Hertzog's request for a general election – even more acute. As Duncan wrote despairingly to his wife, 'I'm inclined to say along with Hamlet, "for my own good part – look you – I'll go pray".'[11]

Earthquake

As the implications of Parliament's decision sank in, it became apparent that South Africa had been shaken by a political earthquake that virtually no one had foreseen or predicted. A front-page report in *Die Burger* summed up the feelings of all concerned – on both sides of the political divide – by describing what had happened as 'so unbelievable that no one in his wildest dreams would have come up with it'. Waves of emotion, euphoria and anger washed over cities and dorps across the country, while telegrams by the hundred rained down on Smuts, Malan and especially Hertzog.[12]

On the morning of Tuesday 5 September, as MPs reassembled on the floor of the House beneath a packed public gallery, there was only one question on everyone's minds: what would Governor-General Duncan decide? Pure anticlimax was to follow. First, the final stages of the Senate Bill had to be formally approved by the House before the measure could be sent to Duncan for signature. That done, the sitting of the House was adjourned for the morning. When MPs gathered after lunch, Hertzog merely proposed that Parliament be prorogued and – in what turned out to be his final act as South African premier – signed a proclamation to that effect.[13]

Unbeknown to anyone, the prime minister had already been privately informed in writing by the governor-general that permission would not be granted for the dissolution of Parliament and the calling of an election. Duncan's reason for denying Hertzog's request was primarily that an election would lead to great bitterness and quite possibly violence, but also that neutrality had been at issue in the election of 1938, only 16 months earlier, when the prime minister had repeatedly declared that Parliament should make the final decision. The House had now delivered its judgement and come down in favour of Smuts's pro-war motion, and if the deputy prime minister were able to form a government, he (Duncan) would not feel justified in dissolving Parliament.

Resignation

On receipt of Duncan's statement, Hertzog had immediately resigned, but the governor-general elected to keep the news to himself until he had invited Smuts to form a government and received a positive answer. The governor-general let it be known, instead, that he would announce his decision the following day, Wednesday 6 September.

At this inopportune moment, the SABC chose to muddy the waters by announcing that Parliament had been prorogued but Hertzog had not yet tendered his resignation – an incorrect report that almost sparked off civil war.[14] Rumours flew that Hertzog was intent on declaring martial law to keep South Africa out of the European conflict, which provoked fury among pro-British loyalists and anti-war Afrikaners alike. Rioters in the Transvaal, attempting to damage properties owned by Germans, were beaten with batons and tear-gassed by anti-war pro-Nationalist policemen[15] before, late in the day, the SABC at last got its facts right. In Johannesburg, the scene of most of the trouble, tempers were calmed when a special edition of *The Star* went on sale on city streets.

War declared

The next morning, it was formally announced that Smuts had accepted the governor-general's invitation to form a government, with himself as prime minister. Later that day, as soon as a coalition cabinet had been sworn in, the new prime minister declared South Africa to be officially at war with Germany and the Axis powers, and took immediate steps to put the country on a war footing. Writing to Isie, and to an American banker friend, Thomas Lamont, that night, Smuts reflected wryly that instead of being kicked out of government as he had expected, he suddenly found himself in command of the country again.[16]

The new coalition ministry of 11 members, a careful balance between Afrikaans- and English-speakers, consisted mostly of leading ex-SAP members of the Fusion government who had supported Smuts over the war issue (Lawrence, Reitz, Sturrock, Stuttaford, Collins, Conroy and Clarkson), plus a returning JH Hofmeyr and Dr Colin Steyn (son of the Free State president MT Steyn), as well as the leaders of the Dominion and Labour parties, Colonel CP Stallard and Walter Madeley, respectively. As Hancock notes, there were some able and energetic men among them

(Hofmeyr, Lawrence, Sturrock and Steyn, in particular) but the rest were elderly, sluggish and backward-looking. Smuts, as always, was the dominant figure in cabinet.[17]

Nationalist fury

Pro-Hertzog Afrikaners were furious at what had transpired. Speaker Jansen, who had remained strictly neutral in the debate, recorded in a private note that no one had expected the leadership of Prime Minister Hertzog to be rejected, or that the Fusion government would disintegrate, or that members of the United Party would join forces with minority parties to vote in favour of war. Nor had Jansen imagined that any government would dare to declare war against the will of so many MPs, and of such a large section of the public. This was dangerous in a country without a homogeneous population and with such a divided past and present, and to do so was simply inexplicable (*onverklaarbaar*). Those like himself who had thought Fusion might enhance the building of 'one nation' had been living in 'a fools' paradise', he noted angrily.[18]

Had Sir Patrick Duncan been constitutionally correct in rejecting the advice of his prime minister and refusing a general election? Many on Hertzog's side thought not. The GNP's mouthpiece, *Die Burger*, declared angrily that the internal situation was not nearly as dangerous as it had been in 1915, and Duncan's reasoning for declining an election was '*bog*' (nonsense). Britain's attorney-general, not the most independent of arbiters, believed the governor-general had acted appropriately, as did many constitutional lawyers,[19] but the matter remains moot to this day.

Strangely, one of those who thought that Duncan had acted within his powers was Hertzog himself. Though bitterly disappointed at the outcome, he understood the governor-general's dilemma. According to the political editor of the *Cape Times*, GH Wilson, whenever the question was raised afterwards, Hertzog 'most generously' admitted that his friend Duncan had acted constitutionally and within his rights in refusing to call an election.[20] With typical courtesy, when writing formally to Hertzog to reject his plea for the dissolution of Parliament, Duncan had enclosed a private note expressing his sorrow at the termination of their official association but hoping that their relationship 'had created a friendship that would outlive any changes in the political scene'.[21]

Hertzog departs

As the new cabinet was being sworn in by Governor-General Duncan, the outgoing United Party premier summoned a meeting between his MPs and the caucus of Malan's Purified National Party, at which he declared the enmity of the past six years to be over. According to Van Wyk, a dejected Hertzog wished to quit politics there and then, but was persuaded by close colleagues to soldier on. That evening, a huge crowd of singing Nationalist Afrikaners gathered at Cape Town's railway station to send off their fallen leader on his journey to the north. Throngs of devoted followers applauded Hertzog at every stop along the route.

Three days later, on Saturday 9 September, at a hurriedly arranged reunification rally on Monument Hill outside Pretoria, Hertzog and Malan solemnly shook hands before a great throng. As Oswald Pirow recorded approvingly, Nationalist Afrikaner reaction to Hertzog's resignation had been 'instantaneous'.[22] At one fell swoop, the white population had reverted to the status quo that had prevailed in the immediate aftermath of the Anglo-Boer War – a situation that both Hertzog and Smuts had striven to overcome.

No majority

Smuts had won the parliamentary vote because he had been able to garner the support of the two minority parties, Dominion and Labour, and the Native Representatives, but it is unlikely he would have won a general election had one been held. The Commonwealth journal, *Round Table*, after observing that generals Smuts and Hertzog had been 'about as happy in harness together as a horse and a zebra', wrote in its December 1939 issue:

> General Smuts has a majority of about seventeen in the House, if we count members who were not present at this momentous debate; but it would be dangerous to assume that he has a majority in the country, or that a general election will return him to power again. If an election or referendum were to be held today, then it is more than probable – especially as regards a general election – that a majority will approve of the policy of the ex-Prime Minister [Hertzog].[23]

As for the majority population of Africans, coloureds and Indians, as usual they were not consulted, and hence – in Bill Nasson's words – showed little inclination to wave flags, sing songs or otherwise react to the war vote: 'As with the Union's expeditionary involvement in an earlier World War, here was another European conflict of that remote sort, as unlikely as the last to show anything by way of recognition and reward to black patriotic service and sacrifice.'[24]

A wider vision

In an open letter to the people of South Africa, Hertzog accused Smuts of having split the United Party irreparably and 'reduced our national freedom to insignificance'.[25] Only by the most determined action on the part of all patriotic Afrikaners, English-speaking as well as Afrikaans-speaking, can that freedom be maintained and we be prevented from being dragged further into the war, the former prime minister insisted.

Not for the first time, Smuts's horizons had proved much wider than Hertzog's. According to Hancock, the new prime minister knew exactly what he was taking on. He understood that going to war would give rise to bitterness and division, and that civil insurrection was likely. But to remain neutral, in his view, would prove even more divisive and damaging to the country's long-term interests. Smuts's line of cleavage, says Hancock, was in a different place to that of Hertzog and Malan. Their concern was the harm that would be caused to white unity. The cleavage Smuts had chosen was the greater national interest and could – he believed – be repaired in the fullness of time.[26]

Smuts harboured no illusions about what war would produce – 'another peace which would be no peace' – but saw no alternative if the growth of Nazism (and Bolshevism) were to be countered and the security and values of the Union defended. The world was a dangerous place for small nations without friends, he often emphasised, which is why he had sought membership of the Commonwealth for South Africa and fought for the organisation's survival: 'For me personally there was no other way. I am a firm believer in the Commonwealth, not only for its own sake and that of South Africa, but as the first tentative beginnings of great things for the future of the world. I was not going to desert or betray that great cause.'[27]

Once again, Smuts realised he was in for a fight on two fronts. Unlike the other Dominion leaders, he had not only to rally a nation wholly unprepared for war, but also to face down internal opponents determined to thwart his every effort, and deeply hostile to the recruitment of non-whites into the armed forces – even as non-combatants. For the duration of the war, the armed resistance of radical Afrikaners would remain the chief impediment to the mobilisation of the civilian population in support of the UDF, or to any deployment of the military outside the country's borders.[28]

One day after the declaration of war on Germany, South Africa's prime minister received a personal message from Britain's newly reappointed First Lord of the Admiralty: 'I rejoice to feel that we are once again on commando together,' wrote a buoyant Winston Churchill.[29]

PART TWO

A Divided Nation

CHAPTER 7

Two Streams

In the saddle again after 15 years, but without the advantage enjoyed by the other Dominion leaders of a popular consensus for taking Britain's side in the war, the almost-70-year-old Smuts sprang into action with characteristic vigour. Although the Fusion defence minister, the pro-Nazi Oswald Pirow, had drawn up a five-year plan for the country's defence in 1934, the Union was still seriously underprepared for any enemy attack. Despite Hertzog's insistence on upholding South Africa's sovereign status, he had left the defence of the country's long coastline – and trade routes – to the Royal Navy. In his defence, it must be said that financial constraints and the British Admiralty's reluctance to delegate 'sovereignty' to a Dominion government were contributory factors. Smuts, on the other hand, had anticipated a struggle for the future of humanity that would span the oceans, into which the Union would inevitably be drawn because of its strategic situation at the foot of Africa.[1]

Yet South Africa was in no fit state to wage war: it had no navy to speak of (only a 970-strong Volunteer Reserve), almost no air defences, a tiny Permanent Force of 349 officers and 5 033 men (almost 2 000 of them in the South African Air Force, SAAF), an Active Citizen Force (ACF) of 918 officers and 12 572 men, and a Special Reserve Battalion of 17 officers and 1 705 men.[2] At UDF headquarters in Pretoria, there was no properly thought-out plan for defending the country's borders on land or at sea. It was time to put one of the Afrikaner's favourite sayings – *"n Boer maak 'n plan'* (a farmer makes a plan) – into practice.

To defend the country's sea lanes, fishing trawlers had to be hurriedly converted into patrol craft and minesweepers. Until fighter and bomber aircraft could be delivered from Britain and the US, the UDF's air arm had to make do with Junkers aircraft commandeered from South African Airways (SAA), and begin recruiting pilots and training air crews. When it came to enlistment in the army, however, the new government had to tread warily. Conscription was out of the question, so a force of volunteers had to be enlisted and readied for service both inside and beyond the country's borders.

Ever reluctant to delegate, the indefatigable Smuts took upon himself the roles of prime minister, minister of defence, minister of external affairs and commander-in-chief of the UDF. An immediate priority was the procurement and manufacture of essential war materials, so he persuaded the highly regarded head of the Iron and Steel Corporation (Iscor), Dr HJ van der Bijl, to accept the appointment as director-general of war supplies. Ironically, only 12 years earlier, as leader of the opposition, Smuts had vigorously opposed the Pact government's plan to establish Iscor; now he was to rely heavily on the parastatal, and its chairman, in the Union's hour of need.[3]

Inspired choice

In appointing the youthful Hendrik van der Bijl as the country's director of war production and wartime supplies, Smuts made an inspired choice. By the time of his premature death at the age of 60, not long after the war, Van der Bijl had left an indelible mark on his country. Born in Pretoria in 1887 and schooled in the Cape, the young Hendrik was one of Victoria College's most brilliant students, graduating with honours in physics, chemistry and mathematics. While furthering his postgraduate studies in Germany in the early 1900s, he was recruited by AT&T and Western Electric in the US to assist in developing new communications technology. He was instrumental in making the US the world leader in radio telephony.

At the height of his career in the US (and by then married to an American), Van der Bijl was lured back to South Africa in 1920 by the then prime minister, Smuts, to become scientific adviser to the SAP government. His master plan, produced in 1922, proposed the establishment of a public utility to generate and provide electricity to industry (and the public) on a non-profit basis. In 1923, aged 36, Van der Bijl became the founding chairman of the Electricity Supply Commission (Escom, later Eskom), the parastatal at the heart of South Africa's power grid. The establishment of Escom, which in its heyday produced the world's cheapest electricity, is regarded as the single biggest factor in South Africa's industrial development during the 20th century.[4]

Aware that no country could industrialise successfully without two basic commodities – cheap power and locally manufactured steel – Van der Bijl went on to establish another key parastatal, Iscor, in 1928, over the determined resistance of steel importers in the private sector. Within five years, South Africa was producing the world's cheapest steel. While director-general of war supplies, for which he refused to draw any salary, he also founded and chaired Amcor (African Metals Corporation) and Vecor (Van der Bijl Engineering Works Corporation), a second steelworks situated at today's Vanderbijlpark.

The scientific honour of which the apolitical Van der Bijl was most proud was being made a Fellow of the Royal Society of London. During his 25 years of service to his country, he took industrial development to a level that no one could have predicted at the start of the war.[5]

Made locally

By the end of 1940, great strides had been made in putting the Union on a war footing. Local heavy industry was successfully manufacturing armoured cars, ammunition, bombs, mortars and other weapons. Uniforms, tents, beds, blankets, food and medical supplies for military use were also produced locally. Notwithstanding the vociferous objections of anti-war Afrikaner Nationalists, 137 000 white ACF volunteers had been put through training at various camps around the country and organised into new units. These volunteers were readily identified by the red-orange flashes on their uniforms, signifying they had taken the Africa Oath for service 'anywhere in Africa'. These red flashes turned out to be a deeply polarising factor: soldiers and policemen who had also taken the 'red oath' found themselves ostracised or victimised by anti-war elements in the armed services, as were opponents of the war in uniform who flatly refused to take the oath under any circumstances.

In July 1940 the UDF created a directorate called the Non-European Army Services (NEAS) to recruit coloureds, Indians and Africans into the military. The NEAS comprised three units: the Cape Corps, the Indian & Malay Corps and the Native Military Corps (NMC). Once again, because of white fears, these units could not be armed and had to be deployed in a variety of noncombatant roles. Recruits to the NMC were used mainly as labourers or security guards, thus freeing up white soldiers for service 'up north'.

According to official statistics, 342 792 volunteers of all races were to serve in the UDF in WWII. Of this number, 217 122 were white, 79 258 African and 46 412 coloured and Indian. In addition, another 63 000 men enlisted in part-time units.[6] Historian DW Krüger commented that 'the creation of the South African army in such a short time and amid so many difficulties was a miracle of achievement, and a personal triumph for Smuts'.[7]

Key contributors to the development of the Union's fighting forces were the steel and munitions industries, which managed to make, within weeks, an ambulance train for South African Railways & Harbours, as well as a complete plant for the manufacture of small arms and ammunition at the Royal Mint in Pretoria.[8] As Smuts had foreseen, it was not long before the country's harbours were full of troop-carrying passenger liners diverted from the Mediterranean around the Cape, as well as warships requiring maintenance and provisioning. South Africa became known as 'the great repair shop of the Middle East'.[9]

In tandem with military preparations, a National Supplies Board was set up to control and regulate imports and exports, raw materials, prices (of food and other essentials), agricultural production and distribution, and rationing. The Treasury was given authority to block any flight of capital and sell the gold and foreign exchange required to finance military operations. As Nasson notes, the wartime economy remained capitalist in essence, but a form of command economy became necessary in priority sectors from munitions and aero-engine manufacture to food canning and railways.[10]

Deep divisions

As the war in Europe began in earnest, the deep ideological gulf between Nazi Germany and opponents of Hitler's aggression was reflected in the divisions within the South African body politic. Whites who had emotional attachments to Britain, or who simply abhorred racial fanaticism of any kind, were wholeheartedly supportive of the Allied war effort. Almost half of those who volunteered for service in the UDF were Afrikaners, many of them poor, not politically aligned, and in search of employment and excitement. Political diehards, on the other hand, who believed that preserving South Africa's race/class structure and exercising the country's constitutional right to control its own destiny were paramount, were determined on neutrality, whereas those enthused by Hitler's racial triumphalism or who had close German affiliations pinned their hopes on a Nazi victory.[11]

The country's communists and their fellow travellers, who regarded the war as a conflict among capitalists, were neutral to begin with, but suddenly became fiercely partisan in June 1941, when Hitler's armies invaded Soviet Russia. Among Africans, coloureds and Indians – who were, of course, not consulted – there was little enthusiasm for fighting another war on behalf of imperial Britain, which was hardly surprising given the lack of appreciation shown for their contribution in WWI.

Within the ranks of Malan-supporting Nationalists, on the other hand, there was genuine outrage at the prospect of having to take the British side once again. Imbued with a renewed spirit of republicanism aroused by the centenary of the Great Trek, thousands of Afrikaners joined extra-parliamentary, pro-Nazi organisations intent on actively hindering the war effort (see Chapter 8). As the first South African forces began departing 'up north', the anti-war lobby became increasingly vociferous. In DW Krüger's words, 'they blamed Smuts, they blamed the British imperialists and they blamed the Jewish capitalists'.[12] Anti-Jewish feeling in right-wing circles proliferated, and the flames of radical white resistance were fanned by broadcasts from Zeesen radio, the German propaganda service – run by Eric Holm, a South African expatriate and Broederbonder – beamed into South African homes in Afrikaans each night.[13]

Nationalists regroup

In the House of Assembly, the 37 Hertzog-supporting MPs had crossed the floor to sit on the opposition benches alongside Malan's Nationalists. And in the country at large, the Afrikaner Broederbond, working behind the scenes as always, was making an all-out effort to forge grass-roots Afrikaner unity. Within a few days of the parliamentary vote, the Broederbond successfully stage-managed a huge rally outside Pretoria to celebrate the *hereniging* (reunification) of Nationalists. Since Fusion, the Afrikaner people had been split, broadly, into two camps, the one seeking white unity based on the equal treatment of the language and cultural rights of both language groups, the other calling for an independent Afrikaner republic, free of British and Jewish capitalist interests. On Saturday 9 September, at the site of the Voortrekker Monument, 70 000 members of the latter camp 'raised their hands and promised never again to break away from one another'.[14]

Equality between the two language groups was not a policy that appealed to younger, hot-headed Nationalists in the Transvaal and Free State. Among those insisting on the establishment of an Afrikaner-led republic as a precondition for white unity were up-and-coming political leaders the likes of JG Strijdom, HF Verwoerd and CR Swart.[15] Their hard-line approach and divisive tactics were anathema to Hertzog, however, whose unbending principle since Union had been equal treatment for both language groups. Pro-republican fervour did not hold much appeal for DF Malan either, whose more immediate aim was to unite Nationalist Afrikanerdom and keep up pressure on the Smuts government to abandon the war against Germany.

Broedertwis

In January 1940, Nationalist enthusiasm was on vivid display once more when a large crowd greeted ex-premier Hertzog on his return to Cape Town for the parliamentary session. Though there were some MPs who still had the temerity to question his adherence to the true faith, Hertzog was quickly elected to lead the reunited Nationalists, now formally known as the Herenigde Nasionale or Volksparty (Reunited National Party or People's Party, HNP). But when Hitler invaded the Low Countries in April, the party's weak-kneed response to the attack on the Netherlands, in particular, alienated many moderate Afrikaners, who deserted its ranks.[16]

Another *broedertwis* (quarrel between brothers) broke out in July when, without asking or informing Hertzog, Free State Nationalists led by Swart and NJ van der Merwe called another rally of Afrikaners in Bloemfontein. The assembly enthusiastically endorsed demands for an Afrikaner republic and single-medium Christian-National education, and denounced the 'British-Jewish-capitalist interests' that had supposedly brought about Fusion. A whispering campaign aimed at undermining Hertzog's credentials as a true-blue (or orange) Nationalist made it apparent to the elderly ex-premier that his tenure as HNP leader was drawing to an end.

With Hitler on the rampage in Europe, Hertzog continued to campaign vigorously against the war. In late August 1940, when it seemed the Nazis were unstoppable, the HNP leader called on Parliament to debate his motion that South Africa should withdraw from the war and make peace with Germany. With characteristic hyperbole, Hertzog described Smuts's decision that South Africa should take part in the conflict as 'the greatest blunder and most fatal mistake ever made by a responsible statesman'.[17] Yet only months earlier, Mussolini's Italy had entered the war on Hitler's side, bringing the prospect of hostilities in North Africa much closer to home and vindicating Smuts's belief that neutrality was a dangerous option. With Smuts able to make the more persuasive case that South Africa's interests were now directly at risk from the Axis powers, Hertzog's pro-neutrality motion was comfortably defeated. The cracks in the HNP ranks began to widen further as Transvaal and Free State MPs became increasingly exasperated at Hertzog's principled insistence on equality between Afrikaans and English. Why, they asked, should he be so concerned with protecting the rights of English-speakers when they had failed so conspicuously as a group to support him over the war issue?

Pirow

Although most, though not all, Fusion MPs who had sided with Hertzog in the war debate rejoined Malan's HNP, a handful of moderate Free Staters chose to form a new Afrikaner Party, under the leadership of Klasie Havenga, to preserve and propagate a more moderate form of Afrikaner nationalism. Seventeen right-wingers, on the other hand, joined Oswald Pirow's New Order for South Africa, an anti-capitalist, anti-Jewish and pro-Christian ginger group within the HNP. While not exclusively Afrikaner-oriented,[18] the New Order was set up to advance the cause of a National Socialist republic modelled along Fascist lines.

The talented Pirow was a colourful individual who blazed a trail across the political firmament for almost two decades until becoming thoroughly discredited for his right-wing views. Born at Aberdeen in the Karoo to German immigrant parents, the talented young Oswald attended Kiel University in northern Germany before furthering his law studies in London. An excellent all-round sportsman in his student days, he was Britain's champion javelin thrower and a trialist for the 1912 Olympics.[19]

As the journalist Piet Meiring observes,[20] Afrikaans-speakers who studied in England tended to become either markedly pro-British or more fervently pro-Afrikaner. Pirow fell into the latter camp, and, on returning to South Africa in 1913, cast in his lot with Hertzog's NP. After two unsuccessful general elections, he became an MP in 1924. Five years later, at the age of 38, he was chosen by Hertzog to succeed Tielman Roos as minister of justice when Roos had to resign due to ill-health. Vowing to 'legislate communism out of existence', Pirow did his best to do so by introducing legislation in 1930 to bar the incitement of anti-white sentiment in South Africa – the first such inroad into the rule of law by any minister of justice. The thrusting young advocate was soon to become Hertzog's most staunch supporter and right hand in government.

Widely regarded as a future party leader, Pirow became minister of defence, as well as minister of railways and harbours, in the Fusion cabinet, where he made a favourable impression on London's *Sunday Times*, which described him – risibly, as it turns out – as 'a brilliant administrator in whose hands the future defence of South Africa would be safe'.[21] BK Long regarded the 'quickly intelligent', irreverent and jovial Pirow as a potential successor to Smuts as party leader. His only rival at that time was JH Hofmeyr. Disillusionment with Pirow set in, however, when his ineptitude as defence minister and extremist views became apparent to his former admirers.[22]

A fervent admirer of all things German, especially Adolf Hitler, whom he described as 'the greatest man of his day, perhaps the greatest of the last thousand years',[23] Pirow was given a free hand by Hertzog to pursue a 'South Africa First' philosophy in order to weaken British influence generally and advance the Union's reach into the white-run colonies of sub-Saharan Africa.[24]

Revisiting his beloved Germany in 1933, Pirow had been beguiled at a meeting with Hitler, and encountered the Führer for a second time in 1936 when he and the future Ossewabrandwag leader, Hans van Rensburg, attended the Berlin Olympics. Throughout the 1930s, Pirow paid official visits to fascist-led countries, meeting Mussolini, Franco, Salazar and the Führer once more, this time at his private retreat at Berchtesgaden. Before his meeting with Hitler in October 1938, he was asked by British prime minister Neville Chamberlain to convey his (Chamberlain's) views on peace and war to the German leader.[25] Yet, of all the dictators Pirow came across, it was the Portuguese dictator, António Salazar, whose nationalist-socialism attracted him most, because of what Salazar had managed to achieve with the limited human and material resources at his disposal.[26]

At Hertzog's urging, Pirow chose to demonstrate the Union's growing regional influence by expanding SAA, whose fleet of Junkers aircraft were acquired from Germany, in order to challenge the services, trade routes and reputation of Britain's financially troubled Imperial Airways. By 1939, SAA, the first national airline in Africa, had won the regional battle for air supremacy.[27]

For most of the economically straitened 1930s, any plans for expanding the country's military capacity was constrained by the Fusion government's lack of enthusiasm for defence expenditure. Mindful of the possibility of attacks from the air, Pirow devoted most of his limited military budget to building up the country's air force. His plans for land defence were far less conventional, however. To protect the northern provinces from possible invasion via Lourenço Marques (today Maputo), he designed a 'bushcart', drawn by oxen, to supplement the UDF's fleet of elderly military lorries, last used in WWI. His invention became the object of universal derision, especially by critics of his pro-Hitler inclinations. Yet, according to Meiring, a motorised version of Pirow's 'bushcart' was used successfully by Springbok troops in the invasion of Italian-held Somaliland.[28] And the military historian Ian van der Waag takes the view that despite or because of Pirow, South Africa's defences reached a peak in 1939 and were in 'a better state of preparation than at any other time in its peacetime history'.[29]

If Pirow's admiration for National Socialism and his authoritarian traits made him deeply suspect in the eyes of pro-war supporters, they failed to endear him to the HNP leadership too. Malan was prepared to tolerate the New Order as a useful pro-republican pressure group within his party caucus, but soon came to regard Pirow's followers as a divisive influence. At the HNP's Transvaal congress in August 1941, Malan forced through a motion stating that membership of another political organisation was no longer permitted. This effectively put an end to the New Order's propagandising within the HNP in favour of a one-party state.[30]

A disenchanted Pirow and his supporters responded by establishing the New Order as a separate political party, while continuing to associate with the HNP and attend its caucus meetings. But after Malan in the Cape and Strijdom in the Transvaal openly denounced the Nazis, the New Order withdrew from the HNP altogether. Pirow declined to stand in the election of 1943, though several of his New Order colleagues did and were heavily defeated. The subsequent collapse of the New Order put an end to the colourful political career of Oswald Pirow.

Hertzog resigns

Strange though it may seem, the principle of English-Afrikaner equality proved to be the rock upon which the HNP's *hereniging* finally foundered. At the party's Free State congress in December 1940, Hertzog's proposed programme of principles – strong on language parity but weak on republicanism – was summarily rejected as the basis for discussion. Realising that the majority of delegates were against him, for the second time in his career, the furious Free Stater stormed out of the party congress, accompanied this time by a small group of followers. In an angry message to his erstwhile supporters, Hertzog warned them not to expect Hitler to bring about their salvation: 'Germany is fighting her own battles. I am not one of those persons who say: "Let the Germans come to South Africa and all will be well." A jingo is always an intolerable person, whether he is English, German or Afrikaans. We must rely on ourselves,'[31] he declared.

Sensing a shift in the wind, Malan chose not to intervene on Hertzog's behalf this time, bringing their temporary alliance in the HNP to an abrupt end. Soon afterwards, a deeply disillusioned Hertzog resigned his parliamentary seat and retired from public life. It must be one of the great ironies of South African political history that the man who had fought so strenuously against all things 'English' all his life had been forced into retirement because of his principled support for the language rights of English-speakers.

Introducing a motion in Parliament that his old foe and colleague be paid a state pension, Prime Minister Smuts said:

> During a great part of my career I was his opponent, but I was always aware of his honesty and uprightness and that he strove always for the good of his country and his people ... In the midst of our bitterest political struggles, our relations were always of the best ... Throughout his political career General Hertzog never thought of himself and never provided for himself. I hope the tradition of General Hertzog will be the tradition of South Africa – a tradition that will guard the country against corruption in public life.[32]

Final twist

Hertzog's career was to take a bizarre final twist. Embittered at being rejected by his own people, he turned his back on democratic politics. Still under Pirow's influence, he declared at a meeting of the Afrikaner Party in October 1941 that National Socialism was most suited to the moral and religious outlook of the Afrikaner. 'Never again and under no circumstances,' he said, 'will I again take part in a political system calculated only to satisfy the vanity, greed and lust for power of individuals and groups of individuals at the expense of national interests. I am still willing to save my country, but apart from the morass of party politics.'[33] Denouncing 'liberal capitalism', with its unrestricted economic competition, as being responsible for the destruction of the Boer republics and the impoverishment of Germany, the elderly leopard made it apparent that he had never really changed his spots.

Little over a year later, on 21 November 1942, a lonely and ailing Hertzog died at the age of 76. Mourned across party lines, he was widely if not universally acclaimed as having been the true leader of Afrikanerdom. As his fellow Afrikaner, DW Krüger, wrote of him, whatever history might say of Hertzog, he had always remained true to his core beliefs throughout his political life, and had led his people from political and cultural inferiority to equality with their fellow (white) South Africans.[34]

Elsewhere in the World

In 1939

13 January	71 people die in Victoria, in one of Australia's worst-ever bush fires
27 January	Hitler orders Plan Z, a five-year expansion plan for the German navy
March	Arab Revolt ends in Palestine
28 March	Francisco Franco takes power in Spain, ending the Spanish Civil War
7 April	Italy invades Albania
23 August	Molotov-Ribbentrop Pact signed between Soviet Union and Germany
1 September	Germany invades Poland
2 September	Britain, France, Australia, New Zealand and India declare war on Germany, followed by Canada on 10 September
17 September	Soviet Union occupies eastern Poland
30 November	Soviet forces invade Finland
13 December	Battle of the River Plate

CHAPTER 8

'By Their Fruits …'

While one section of white South Africa prepared feverishly for involvement in the war, the other section was caught up in a fratricidal struggle for the soul of Afrikanerdom. Of particular concern to the Smuts government – and eventually to Malan's HNP – was the upsurge in support for the paramilitary, pro-German Ossewabrandwag (Ox-Wagon Sentinels, OB). Unwilling to wait for a German victory that would put an end to South Africa's ties with Britain and hasten the advance of an Afrikaner-led republic, thousands of militant Afrikaners joined the OB in the hope of bringing about the downfall of the Smuts government.[1]

Founded in early 1939, a few months before the outbreak of war, the OB's ostensible purpose was to promote and enhance Afrikaner culture: its true aim, however, was to bring about a one-party, National-Socialist republic. From the outset, the organisation's cultural and political activities were inextricably intertwined. Hand in hand with the nurturing of patriotism through festivals, homage to heroes, youth camps, public lectures and jukskei tournaments went active resistance to the UDF's recruitment of young Afrikaners to fight for their country. In October 1940, in response to Nationalist concerns about its activities, the OB came to a modus vivendi with Malan – known as the Cradock Agreement – that the HNP would function as a political party and the OB would keep out of politics.[2] The agreement was to be honoured more in the breach than in the observance.

Torchlight parade by the Ossewabrandwag, led by Commandant-General JF 'Hans' van Rensburg (centre).
STELLENBOSCH UNIVERSITY

Though claiming to be a 'cultural organisation', the OB based its activities on the old Boer commando system. Its 'commandant-general' was supported by an array of 'officers' who oversaw a pseudo-military structure that included separate men's, women's and youth wings. Such was the enthusiasm for the OB that at its peak it had a membership of well over 300 000 (more than twice the number of UDF volunteers), with branches in every corner of South Africa.[3]

The OB's first commandant-general was Colonel JC Laas, a farmer, part-time soldier and devotee of Adolf Hitler. Widely considered to be out of his depth, Laas was replaced before long by a far more substantial figure, the 43-year-old Dr JFJ (Hans) van Rensburg. As a 16-year-old, Van Rensburg had taken the government's side in the Afrikaner rebellion of 1914, but the appalling spectacle of Afrikaner shooting Afrikaner had made him determined that such a tragedy should never happen again.[4]

A brilliant academic with a magnetic personality, Van Rensburg was just 37 when he was appointed provincial administrator of the Orange

Free State by the Fusion government. At the outbreak of war, he was also the part-time commanding officer of a brigade in the UDF. Yet as a fervent believer in National Socialism, he was not prepared to serve under a Smuts-led government; and so, after biding his time, he resigned as Free State administrator and as a member of the UDF in order to become commandant-general of the OB on 1 January 1941.

Despite some OB members, especially in the Cape, being more anti-British than pro-German and not in favour of violent subversion or sabotage, under Van Rensburg's leadership the organisation became more politically active and militant. At the heart of its operations, under the overall authority of the commandant-general, were the Stormjaers (Stormtroopers), an avowedly terrorist unit that embarked on a campaign of violent civic disruption, which included the bombing of post offices, electricity pylons, power lines, banks and shops, and the beating up of Jews and UDF soldiers. The unit's head, for a time, was one Steve Hofmeyr, former captain of the University of Cape Town's first rugby team, Rhodes Scholar and Oxford Blue, and grandfather of the current pop singer of the same name. The multitalented and secretive Hofmeyr was regarded with awe by Van Rensburg, as much for his cold-eyed fearlessness as his ability to mix easily with unsuspecting English-speaking civil servants at the Pretoria Club.[5]

Internment

Given his experience at the hands of pro-republican Afrikaner rebels in 1914, Smuts was taking no chances this time. Within days of becoming minister of defence, and without obtaining parliamentary approval, he announced emergency regulations empowering him to detain any person suspected of being a threat to state security. To further discourage insurrection, all rifles in private hands had to be handed in immediately to the authorities, a precaution that resulted in the confiscation, within a few months, of almost 90 000 firearms. These regulations were approved retrospectively – in the face of furious HNP protests – once Parliament reconvened in early 1940.

An American secret agent, quoted by Keith Shear, observed that no

A propaganda poster in support of the war effort.
DITSONG MUSEUM OF MILITARY HISTORY, JOHANNESBURG

department posed a greater threat to the Smuts government than the body primarily tasked with upholding law and order, the South African Police (SAP): 'Many lower-ranking white policemen, a large majority of whom were Afrikaners, were anti-war, but many more resented unpopular duties like executing internment orders.' Police officers were often involved in shielding fifth-column activities.[6]

Internment revived memories of Kitchener's concentration camps during the Anglo-Boer War, and aroused strong emotions among anti-British Afrikaners. Yet it was the government's primary duty to maintain law and order, and it had no other effective counter to the undermining and sabotaging of the country's war effort, not only by militant Afrikaners but also by German spies, agents and provocateurs. Far more was at stake than just white South African unity: while an embattled Britain struggled to keep the Germans at bay in Europe, the Union's mineral wealth and the security of the Cape sea route were crucial to the Allies, and had at all costs to be kept out of pro-Nazi hands.

By September 1941, approximately 4 000 militants and enemy nationals were being held in five internment camps in the Transvaal and Free State. The largest of these was at Koffiefontein, which housed 800 anti-war militants. Among the internees were the future Nationalist prime minister BJ (John) Vorster; his younger brother Koot, a Dutch Reformed minister later jailed for three years under the Official Secrets Act; and the future Bureau of State Security chief in the 1970s, Hendrik van den Bergh.

John Vorster at the time was a leading figure in both the Afrikaner Broederbond and the Ossewabrandwag. In 1942, he declared unambiguously: 'We stand for Christian Nationalism which is an ally of National Socialism (Nazism). You can call such an anti-democratic system a dictatorship if you like. In Italy it is called Fascism, in Germany National Socialism and in South Africa "Christian Nationalism".'[7] Denouncing Britain as the enemy, the truculent eastern Cape lawyer called for closer ties with the Third Reich.[8] In the 1948 election, he would be rejected as an HNP candidate because of his extreme views.

Vorster's experience in detention obviously taught him well: two decades later, as HF Verwoerd's minister of justice, it was Vorster who put the pernicious 90-day and 180-day detention-without-trial laws on the South African statute book.

Violence and sabotage

In platteland towns and on city streets, the outbreak of war had brought about a tense, highly charged atmosphere in which outbursts of fighting between white civilians and random acts of violence and sabotage were commonplace. For that, the activities of the OB, and particularly the Stormjaers, were primarily responsible. According to Albert Blake's *Wit*

Terroriste, the extremist wing of the OB had as many as 9 000 members, some 8 000 based in the Transvaal, 850 in the Free State and a handful in Natal and the Cape.[9] Its leaders rationalised their treasonous activities by claiming that, in forcing the government to keep many hundreds of UDF soldiers at home to counter disruption, the OB was actually saving the lives of Afrikaners who might otherwise be sent to the front.[10]

The OB's sabotage campaign reached its peak in 1942, when two OB members were sentenced to death for blowing up the Benoni post office, causing the death of a passer-by.[11] The pair were spared the noose by Smuts, who wisely decided against giving any further boost to Afrikaner martyrdom, having learnt his lesson from the execution of Captain Jopie Fourie in the Afrikaner rebellion of 1914–1915. As soon as the Nationalists came to power in 1948, the two men were released from prison.[12]

The 'Shirts'

The war had also brought new recruits to the various far-right 'Shirt' movements, which had emerged in the 1930s when disoriented and openly anti-Semitic right-wing Afrikaners, impatient with parliamentary democracy and dismayed by Fusion, set out to 'replace nationalism with fascist and racist ideologies'.[13] Their ranks included Manie Wessels's Blackshirts, popular among poor Afrikaners in the Transvaal, and Louis Weichardt's better-known Greyshirts, a Christian National Socialist organisation, never more than 2 000 strong, whose logo was a swastika in the colours of the South African flag. Allied fringe groups included the South African Fascists, led by former Greyshirt leader Johannes Strauss von Moltke, who had broken from the organisation after being accused of financial irregularities and consorting with a Jewish woman,[14] and Cape National Party secretary FC Erasmus's Oranjehemde (Orange shirts), a 'militant shock troop' of young Afrikaners.[15]

The 'Shirt' movements, according to ES Munger, had 'a superficial quality, their vitality vitiated by their distance from the source in Europe'.[16] Their significance lay not in their numbers but in their members' attempts to present themselves as the torchbearers of Afrikaner Nationalism, and in the pressure they exerted on the right wing of Malan's HNP, whose Transvaal caucus had gone so far as to ban Jews from party membership in 1937.[17] Attempts by the Greyshirts in the early stages of the war to forge a 'national, anti-liberal, anti-communist front'[18] with the HNP foundered on Malan's fears of being tainted by Nazism, and his determination to remain loyal to the country's parliamentary system.

The OB wanes

The OB's commitment to armed subversion and its rapid growth among young Afrikaners became a cause of real concern to Malan and the HNP, which found itself, ironically, having to defend the democratic system that many Nationalist spokesmen denounced for having been captured by 'British-Jewish-Capitalist-Imperialist-Masonic influences'.[19] Though initially sympathetic to the OB's broad aims, Malan soon came to regard the organisation (and Pirow's New Order) with aversion – and mounting alarm. He not only disliked their fascist leanings but also suspected, rightly, that OB leaders were out to displace the HNP as the political home of Afrikanerdom.[20]

In what Malan described as one of the three most difficult decisions of his life (the others being choosing to leave the church for politics and whether or not to support Fusion), he decided to bring the OB to heel.[21] After Van Rensburg reneged on his undertaking not to engage in politics and expressed his contempt for Parliament, the HNP leader brought matters to a head at the party's Transvaal congress in 1941, demanding that the OB cease its politicking forthwith. When Van Rensburg pointedly refused, the HNP hierarchy decided that office bearers of the party could no longer be members of the OB, and ordered members to resign from a movement 'tinged with foreign ideologies'.[22] In branding the OB's ideas as un-Afrikaans, Malan found ready support from Calvinist conservatives in the Dutch Reformed Church and from HNP-supporting newspapers.[23] It was not long before enthusiasm for the OB began to wane, especially after the fortunes of war began to turn against Hitler.

Robey Leibbrandt

Afrikaner anger at Smuts, and the widespread belief in 1940–1941 that a German victory was imminent, induced many Nationalist MPs to use the kind of inflammatory language in public that most countries would regard as being treasonous.[24] It also led to right-wing subversion becoming accepted as a means of demonstrating opposition to the beleaguered government. The most extreme example was Operation Weissdorn (Hawthorn), a plot hatched by German intelligence attempt, involving one Robey Leibbrandt, to assassinate Smuts and other leading politicians and industrialists – including Sir Ernest Oppenheimer – and stage a military coup with the assistance of the OB's Stormjaers.[25]

Robey Leibbrandt was born to an Afrikaner father of German descent who had fought alongside Smuts in the Anglo-Boer War, and an Irish mother. Adventurous and seemingly fearless as a boy, the young Robey matriculated at Grey College in Bloemfontein, where he excelled at various sports, most notably boxing. After school, he underwent training in the police, army and railway police.[26] Chosen to box for South Africa at the Berlin Olympics in 1936, he was mesmerised by the oratory of Hitler during the opening ceremony. As Hans Strydom records, '[Leibbrandt] would never forget the day he marched past the Führer. "I don't know what happened to me at that moment," he said years later, "but an hypnotic power controlled me. At the sight of Adolf Hitler, it felt as if my Irish-German blood exploded in my Afrikaner heart."'[27] Returning after the Olympics to study at the Reich Academy for Gymnastics in Berlin, he became a fanatical supporter of National Socialism.

Having chosen to remain in Germany after war broke out, Leibbrandt volunteered for service in the Wehrmacht (armed forces), becoming a paratrooper and glider pilot – the first South African to do so.[28] He was also given training in irregular warfare and sabotage before being persuaded to return to South Africa to take part in Operation Weissdorn. In June 1941, Leibbrandt was landed on the remote Namaqualand coast by rubber boat from a captured French sailing yacht. Going under the name Walter Kempf, he soon established links with the Stormjaers, and had no fewer than three meetings with an unsympathetic Hans van Rensburg, whom he threatened with assault at their final meeting.[29]

Snubbed by Van Rensburg, who drew the line at a German-inspired civil insurrection, Leibbrandt successfully recruited to his side some 60 of the most fanatical Stormjaers, whom he formed into a paramilitary force, the Nationalist Socialist Rebels (NSR), which successfully sabotaged power lines, railway tracks and other infrastructure targets across South Africa. Fearing that the rebels' activities might force the authorities into taking drastic action against the OB, Van Rensburg decided to inform the government, secretly, of Leibbrandt's presence in South Africa, and to reveal the latter's aims and intentions.[30]

An unattractive and bombastic personality, Leibbrandt revelled in his role as the undercover leader of the NSR, publishing inflammatory pamphlets and daring the authorities to catch him. But his recklessness put off even some of his own followers, who began to suspect he was out to take over the Stormjaers and even the OB.[31] By now, his plans to assassinate Smuts and spark off a national uprising had become known to the police, some of whom were Stormjaer sympathisers and showed little inclination to track down Leibbrandt and arrest him. But loyalists within the police, notably the intrepid Captain Jan Taillard, were given orders to uncover the NSR's formidable stockpile of weapons, guard Smuts, and capture Leibbrandt before he could embark on an audacious campaign to sabotage the nation's railway communications, due to begin in 1942.

Leibbrandt's recklessness was to prove his undoing. Taillard, one of the few senior policemen whom Smuts knew he could trust, had been instructed earlier to resign from the SAP, ostensibly because of his opposition to the war, but actually to prepare himself for counterinsurgency operations should they become necessary.[32] Working his way – at great personal risk – into Leibbrandt's confidence, Taillard eventually led the unsuspecting rebel leader into a police trap outside Pretoria on Christmas Eve 1941. At his trial in the Pretoria Supreme Court, Leibbrandt refused to give evidence. He was convicted of treason and sentenced to death. Smuts commuted the sentence to life imprisonment on the grounds that he had fought alongside Leibbrandt's father, Meider, one of the bravest of his comrades in the Anglo-Boer War.

By now, Van Rensburg's disapproval of the unauthorised activities of the Stormjaers, and of Leibbrandt's NSR, had made him suspect in the eyes of Afrikaner right-wingers, who regarded it as odd that the organisation had not been banned and its leader interned, especially after the HNP and the OB had parted ways. The United States also found the government's forbearance hard to understand. 'The most striking of many anomalies of the Union of South Africa,' an intelligence report noted, 'is the fact that while it is allied with the other United Nations in the fight to the finish against Hitler, it permits its local brand of Hitlerism to thrive virtually unchecked. Still on the loose are its local "fuehrer" and all but a few of his followers, although their declared objective is the overthrow by revolutionary means of the government now in power.'[33]

The government's tolerance of the OB may be attributed to Smuts's shrewdness in not overplaying his hand against Van Rensburg.[34] Such was the depth of HNP enmity towards the OB that once the party's formidable propaganda machine had turned against the organisation, there was no longer any need to outlaw the fringe organisation or intern its leader. As Harry Lawrence famously declared, 'Instead of the government having to ban the OB, Dr Malan has done it for us.'[35]

In due course, the end of the war was to take Van Rensburg completely by surprise. His faith in the size and precision of the German military machine had led him (and his followers) to believe in the certainty of a German victory. Hitler's eventual capitulation and the rout of the German armed forces were to come as a devastating shock to him and what remained of the Ossewabrandwag.[36]

Elsewhere in the World

In 1940

8 January	Food rationing begins in Britain
5 March	Massacre of 22 000 Polish officers and intellectuals by Soviet secret police at Katyn
9 April	German troops occupy Denmark and invade Norway
10 May	Winston Churchill succeeds Neville Chamberlain as British prime minister
11 May	German forces invade Belgium, Netherlands and France
27 May–4 June	340 000 Allied troops evacuated from Dunkirk
10 June	Italy declares war on Britain and France
22 June	France and Germany sign armistice: France is divided into occupied and unoccupied zones
July	1 SA Infantry Brigade under Brigadier Dan Pienaar leaves for East Africa
July–August	Battle of Britain
20–21 August	Leon Trotsky assassinated
8 November	Franklin D Roosevelt defeats Wendell Wilkie in US presidential election
15 October	Charlie Chaplin's wartime satire *The Great Dictator* is released

CHAPTER 9

Fights and Strikes

In early 1941, Britain stood alone in Europe. The Low Countries, Denmark, Norway and much of Eastern Europe had succumbed to Hitler. Half of France was occupied by the Germans and the other half governed by Marshal Pétain's collaborationist Vichy regime. France's cave-in to Germany and the entry of Italy into the war had tilted the balance of military power in favour of the Axis countries. Hitler now had treaties guarding his flanks with the Soviet Union, along the Mediterranean and in Spain. In the Far East, Britain's possessions were under threat from an aggressive, expansionist Japan.

The British had been counting on the French as an essential partner in North Africa as much as in Europe.[1] In France's absence, Britain's military presence in Egypt and East Africa was now being threatened by the much larger Italian forces stationed there. For South Africa, a once-distant conflict had moved disconcertingly close: its northern provinces – and gold mines – were now within reach of Mussolini's medium-range bombers.[2] The UDF found itself having to take the lead in neutralising the Italian presence in Africa.

Smuts took up the challenge with relish: the preceding year had given him time to repair some of the country's woeful military deficiencies. His untiring efforts, coupled with a rapidly industrialising economy, enabled the UDF to send a credible force of 27 000 men – one division and two brigades – fully equipped with South African-manufactured tanks, armoured cars, trucks and motorcycles, to take on the Italians in East Africa.³ The motorised brigade was a successor in kind to the mounted and highly mobile Boer commandos of old.⁴

In December 1940, shortly before a British-led counteroffensive against Italian forces in Abyssinia and Somaliland could get under way, Brigadier Dan Pienaar's 1st South African Infantry Brigade joined forces with troops from the Gold Coast to overrun El Wak, a key fortress along the border between Italian Somaliland and Kenya. In simultaneous engagements with a much larger Italian air force, the SAAF inflicted serious damage on enemy aircraft and ground installations nearby.

From Kenya, Pienaar's men – accompanied by other African units – advanced swiftly through Somaliland and the Sudan into Abyssinia, whose capital, Addis Ababa, was captured on 5 April. Several thousand Italians were taken prisoner and transported back to South Africa. Having broken the back of Axis power in East Africa by mid-year, the UDF command turned its attention to the North African desert, where the British Eighth Army was preparing for battle with Rommel's Afrika Korps, which had been forced to come to the aid of the embattled Italians.

Back home, pro- and anti-war sentiment often ran high as news filtered back from the war front. There were clashes countrywide as frustrated soldiers, kept on standby to quell any incipient revolt by anti-war elements, ran up against university students spoiling for a scrap in places like Potchefstroom, Pretoria and Port Elizabeth. The firing of the noon-day gun in Cape Town, at which citizens were asked to observe a two-minute silence and pray for an Allied victory, caused particular offence to Nationalist supporters and sparked off intermittent clashes between soldiers, policemen and students of Stellenbosch University.

One such incident was the 30-minute outbreak of fighting that erupted in central Cape Town when two Maties students provocatively ignored the two-minute silence and were set upon by soldiers. It had an ugly sequel in Stellenbosch later that night. Some local coloureds allegedly jumped the

Italian prisoners of war march past South African troops following the fall of Amba Alagi, the last Italian stronghold in Eritrea, May 1941.
MIRRORPIX/MIRRORPIX VIA GETTY IMAGES

queue outside a cafe awaiting delivery of the evening newspaper carrying a report of the fracas. Furious students, full of beer and armed with bricks and stones, went on a rampage against coloured people in the town, invading homes, whipping children and inflicting heavy damage on property and vehicles. The coloureds retaliated in kind and what became known as the 'Battle of Andringa Street' raged into the early hours of the next morning, until brought to an end by police reinforcements. An embarrassed university administration apologised and made attempts to mend the badly damaged relations with the community, but paid only a miserly £25 (around R25 000) by way of compensation to a messenger injured in the fighting. It was, recounts Hermann Giliomee in his autobiography, a 'shameful' episode.[5]

Screenings of pro-war propaganda newsreels in cinemas in country towns, such as 'General Smuts at the Front' or 'Springboks in the North', also sparked off outbreaks of fighting, which the police (hardly impartial themselves) struggled to contain. In retaliation for attacks by pro-war zealots on the offices of Afrikaans newspapers, German- and Jewish-owned businesses were attacked or set on fire. In Johannesburg on 31 January 1941, a pitched battle between soldiers and civilians outside the City Hall brought traffic in the city centre to a virtual standstill.[6]

Price controls

A more enduring problem throughout the war years was monetary inflation. As the inevitable shortages occurred, so prices increased.[7] In 1941, price controls were introduced for the first time in an attempt to counter the rapid rise in the cost of living. The process itself was arbitrary: the authorities would become aware of a looming shortage of a product and a price controller would then be appointed to freeze stocks and issue permits for purchase and sale.[8] Despite the stabilisation of producer prices by state intervention, the cost to consumers continued to rise as a result of a heightened demand for scarce goods, materials and war-related products and services. The importance of food meant that agriculture had to be afforded special protection: farmers were subsidised and agricultural marketing boards established to set minimum prices for wheat, maize, dairy produce, citrus and wine.[9]

Within a year, there were controls on petrol, oil, rubber, tin, paper, iron and steel, vehicles, soaps and oils, foodstuffs, building materials, non-ferrous metals, agricultural implements, machine tools, alcohol, glass, leather, medical requisites, timber and textiles. The general public, exhorted to make sacrifices for the war effort, grumbled unceasingly, and the government wisely decided not to try people's patience any further by enforcing food rationing.[10] If truth be told, though, South Africa was actually far better off than many other countries during the war: children evacuated from Britain wrote home to tell their parents about the plentiful diet of meat, vegetables and fruit they were enjoying in the Union.

Worker militancy

Another of the war's far-reaching consequences was the growing militancy – and political influence – of the African workforce, chiefly on the Witwatersrand but in the Cape and Natal as well. Labour unions, organised mainly by activists who were either orthodox communists (maintaining that revolutionary methods might differ from country to country, depending on circumstances) or Trotskyites (who believed in universal working-class solidarity and permanent worker-led revolution against the capitalist classes), had a radicalising influence on non-white political organisations that was most evident in Johannesburg and the other major cities. Most of the important African and coloured trade unions – on the mines, railways and municipalities and in the flour-milling, saw-milling and wholesaling industries – were affiliated to the Council of Non-European Trade Unions (CNETU), established in 1941.

Immediately after its formation, the CNETU embarked on a national campaign to increase its membership among trade unions large and small. From an initial membership of 37 000 workers in 25 affiliated unions, membership grew within five years to 158 000, from 119 affiliated unions countrywide.[11] Fortunately for the wartime economy, the CNETU was somewhat constrained by the Communist Party's reluctance to disrupt production after the entry of the Soviet Union into the war on the Allied side (see Chapter 12).

The labour union with the greatest political influence during the war years was the African Mine Workers' Union (AMWU), founded in 1941 by Gaur Radebe (a close friend of Nelson Mandela's) and Edwin Mofutsanyana. The AMWU's first president was the popular ex-teacher JB Marks, an executive member of both the ANC and the CPSA. Within three years, the AMWU's membership had reached 25 000, in spite of constant harassment by mine officials.

Mineworkers, as Tom Lodge points out, were one of the most difficult groups within the industrial labour movement to organise. Mostly migrants, recruited in their thousands from South Africa's tribal reserves and adjacent African territories, they were housed in tightly controlled compounds and locked into a labour market in which one employer, the Chamber of Mines, effectively controlled both recruitment and wages. As a result, pay levels were low, and the fixed price of gold and high capital cost of its extraction 'served to further rationalise the low-wage structure of the mining industry'.[12]

Not all industrial action was union-inspired. Despite being declared illegal in 1942, many strikes on the Witwatersrand were the result of general worker dissatisfaction at the decline in the real value of their wages because of increases in the cost of living. Labour unrest caused many employers to appreciate, for the first time, the value of trade unions as a preferable alternative to industrial anarchy. Ever since WWII, issues of union recognition, wage levels and working conditions have lain at the heart of every dispute between government, employers and workers in all sectors of the economy, and are still a staple of our politics today. It took the war to give the trade unions an influence over the economic life of South Africa that has never been relinquished.

War becomes real

Japan's entry into the war in late 1941 and the threat of its navy's penetration of Indian Ocean waters brought the reality of war – including possible invasion – much closer to home. By this time, the danger to shipping in the Mediterranean posed by the Axis powers had significantly increased the importance, to the Allies, of the Cape sea route. Naval defences along the South African coast were strengthened and nightly blackouts were enforced by wardens in every seaside town and harbour city. An American request to establish a naval base at Saldanha was turned down by Smuts, but a Seaward Defence Force was established at Saldanha Bay to carry out the difficult and hazardous task of clearing enemy mines laid along the main shipping route around the Cape.[13]

The threat of possible invasion gave added impetus to the governor-general's National War Fund. The Fund's purpose was to provide financial assistance

Pull together! – a wartime propaganda poster emphasises the shared nature of the war effort.
DITSONG MUSEUM OF MILITARY HISTORY, JOHANNESBURG

to the families of men fighting 'up north', to assist with their children's education, to help returning soldiers get back on their feet, and to sustain bereaved families. As Vera Back, one of 9 000 Women's Auxiliaries helping to support the war effort, recorded: 'Money was raised in the usual ways: bingo, cake sales, street collections, fairs, morning markets – and gambling.'[14]

South Africans of all races need little encouragement to gamble – especially when doing so was 'in the national interest'. Before the war, gambling in the Union (except for horse racing) was prohibited, but during the war years, the nationwide (and widely ignored) ban was unofficially lifted. Well-heeled patriots, especially in Johannesburg, rushed to the tables with enthusiasm. Roulette parties were held in clubs and private homes and sweepstakes of all kinds organised. Officialdom turned a blind eye to the fun and games as long as the profits (or most of them) went into the National War Fund.[15]

Holding the fort

As minister of defence, Smuts had to leave South Africa at regular intervals to visit troops in East and North Africa and confer with Allied military

Minister of Finance JH Hofmeyr ('Jan Tax') preparing to deliver a budget speech.
HISTORY AND ART COLLECTION/ALAMY STOCK PHOTO

chiefs. He could not have done so without the resolute support and exceptional administrative capabilities of his stand-in as minister of finance and acting prime minister, Jan Hendrik Hofmeyr, one of Afrikanerdom's most remarkable – and contentious – figures.

Born in Cape Town in 1894, Hofmeyr was a child prodigy, able to read Dutch and English by the time he was five. Matriculating at the age of 12, he was awarded a BA with first-class honours from the South African College (later the University of Cape Town) only three years later, coming first in the examination. For this achievement, he was awarded a Rhodes Scholarship, which he was unable to take up until he was 18. In the meantime, he read for a master's degree in classical studies.

After a brilliant academic career at Oxford, during which he won a double first, Hofmeyr returned to South Africa and in 1917 took up a professorship at the South African School of Mines and Technology, which in 1922 became the University of the Witwatersrand (Wits). Two years later, at only 24, he was chosen as the first principal of Wits. After five years in office, he was persuaded by the then prime minister Smuts to enter politics, and in 1924 was appointed as provincial administrator of the Transvaal at the age of 29. When Smuts was defeated later in the year, the incoming prime minister, Hertzog, invited Hofmeyr – who up to then had disdained party politics – to remain in office.

Parliamentary star

After a notably successful five-year term as provincial administrator, and as a firm believer in the need for closer Anglo-Afrikaner solidarity, Hofmeyr stood successfully for Parliament in 1930 on the ticket of Smuts's SAP. According to his colleague and friend Leslie Blackwell, 'No man, not even Botha or Smuts, entered Parliament with more prestige and panache than Hofmeyr.' His reputation for independence of mind was to make him a key figure in the coalition negotiations between Hertzog and Smuts in 1933, and the formation of the 'fused' United Party. It was not long before the neophyte politician was known as Parliament's most polished speaker and hardest worker.[16]

The high regard in which Hofmeyr was held is evident from his appointment by Hertzog to no fewer than three portfolios – education, interior and public health – in the new Fusion government. Within a matter of days, his exceptional administrative abilities and capacity for hard work had enabled him to master the business of running the three departments he had been given.[17]

As a politician, Hofmeyr was both the hope and despair of the small coterie of white liberals in South Africa.[18] A believer from his young days in the virtues of 'trusteeship', he once described the nation's core racial problem as 'the white man's fear of the economic advance of the black man, and of the growth of his political rights; the fear of black revenge, which prevents him from making any concession of power, [and] the fear that one day little brown children will play among the ruins of the Union

Buildings'. The key challenge, as he saw it, was to make 'South Africa safe for European civilisation without paying the price of dishonour to the highest ideals of that civilisation'.[19]

Hertzog's Native Bills of 1936, which put an end to the Cape African franchise, presented Hofmeyr with his first serious crisis of conscience. A chorus of protesters, which included the multiracial All African Convention (AAC), gathered in Bloemfontein; church leaders and white members of the public led by Sir James Rose-Innes, former chief justice of the Union, condemned the proposals out of hand and looked to Hofmeyr, the Fusion government's most liberal minister, to take the lead.

Hofmeyr did not let them down, speaking out strongly against the legislation in Parliament and refusing to vote in its favour. Hertzog, who did not like to be crossed, could not afford to dispense with Hofmeyr, however. Declaring that he would not regard opposition to his Bills as a vote of no confidence, the prime minister agreed to keep Hofmeyr in the cabinet, and Hofmeyr, rather surprisingly, said he was prepared to stay. A 'very much disturbed' Smuts made no effort to dissuade his protégé from speaking out against the Bills, but voted in favour of them himself.[20]

Speaking on the legislation in Parliament, Hofmeyr had this to say: 'I have always regarded trusteeship as implying that at some stage or another, the trustee is prepared to hand over the trust to his ward. I have yet to learn that the European trustee in South Africa contemplates any such possibility.' The legislation before the House, he asserted, was born of fear, of the desire to achieve (white) self-preservation, but he did not believe himself that self-preservation could be attained in such a way. White civilisation could only be preserved with the consent and goodwill of the non-European people: 'I know perfectly well that I am speaking against the feeling of the overwhelming majority of the members of this House. I know that I am speaking against the feelings of the great mass of the people of this country ... But these are matters on which the future must be left to judge.'[21]

As Paton records, Hofmeyr sat down in near silence. Members of his own party rose immediately to attack him.[22]

Three years later, Hofmeyr did eventually resign from the Fusion cabinet, over the nomination of one AP Fourie as a Native Representative to the Senate. 'Always a purist in matters constitutional',[23] he believed that Fourie was wholly unqualified for the position and his appointment was a gross violation of the spirit of the Union constitution. In September 1939, during the war vote, Hofmeyr was still on the UP backbenches and did not participate in the momentous debate. But no sooner had Smuts accepted Duncan's invitation to form a cabinet than the first person he turned to was Hofmeyr.

Knowing the younger man was as hard a worker as himself, Smuts imposed on Hofmeyr a heavy administrative burden, making him minister of finance, minister of education and, in due course, deputy prime minister. During the war, Hofmeyr sometimes held as many as six portfolios and never fewer than two. In Smuts's absence, he managed the government virtually single-handedly, freeing up the prime minister to concentrate on military matters and external affairs.[24] From 1941 to 1945, Hofmeyr was responsible for no fewer than 112 of the 241 Bills passed by Parliament. By the end of the war, the pressure had exacted a severe toll on his health.[25]

Parsimonious by nature, as finance minister Hofmeyr kept a tight control over government spending, which made him more enemies than friends. He found it intolerable that social-welfare schemes should apply to white people only, and increased expenditure on the other races wherever he could. His detractors claimed he did not spend enough, during his tenure, on the acquisition of more land for African settlement, and criticised him for extending benefits on a racially discriminatory scale. His supporters countered that, without Hofmeyr, none of these additional benefits would have been granted.[26]

For the duration of the war, Hofmeyr had effectively to prepare two budgets each year – one to fight the war, the other to combat and pacify an internal opposition that saw no need for war and thought the domestic interests of the Union itself were all that mattered.[27] Fortunately, the gold reserves of South Africa enabled the economy to withstand the strain of waging war on more than one front.

Elsewhere in the World

In 1941	
20 January	Franklin Roosevelt sworn in for third term as US president
1 March	Bulgaria joins the Axis Powers
11 March	US Congress passes Lend-Lease Act
6 April	Germany invades Yugoslavia and Greece
6 April	UDF forces under Major-General Brink occupy Addis Ababa; Dan Pienaar's troops sweep into Italian Somaliland
30 June	Hitler launches Operation Barbarossa – the invasion of the Soviet Union
1–2 July	South African divisions join Eighth Army in Egypt
14 August	Atlantic Charter signed by Franklin Roosevelt and Winston Churchill
8 September	Siege of Leningrad begins
12 November	Battle of Moscow begins
23 November	5th South African Infantry Brigade destroyed at Sidi Rezegh
7 December	Japanese surprise attack on US fleet at Pearl Harbor, Hawaii
8 December	USA declares war on Japan and Germany

CHAPTER 10

The ANC Awakens

Black South Africa found its political voice for the first time during the war years. A combination of circumstances, among them the social turmoil triggered by the war, the political demise of Hertzog – architect of the much-resented Native Bills of 1936 – and the signing of the Atlantic Charter by Franklin Roosevelt and Winston Churchill in August 1941, resulted in a more vehement condemnation of racial discrimination by a variety of organisations representing Africans, coloureds and Indians.[1] The ANC, reinvigorated by its new president, Dr AB Xuma, was the first to come forward with a series of policy proposals for postwar reconstruction that offered a radical alternative to white trusteeship, segregation and the prospect of apartheid.[2]

Throughout the 1940s, African nationalism metamorphosed steadily from ineffective protest motions into a political movement confident enough to challenge and resist the actions of the government of the day. The transformation was brought about by the efforts of trade unionists, the emergence of a younger and more militant generation of African leaders, and the infusion of new ideas from within the Union and abroad – as well as by the inability of white political parties to respond effectively to black demands and protests.[3]

On the eve of WWII, some 80 to 85 per cent of Africans, out of a population of 6.6 million, lived on the land. Around two million were labourers on white farms, while the majority eked out an existence in the impoverished native reserves.[4] In the late 1930s, this rural peasant class was for the most part 'thoroughly uninterested in the social and political causes that were increasingly capturing the attention of urban Africans'.[5] Political awareness was limited, too, among the swelling number of migrant and semi-migrant Africans looking for work in the towns and cities. Their primary focus was day-to-day survival in an environment hostile to their presence.[6]

Yet, thanks to mission schools and colleges scattered throughout the country, an African middle class had begun to emerge whose political loyalties lay mainly with the ANC. As Lodge writes, in contrast to the political lethargy of the previous decade, the 1940s were a period of political ferment, brought about by the upheavals that accompanied the 'massive' wartime expansion of the African working class.[7]

At this stage, most middle- to upper-class Africans, steeped in non-violent, Christian assumptions and having a broadly optimistic liberal faith in the inevitably of progress, still believed in the superiority of European culture, and in the goal of assimilation between white and black.[8] But their patience and confidence in the good intentions of whites had been sorely tested by the Hertzog legislation of 1936. Unlike during WWI, when the ANC had suspended agitation against the white government's policies and agreed to support the war effort, this time its attitude was less conciliatory. While support for Britain against Hitler's Germany was unequivocal – the Smuts-led government being regarded as a 'bulwark against an incipient pro-Nazi Afrikaner rebellion'[9] and thus the lesser of two evils – the ANC's backing for the UDF in WWII was made conditional on policy reforms. Recruiting for the armed forces was encouraged less than wholeheartedly. Yet Xuma and the ANC 'old guard' still nurtured the hope that if enough Africans demonstrated their loyalty to the flag, the government would duly respond in kind.

The All African Convention

The Native Bills of 1936, which removed Africans from the common roll in the Cape and entrenched the unequal distribution of land throughout South Africa, had created a segregated electoral system that made provision for three (white) Native Representatives in Parliament and a separate, 12-member elected Native Representative Council (NRC) with advisory powers. African reaction to the legislation was immediate but not very effective. In 1935, an attempt was made to unite black opposition to the impending legislation by launching an umbrella organisation, the All African Convention – in Bloemfontein once again – under the direction of the university professor and lay preacher Dr Davidson Don Tengo (DDT) Jabavu.

The AAC was intended to be a federation of African political, educational, business and cultural groups whose declared aim was 'to render all segregatory legislation unworkable'.[10] It brought together 'an astonishing coalition – ranging from elderly conservative rural African chiefs to young "coloured" Trotskyites from the Western Cape'.[11] For a time, the AAC was widely accepted by urban Africans as the 'political mouthpiece of the African people' and enjoyed the support of the ANC and the CPSA. But the movement was to founder over disagreements around strategy and the unwillingness of its leading members to shun the new political structures and venture beyond 'wordy protests, delegations and vague calls for African unity and days of prayer'.[12] The two organisations to benefit most from the AAC's lack of focus were the ANC and the Cape-based Non-European Unity Movement (NEUM).

A moderate voice

DDT Jabavu, South Africa's first black professor and for many years one of the country's foremost African spokesmen, was the son of the famous Tengo Jabavu, a prominent supporter of Cape politician WP Schreiner's protest in London at the provisions of the Union of South Africa Act of 1909. Educated at a Quaker school in the UK and at the University of London, in 1916 DDT Jabavu was appointed as the first member of staff at the University College of Fort Hare (later the University of Fort Hare), where he remained as professor of Bantu languages until his retirement in 1948. He also taught Latin, history and anthropology at the college.

Politically, Jabavu was a gradualist who accepted the principle of a qualified franchise for Africans as the stepping stone toward full citizenship on a common voters' roll. Such an outcome, he believed, would be achieved over time through persuasion and rational argument rather than confrontation and mass action. DDT was an outspoken opponent, however, of any steps to remove Africans from the voters' roll, and in 1935 joined Pixley ka Isaka Seme of the ANC in convening the AAC to coordinate opposition to Hertzog's proposed Native Bills.

In early 1936, Jabavu and a deputation from the AAC (which included AB Xuma) met on several occasions with Hertzog in Cape Town to discuss the pending 'Native legislation'. The delegation was firmly opposed to the abolition of the Cape franchise, but some members apparently agreed that a separate roll was preferable to the total abolition of the African vote. This led to Jabavu's being accused of endorsing the principle of a separate roll for Africans, an allegation that was to damage him politically, and one he always denied.

As a proponent of unity among all non-white people, Jabavu forged close links with coloured and Indian leaders, serving for a time as chairman of the NEUM. Like his father, he kept his distance from the ANC, but when the AAC and ANC became rivals for the votes of Africans, Jabavu was always among those in favour of reconciliation between the two organisations.[13]

Liftoff

Though its members would never admit it, the AAC's most significant political achievement was to reawaken a somnolent ANC, which had become almost moribund by the 1930s. At a Jubilee Conference in 1937, a small group of ANC activists, prominent among them its diligent secretary-general, the Reverend James Calata of Cradock, as well as the communists JB Marks and Moses Kotane, had inspired a revival in the organisation founded in 1912. Their efforts received the active support of the white Native Representatives in Parliament, the redoubtable trio of Margaret Ballinger, Donald Molteno and Edgar Brookes, all of whom shared the ANC's embracing of multiracial equality.[14]

Liftoff for the ANC really began in 1940, with the election of the 'intelligent, efficient and charming'[15] AB Xuma, a medical doctor, as president-general. Xuma gradually transformed what had been a run-down and dispirited organisation – whose main activity had been holding an annual conference – into an effective political movement.[16] Using some of his own money, he improved the ANC's financial position, drew the black intelligentsia into the movement, and established membership branches at grassroots around the country. Aiming to attract mass support among Africans, Xuma's special strengths were his organisational skills and determination to turn the ANC into a more tightly focused operation.

AB Xuma

Alfred Bitini Xuma was born in the then Transkei on 8 March 1893 and schooled at the Wesleyan mission school, Clarkebury. Helped by the Methodists, he left South Africa in 1913 to study in the USA. Working in menial jobs in the evenings to pay for his studies and upkeep, he gained a BSc from the University of Minnesota in 1920, and won admission to medical school in Milwaukee where he was the only black in the first-year intake. After two years there, he completed his medical studies at Northwestern University in Chicago. Without the financial help of white Americans, however, Xuma would never have been able to fund his studies, an experience that made him a lifelong believer in the value of multiracial cooperation.

After qualifying as a doctor in Britain as well, Xuma set sail in 1927 for South Africa, where he opened a practice in Sophiatown, Johannesburg, his home for the next 30 years. He quickly established links with the white liberal community, one of whose pillars, JD Rheinallt Jones, founder of the South African Institute of Race Relations, took a keen interest in his

Dr AB Xuma, who reinvigorated the African National Congress during the 1940s.
GETTY IMAGES

welfare.[17] Described by Heidi Holland as 'a stocky, autocratic man with a dynamic personality and a rags-to-riches history',[18] Xuma had married a vivacious and upwardly mobile African American, Madie Hall, who became the first president of the ANC's newly formed Women's League, which she headed from 1943 to 1948.

As Xuma's medical practice grew, so too did his political consciousness. Adamant that Western medicine was superior to African traditional healing, he defied local convention by treating white patients as well as Africans. He began also to participate actively in multiracial discussion groups, and his reputation as a leader among the black elite was boosted by a speech to a Christian students' conference at Fort Hare in 1930, in which he called on the Hertzog government to abandon racial segregation and introduce a common citizenship for all South Africans, whatever their race.[19] (At this time, it was generally accepted that a non-racial franchise would still be a qualified franchise.) Arguing for a multiracial dialogue in

South Africa, he proposed that educated Africans should take a leading part in the discussions.

Although also a deputy president of DDT Jabavu's AAC, Xuma felt far more attuned to the ideals of the ANC. Proposed by Calata, he stood successfully for election as the Congress's president-general at its annual conference in December 1940, winning narrowly by 21 votes to 20 over the incumbent, the Reverend ZR Mahabane. Under his leadership, a 'plaintive' ANC immediately began to assert more aggressively and confidently that every individual had rights, irrespective of colour.[20]

Not long after taking office, Xuma outlined his vision for the ANC in a manifesto entitled *The Policy and Platform of the African National Congress*. The document declared the ANC to be the mouthpiece of the African people of South Africa, and its aim 'to stand for racial unity and mutual helpfulness and for the improvement of the African people politically, economically, socially, educationally and industrially'.[21] Dismissed by implication was any notion that South Africa was a whites-only country.

The NRC

To Xuma and his followers in the ANC, the early years of the war offered fresh hope after decades of disillusionment.[22] For a brief period from late 1941, it seemed that the gap between African demands and government policy was at last narrowing. The early successes of the Axis powers had made the UP government aware that it might need black support, and Smuts and his like-minded ministerial colleague Deneys Reitz defied conservative white opinion by relaxing curbs on the movement of Africans and promising to arm black soldiers should circumstances demand it.[23] To Nationalist outrage, Smuts went even further by vowing to 'arm every Coloured and Native' if the country was threatened by a Japanese invasion.

During the early stages of the war, both the AAC and the ANC took a wait-and-see approach to the new arrangements for African political representation. Though opposed in principle to the system, both organisations understood they were competing for the allegiance of a relatively small elite. Some of the cream of the black intelligentsia – individuals such as Dr John Dube, first president of the ANC, the newspaper editors Selope Thema and RH Godlo, and the veteran Natal trade unionist AWG Champion – had already decided (back in 1937) to explore the possibilities offered by the Native Representative Council and stood successfully for election. Since then, the NRC had become regarded as the de facto third chamber of Parliament, its members adding the letters 'NRC' after their names in the same way that MPs did. According to Roth, ordinary Africans attached more status to the NRC than to any black organisation of that time, including the ANC.[24] Xuma himself declined nomination for the NRC, being unwilling to lend his support to a segregated institution.

In 1942, the NRC's ranks were significantly strengthened by the addition of Professor ZK Matthews of the law faculty at Fort Hare, and the outspoken Free State businessman Paul Mosaka. In the white Parliament, the liberals, Ballinger, Brookes and Molteno, had transformed the debate about 'native policy' from how the authorities should *control* Africans into how to *improve* the immediate and future welfare of Africans. Taken together, the new political arrangements meant that, for the first time in history and in a way that Hertzog never anticipated, African demands were 'continuously and accurately put' before the parliamentary representatives of white voters.[25]

Better days

Committed though he was to the policy of segregation, Smuts was prepared to heed Ballinger and her colleagues and consider policy reforms – and to bend the rules where necessary. Enhancing social-welfare benefits, he believed, would be easier than dealing with the more explosive issues of political reform and the recognition of trade unions.[26] The prime minister was also eager to secure more African support for the war effort. 'Native' policy was implemented with a new flexibility and influx controls relaxed for a short period in 1942, during which there was a dramatic fall in the number of pass law arrests. The secretary for native affairs, Douglas Smit, took it upon himself to call publicly for the elimination of the economic colour bar, declaring that whites and blacks in the country were so intertwined that a policy of segregation could never be carried out to its logical conclusion.[27]

At the same time, the government-appointed Social and Economic Planning Council (SEPC) began to devise plans for post-war reform, and a commission was set up under Smit's chairmanship to examine the socio-economic, educational and health conditions of urban Africans. Midway through the war, the Smuts government announced that black people would henceforth be included in all social-security schemes, and expenditure increased on African education, old-age pensions and unemployment insurance.[28] With real wages in the manufacturing sector rising sharply, black South Africans were enjoying greater freedom than ever before.[29] Moderate African leaders at last had grounds for optimism that political reforms might come through constitutional channels rather than demonstrations and mass protests.[30]

Atlantic Charter

In August 1941, Franklin Roosevelt and Winston Churchill signed the Atlantic Charter aboard the cruiser USS *Augusta*, off the coast of Newfoundland. Intended to pave the way for the US to enter the war, the Charter offered 'a blueprint for the future peace and security of the world' once the Nazis had been defeated. Among the Charter's eight principal points was the right of all people to self-determination. Though Churchill quickly backtracked on the anti-colonial implications of the Charter (principally because of its potential effect on India), arguing that it applied only to countries under German occupation, the declaration was taken at face value by black South Africa and had an immediate impact on the political debate.

Hoping it might provide the basis for an alternative to segregation, the ANC leadership seized upon the Charter at its 1942 conference, setting up a committee of 30 leading African intellectuals under the chairmanship of Professor ZK Matthews to examine its ramifications. Other significant decisions taken at the conference were to establish a youth wing of the organisation and launch a one-million-member recruitment campaign.

The ANC's Charter committee came to two main conclusions: first, that all people in South Africa had the right to choose the form of government under which they lived; and second, that the Charter's provisions applied as much to the blacks of South Africa as they did to people elsewhere in the world.[31] The ANC's formal response was set out in a comprehensive document entitled *African Claims in South Africa*, in two sections – 'The Atlantic Charter from the Standpoint of Africans within the Union of South Africa' and a 'Bill of Rights'. The latter called on a post-war South African government to abolish racial discrimination and grant Africans full franchise rights, freedom of movement, equal education, equal pay and access to property and social services.

On economic issues, it was acknowledged that African development involved more than direct political representation, the emergence of a black 'middle class' and the furtherance of trade unionism.[32] *African Claims* declared that a primary obligation of any government was 'to promote the economic advancement of the people under its charge'. As Walshe points out, no doctrinaire concerns were expressed about either socialism or nationalisation, but an explicit reference was made to nationalising the armaments industry.[33]

African Claims was subsequently adopted as the ANC's official policy at its annual conference of 1943, at which Xuma was re-elected to another three-year term as president.

Smuts's bind

The Atlantic Charter put Smuts, the much-respected internationalist, in a bind. He did not accept that the Charter was intended to regulate the *internal* affairs of sovereign countries, and was unable to reconcile its provisions with his fundamental belief in the merits of white 'trusteeship' in

South Africa. But in calling for a united war effort, and urging people of all races to 'stand together in the hour of danger', he acknowledged the need for post-war change. In a landmark speech to the Institute of Race Relations in early 1942 – widely reported in the black press – he accepted the permanence of Africans in the urban centres of South Africa. 'Isolation' had gone, he averred, and in failing to halt the influx of Africans into cities and towns, segregation had 'fallen on evil days … You might as well try to sweep the ocean back with a broom,' he declared.[34]

Social improvements had to be extended to all races, Smuts continued. It was 'an outrage' to speak as his Nationalist opponents did of a South African population of two million, when the country had over ten million people: 'That outlook which treats the African and native as not counting is making the ghastliest mistake possible … the native is the beast of burden; he is the worker when you need him; he is carrying this country on his back.' The concept of 'trusteeship' still had to be worked out, Smuts conceded, 'but it offered the only route to harmonious race relations'.[35]

In speaking so frankly, Smuts was making yet another rod for his back. His Nationalist opponents seized on his references to the failures of segregation as proof of his intention to encourage racial integration in the major cities. Liberal white and African leaders, on the other hand, challenged him to stand by his bold words and bring about political reform.[36] As Barber observes, the dilemma for the Smuts government was whether to abandon the concept of a white-dominated state, or to move slowly in the direction of a multiracial society with equal rights for all. Knowing that white voters would never countenance the latter, Smuts resorted to the frequent expression of liberal ideals without ever actually committing to them. While believing genuinely in the community of the world, it seems that some deep instinct within his psyche prevented him from believing in the community of black and white in South Africa.[37]

Elsewhere in the World

In 1942	
January	Japanese forces invade Burma
7–15 February	Fall of Singapore
May	SAAF and UDF take part in Allied invasion of Madagascar
6 May	US forces in the Philippines surrender to the Japanese
4 June	Battle of Midway
21 June	Fall of Tobruk; 10 000 South Africans taken prisoner
6–7 August	US Marines land on Guadalcanal in the Solomon Islands
23 August	Battle of Stalingrad begins
23 October–3 November	Montgomery's Eighth Army defeats Rommel at second battle of El Alamein
8–16 November	Operation Torch: Allied amphibious landings in French North Africa
22 November	Red Army completes encirclement of German troops at Stalingrad
2 December	Enrico Fermi, Edward Teller and Leo Szilard produce first self-sustaining nuclear chain reaction at the University of Chicago

CHAPTER 11

Seismic Shifts

In the 1940s, South Africa experienced its second Great Trek: the mass movement of thousands of Africans from the tribal reserves to urban areas in search of work. There was a simultaneous migration of job-seeking Afrikaners from the platteland to the mines. This seismic social upheaval, which began in 1935 and accelerated rapidly in the early 1940s after South Africa had gone to war, brought with it severe and seemingly intractable social problems[1] that would have imposed severe strains on any peacetime government, let alone one fighting on two fronts.

In the rural areas, black opposition to the Native Trust and Land Act of 1936, which prohibited the purchase of land outside the reserves, simmered on, encouraged by trade unionists in the CPSA and ANC. In the cities, tenants' organisations and squatter movements mobilised against rent-seeking landlords and local authorities, while transport companies were confronted by boycotting commuters. Afrikaner workers were especially unsettled by having to compete for lower-paid jobs on the mines, and for living space in the increasingly crowded cities. Protests, demonstrations and (illegal) strikes became commonplace.

As Dubow reflects, a consequence of this social disorder was the search it inspired for a 'new' South Africa, not only among Afrikaner and African nationalists but also among a third group – liberal or social democratic opponents of nationalism and fascism, whose ranks included 'intellectuals, reform-minded politicians and bureaucrats, as well as servicemen and -women'.[2] The growth in urban slums, squatting and crime, on the other hand, fired up political scientists and social engineers, especially the proponents of tighter segregation.

By early 1942, South Africa's economy was running fairly smoothly, despite shortages of some goods and materials. Gold production was still on the rise, and hundreds of new factories were turning out products for war use inside the country and abroad. As DW Krüger noted, 'the urge to produce served as a great impulse to industrial development'.[3]

Although agriculture was holding up quite well – except in the reserves – certain consumer items were in short supply, causing the government to redouble its efforts to persuade people to live more frugally. A shortage of wheat on the world market meant a prohibition on the baking of white bread – except in military and civilian hospitals – and the production of a coarser, unpopular 'standard loaf', which required less wheat. A subsidy on bread, introduced at the time, endures to this day.

Inexplicably, farmers were allowed to export sugar and maize – staples of the poor – notwithstanding the scarcity of both at home: the new agricultural boards were blamed. The greatest annoyance, however, was the shortage of meat, often unobtainable in the cities due to price controls but available in rural areas. In an attempt to alleviate the problem, the authorities tried in vain to persuade people to observe one day each week as a 'meatless day'.[4]

By now, hardly any aspect of South African life was unaffected by the war in one way or another. People's freedom of movement was restricted by a coupon-based system of petrol rationing, which limited car travel to 400 miles (640 kilometres) a month, while the building of private houses was discouraged.[5] To cap it all, thirsty drinkers were told that because of the country's duty to supply visiting convoys as well as the 'boys in the desert', sales of beer had to be cut by half.[6] The man in the street, unused to making material sacrifices, came to realise that every war has its price, and even staunch Smuts supporters were heard to grumble.

War at sea

During the war, an estimated 400 Allied convoys, numbering some 50 000 ships and carrying six million troops, rounded the Cape and called in at one of South Africa's seaports.[7] Cape Town's busy harbour was only one of several stopping-off points in South Africa for merchant shipping sailing up the Atlantic coast to Freetown, in Sierra Leone, the main assembly point in Africa for vessels bringing critical war materiel from the British Commonwealth – especially India.[8]

Worried about the effectiveness of the Allies' anti-U-boat measures in the North Atlantic and Mediterranean, the German command decided it had to disperse its navy in an attempt to slow down the worldwide movement of the enemy's seaborne supplies.[9] One way of doing so was to attack merchant-shipping lanes off the South African and Mozambican coasts. A secondary German naval objective was to complement the activities of Japanese submarines in the Indian Ocean.

German submarine attacks in South African waters began in mid-1942 and led to the sinking of nine merchant ships in two days.[10] Three months later, a more concerted U-boat offensive, Operation Eisbär (Polar Bear), got under way. By December 1942, eight U-boats had claimed no fewer than 53 Allied ships, weighing 310 364 gross tons.[11] The success of Eisbär led to further U-boat activity off Durban, as well as occasional opportunistic attacks by German submarines making their way via the Mozambique Channel to support Japan in Far Eastern waters.

By early 1943, effective countermeasures by the South African Navy and Royal Navy – aided by SAAF and Royal Air Force (RAF) aircraft – had persuaded the German naval commander, Admiral Karl Dönitz, that because of its remoteness from the main naval theatre in the North Atlantic, the southern African coast was not really a viable operational area. The result was a drastic reduction in U-boat activity. Nonetheless, by the war's end, German submarines operating in or near South African waters had sunk 114 Allied naval vessels and merchant ships, weighing a total of 667 543 gross tons. As Kleynhans notes, for a brief while, German

U-boats succeeded in throwing shipping off the coast of South Africa into confusion and disarray.[12]

The Italians

The influx of Italian prisoners of war (POWs) into South Africa, beginning in early 1941 with the arrival of 10 000 captives from East Africa, became a flood in 1942–1943 after the fall of bases in Somalia, Abyssinia and Libya to the Allies. The Italian POWs could not be taken to Britain because of the danger of sea travel through the Mediterranean, nor could they be housed in Egypt, so they were sent down the East African coast to South Africa, to be detained in camps vacated by UDF soldiers departing for the front. The largest of these camps was at Zonderwater, east of Pretoria, which became the biggest detention camp built by the Allies in WWII, and home to more than 100 000 Italian captives.[13]

Beginning as a temporary tented encampment, Zonderwater was rapidly transformed into a huge red-brick and wooden mini-city of 14 separate 'blocks', each containing four camps of 8 000 men. When completed, Zonderwater could accommodate a total of 112 000 POWs and contained 30 kilometres of roads, mess halls, theatres, schools, gyms, sports fields and other recreational facilities, as well a hospital with more than 3 000 beds.

The man who oversaw the construction and operations of Zonderwater was its commanding officer, Colonel Hendrik F Prinsloo, a close associate of Smuts who had been interned in a British concentration camp as a 12-year-old during the Anglo-Boer War. Prinsloo was aptly described as 'an officer gifted with extreme competence and humility'.[14] He ensured that the letter and spirit of the Geneva Convention were adhered to and allowed representatives of the Red Cross to visit the camp regularly. Thanks primarily to Prinsloo, who was decorated by the post-war Italian government, Zonderwater was a model of its kind.

A new idealism

Another noticeable feature of wartime South Africa, as Paton and others noted, was an upsurge in idealism. Men and women had concluded that the old world was not good enough and determined to build a better one. With Smuts's encouragement, an Army Education Service (AES), headed by the director of military intelligence, Dr EG Malherbe, a future principal of the University of Natal, and Leo Marquard, founder of the National Union of South African Students (Nusas), was established to impress upon soldiers not only what they were fighting *against*, but, more importantly, what they were fighting *for*.[15]

According to Malherbe, the AES sought to alleviate the boredom of wartime service by making troops aware of their country's many cultural, political and social assets, 'for the preservation of which they were prepared to sacrifice their lives'.[16] Michael Cardo reflects that the AES never sought to promote 'a sense of cultural imperialism'. It aimed rather to strengthen ties between moderate English- and Afrikaans-speakers, in the hope of diluting the exclusivist appeal of Afrikaner Nationalists imbued with fascist sympathies.[17]

The war had a profound impact on those soldiers, white and black, who went 'up north' to fight against Nazism and Fascism. For blacks, the experience of travelling outside segregated South Africa was 'profoundly liberating', while for many whites their encounter with a world far richer in culture than they had ever dreamt of 'made the social structures at home seem both mean and petty'.[18] The AES, in Paton's judgement, was highly successful in changing preconceived ideas and racial attitudes: 'Many white soldiers and civilians saw for the first time what white supremacy really did to black men and their hopes and aspirations'[19] and came to realise that non-white people were men and women of their own kind. 'It seemed,' wrote Paton, 'as though in fighting against evil, they could see more clearly the evil in themselves and society.'[20]

Not all men in uniform were converted, however: some emerged blinder and more colour-prejudiced than before.[21] Yet many more were to be found, in the 1950s, in anti-Nationalist (if not necessarily anti-segregation) movements such as the short-lived Torch Commando.

Wage demands

Responding to the demands of an increasingly urbanising population, AB Xuma's ANC began to press more insistently for opportunities for black workers in skilled and semi-skilled occupations, an abandonment of wage rates geared to migrant labour, and the payment of a living family wage. The ANC claimed, justifiably, that the low-wage structure of the gold mines and the persistent reliance on migrant labour was serving to depress wage levels in other sectors of the economy.

As usual, unskilled wage rates varied greatly between Cape Town, Durban and Johannesburg, each a centre of simmering industrial unrest. In response to worker protests, the government set up a series of Wage Board investigations in particular regions and industries – a development welcomed initially by the ANC as 'a progressive step'.[22] Although there were short-term gains in real incomes, before long wages began to lag behind the cost of living and a series of strikes broke out on the Rand and in Natal. Besides miners, these strikes involved municipal workers, milk distributors, coal transporters, and railway and dock workers. Instead of calling for further Wage Board investigations, the ANC resolved to press for a national minimum wage of £2 per week.[23]

Goaded by Nationalist allegations that 'communist-inspired' unrest and a rising crime rate were putting safety and security in the entire country at risk, and with elections looming, the Smuts government responded by toughening its stance. The War Measures Act of 1942 banned strikes and lockouts and allowed the minister of labour to intervene in any dispute deemed harmful to the war effort.[24]

Tobruk

If the enemy threat along the country's coastline was not evidence enough, the fall of Tobruk in the North African desert in June 1942 brought the harsh reality of the war home to South Africans. A few months earlier, two UDF divisions had been sent to reinforce the Allied Eighth Army, on the offensive against Axis forces led by Rommel along the Egyptian-Libyan border. The port and garrison fortress of Tobruk, a key Allied military stronghold on the Libyan seaboard, was defended by some 33 000 troops under the command of South Africa's Major-General HB Klopper.

Earlier in the desert war, a besieged Tobruk had been bravely held, mainly by Australians, against repeated attacks by Rommel's Afrika Korps. The port and military base had since become a symbol of spirited Allied resistance to the Axis armies. But the Allied military command had come to the conclusion that it was not in the Eighth Army's interests to hold on to Tobruk at too high a cost if it were to be encircled for a second time.[25] On 20–21 June, a surprise assault by Rommel – with far fewer men – by air, land and sea on the large Allied garrison at Tobruk forced Klopper and more than 30 000 Commonwealth troops, 10 000 of them South African, into a humiliating capitulation. Tobruk's huge fuel and ammunition dumps were now in German hands.[26]

The surrender of Tobruk was a devastating reverse for the Allies, both militarily and psychologically. Winston Churchill, visiting President Roosevelt in the White House at the time, was stunned and embarrassed by news of the loss, which he ranked alongside the fall of Singapore as one of the greatest Allied setbacks in the war.[27] Instinctively, he blamed Klopper, who, he grumbled, had 'got cold feet and waved the white flag twenty-four hours after the German attack began'.[28]

The surrender of Tobruk dealt a huge blow to South Africa's military prestige, for an entire division, containing some of the country's finest young men, had been lost to the enemy. Making matters worse, for many agonising months their families back home had no news of whether their fathers or sons were missing, captured or dead.[29]

Hard hit by this unexpected 'thunderbolt from the north', a dismayed Smuts 'took the news like a soldier'.[30] His Nationalist opponents, on the other hand, were elated: the Allies were on the back foot in the North

Atlantic, in Soviet Russia and now in North Africa – and a German victory in the war looked inevitable.

As Krüger records, the bad news from Tobruk had an immediate effect on the political atmosphere in South Africa. Supporters of the war became angrier, more determined, and more conscious of the presence of fifth columnists in their midst,[31] while their diehard opponents 'combined their sneers at Smuts with cheers for the Germans'.[32] The bitterness between the two sides intensified as soldiers and policemen who had taken the 'red oath' were mocked and jeered at by Nationalists for betraying their Afrikaner heritage.

No stranger to setbacks, Smuts turned crisis into opportunity. Two weeks after the fall of Tobruk, South Africa's most popular horse race, the Durban July, went ahead as scheduled. As soon as the day's racing was over, a squadron of armoured cars drove around the Greyville racecourse carrying placards proclaiming, 'AVENGE TOBRUK'. Loudspeakers and radio transmitters broadcast a message from the prime minister calling for volunteers to make good the UDF's losses in North Africa. There were bigger races ahead in Egypt, Smuts declared, and at stake was the future of South Africa itself.[33] His appeal produced immediate results: within a week, 5 000 more men had volunteered for active service. Soon after that, Smuts flew off to Cairo for a high-level Tobruk post-mortem and planning conference with Churchill.

Madagascar campaign

A military operation with a more positive outcome for the Allies in mid-1942 was the capture of Madagascar, an amphibious operation in which South African forces played a limited though important part. The huge and strategically important Indian Ocean island, a French colony under the control of the Vichy government, was regarded by Allied planners as an inviting target for the Japanese. Aided by SAAF aircraft based in Kenya, British forces seized the natural harbour and naval base of Diego Garcia on the northern tip of Madagascar in May, and were assisted by South

African infantry to overcome the Vichy forces holding out in the southern half of the island. Churchill described the success of the Madagascar operation as 'a model for amphibious descents' of this kind.[34]

The tide turns

As 1942 neared its end, the tide of war began to turn gradually but ineluctably in favour of the Allies. In October, Montgomery's Eighth Army, which included the 1st South African Infantry Division under the command of Major-General Dan Pienaar, inflicted a decisive defeat on the Axis forces at El Alamein; in Russia, the German advance was halted at Stalingrad; and in the Far East, an effective American counterattack against the Japanese was under way. As the confidence of the Axis powers began to wane, so too did right-wing Afrikaner hopes of a German victory. Nationalist Afrikaners, wrote DW Krüger, 'unwillingly realised they had placed their trust in false gods'.[35] Hitler's setbacks were bringing an untimely end to their wartime republican dream.[36]

CHAPTER 12

Opposed to Racism

The war rescued the tiny Communist Party of South Africa from irrelevance and obscurity. Wracked by internal dissension and rejected by black and white activists alike, by the early 1940s the CPSA's membership had plunged to fewer than 300 of the faithful. Founded in 1921 in the aftermath of the Bolshevik Revolution by radical working-class émigrés from Eastern Europe, the party was small but well focused, with a centralised, Leninist-style operating structure. Membership was confined initially to whites, and during the Rand mineworkers' revolt of 1922 the party's posters exhorted workers of the world to join in 'the fight for a White South Africa'. At its 1924 conference, the CPSA thought better of its racism, however, deciding that its revolutionary future lay among 'the natives',[1] on the premise that working-class unity transcended racial divisions.

Before long, the party had more black members than white and was putting out feelers to the more established ANC, led by Josiah Gumede. A socialist, deeply impressed by his encounter with the Soviet system, Gumede also believed in black pride and racial exclusivity. Until 1928, by which time three members of the party's central committee were black, the CPSA had put the emphasis on class solidarity. But in that year, the Comintern – the organisation founded in Soviet Russia in 1919 to advance the cause of revolution worldwide – decreed that South Africa represented a 'special type of colonialism', one in which the white capitalist class were not transient migrants but permanent settlers. A prerequisite for 'socialism', therefore, was the overthrow of white rule and its replacement by black majority rule. South African communists were directed by the Comintern to work with (and within) the ANC in order to transform it into a 'fighting nationalist revolutionary organisation against the white bourgeoisie and British imperialists'.[2]

This was more easily said than done. Unlike Gumede, many ANC leaders were most uncomfortable with a party founded on an alien ideology, which took its orders from the Kremlin and regarded its association with Africans as a means to the end of a communist (and anti-Christian) society. They may also have been deterred by the fate of CPSA activists who had fallen foul of Stalin's paranoid belief that the Comintern was riddled with spies from other countries. According to the future Kenyan leader, Jomo Kenyatta, the first black general-secretary of the CPSA, the 28-year-old Albert Nzula, had been dragged out of a meeting in Moscow at which Kenyatta was present, and put to death by Stalin's secret police.[3] The Soviet authorities attributed Nzula's death to pneumonia contracted while lying, inebriated and undetected, in the snow. Others believed he had become another of Stalin's millions of victims.[4]

A similar fate had befallen two white CPSA members, Maurice and Paul Richter, who went to Moscow to seek international support for revolution in the Union and never returned.[5] It took another 50 years before the SACP (as the CPSA had become) revealed what had happened to the brothers.[6] In the long run, despite frequent disagreements – some of them violent – the differences between the ANC and CPSA were subsumed in the common struggle against white supremacy, and the rivalry between the two became less important than the common ground between them.

In 1930, after urging his supporters to campaign in favour of a black republic, Josiah Gumede was replaced as ANC president by the ultra-cautious Pixley ka Seme. As ideological differences between 'nationalists' and 'socialists' grew during the worldwide economic depression of the

1930s, the ANC became almost moribund.⁷ And by 1940 the CPSA's influence had also declined markedly. Harassment by the state, especially by Hertzog's justice minister, Oswald Pirow, and attempts by Afrikaner workers and 'fascists' to capture the white labour movement hampered the party, which lost some of its recently acquired black supporters. The party moved its headquarters to Cape Town, which became the centre of communist activities – such as they were – in the country. But the ANC was in no better shape itself. Also riven by internal leadership disputes, by the end of the 1930s the organisation had virtually abandoned its opposition to Hertzog's segregationist legislation to the rival All African Convention.

Strained relations

As Philip Bonner points out, it was trade unionists rather than politicians who, in the 1930s, had spearheaded opposition to the Fusion government.⁸ In 1938, tired of working with white unionists, black trade-union leaders took the initiative in forming the pro-Africanist Council of Non-European Trade Unions. Three years later the AMWU was formed, under the leadership of JB Marks, a member of the executive of both the ANC and SACP. Along with fellow communists Moses Kotane and Dan Tloome, Marks persuaded a reluctant ANC to campaign more vigorously for a repeal of the pass laws and for a common franchise. The growing influence of the trio antagonised moderate Africanists within the ANC, however, who made unavailing attempts to have communists expelled from the organisation.⁹

Events in Europe put further strain on the relationship between the ANC and the CPSA: black South Africans were far more concerned with making ends meet than the looming threat of war on a far-off continent. Taking its cue from Moscow as usual, the CPSA roundly condemned the hostilities between Britain and Germany as 'an acute form of capitalist rivalry between British imperialism and Nazi Germany … for power, markets and colonies'.¹⁰ In so doing, the CPSA found itself in the disreputable company of the pro-Nazi Ossewabrandwag and the 'Shirt' movements, and party membership dwindled.[11]

The CPSA's anti-imperialist tune changed abruptly in mid-1941, when Hitler tore up the Molotov-Ribbentrop pact of 1939 and launched Operation Barbarossa, the military invasion of the socialist motherland. At this point, the Smuts government, Stalin's Soviet Union and the CPSA suddenly became unlikely bedfellows. With the CPSA switching to supporting the activities of the UDF, and whites having to welcome (and in some cases praise) their new ally, communism in the country took off as never before.[12]

Within a year, Moscow had established a diplomatic and commercial presence in South Africa, and members of a group calling itself the Friends of the Soviet Union (FSU) were addressing 'Defend South Africa' rallies across the country. In its recruitment drive for the UDF, the Springbok Legion, a servicemen's union that became radicalised by the communists, frequently shared a platform with the FSU and Medical Aid for Russia, both of which had close links to the CPSA.[13] Smuts's justice minister, Dr Colin Steyn, was persuaded to become a patron of the FSU, despite his sister Emmie's being head of the women's section of the Ossewabrandwag in the Cape, and turned down a request from the Dutch Reformed Church that the CPSA be banned altogether.[14] Even the SABC was caught up in the enthusiasm, allowing the communist anthem, 'The Internationale', to be aired on radio and a speech by CPSA leader Bill Andrews broadcast on May Day 1942.[15]

'Red peril'

Malan's HNP and their fellow travellers let no opportunity go by to exploit the 'red peril' for electioneering purposes, warning of the danger of allowing communism to 'spread like wildfire among our millions of natives'.[16] By late 1942, sporadic bus boycotts, labour strikes (frequently communist-inspired) and urban riots outside Pretoria and in Natal, in which black and white lives were lost, had forced the Smuts government onto the defensive. As the general election drew closer, pass law arrests resumed with greater frequency.

The CPSA's new-found respectability among whites brought about a rapid spurt in membership, which encouraged the party to contest elections for the first time since the 1920s. The party had to project a Janus-faced image, however, attempting to convince whites of its moderation while continuing to recruit black Africans into its ranks. Its policies were necessarily vague and ambiguous: in one extraordinary pamphlet entitled 'We South Africans', the CPSA went so far as to suggest confusingly that 'Africans may prefer a policy of total segregation under a socialist state'.[17]

An election looms

Optimism among African leaders that the Smuts government had become more 'liberal-minded' in 1941–1942 was brought to an end by the election campaign of 1943.[18] It was wartime, and besides the racial fears whipped up by the Nationalists, sharply rising prices and shortages of food, building materials and petrol were aggravating to white voters. On 19 January, Malan – by now the undisputed *Volksleier* (Nationalist Afrikaner leader) – went on the attack in Parliament, focusing on issues of economics and race and calling for any socio-economic improvements for other race groups to be accompanied by tighter segregation.[19] White unity had to be maintained and preserved in the interests of the whole population, the HNP leader claimed.

Smuts, whose conception of white trusteeship went much wider than Malan's, had to measure his response carefully. Knowing the majority of white voters would never agree to dismantle the segregationist system in operation since 1910, and still committed personally, even if uneasily, to Hertzog's 1936 legislation, he temporised once more, arguing that the material lives of black Africans could be substantially improved without any far-reaching extension of their political rights. In an interview with the Christian Council in early 1943, he professed great sympathy for Africans but spoke of the 'tremendous snags' involved in granting blacks parliamentary representation and asked the delegation 'to accept the will for the deed'.[20] To ANC leaders like Xuma, it was clear that prime minister and party were edging away from any significant reconsideration of 'native policy'. The legislative status quo was to be preserved, but there would be improved social welfare benefits for Africans.

Margaret Ballinger

In March 1943, the issue of race was put squarely before Parliament by the redoubtable Margaret Ballinger, as outspoken and courageous a politician as one Helen Suzman of a later time. Born in Scotland in 1896, Margaret came to South Africa eight years later – to Bloemfontein, where her father, John Hodgson, fought as a burgher against the British. Proud of her Free State heritage, Margaret Hodgson studied at Rhodes and Cambridge universities, before going on to teach history at Rhodes and Wits. Her academic career came to an end with her marriage to William Ballinger, a trade-union organiser sent out from Britain in 1928 to assist Clements Kadalie's Industrial and Commercial Workers' Union.

Elected as one of three Native Representatives to Parliament under Hertzog's segregationist legislation of 1936, Margaret Ballinger was a lifelong liberal who believed that a common society was the only route to long-lasting peace in South Africa. An eloquent speaker, always well prepared and in command of her facts, she and her colleagues Edgar Brookes and Donald Molteno had a political impact out of all proportion to their numbers, and 'stood head and shoulders above the great majority of their fellow parliamentarians'.[21] For the first time ever, members of the House had to listen to sustained criticism of the pass laws, the migrant-labour system, the paltry spend on African pensions, education and child welfare, and discriminatory pay scales based on race. And they did not like to hear it.

As her admiring colleague Dr Oscar Wollheim wrote in tribute: 'For 23 of her 86 years, Margaret Ballinger sat stoically and heroically through six months of every year … having to endure abuse, calumny, distortion of her words and often venomous attacks upon her personality. The worst moments must surely have been … when her well-reasoned, well-researched and documented approach to a question was completely ignored and answered by a torrent of emotional and racialistic prejudice … [She] was one of the brightest stars to shine in the intellectual and political ferment of South Africa.'[22]

Speaking in the House on behalf of the ANC and the NRC, in support of the findings of the Smit report into the socio-economic, educational and health conditions of urban Africans, Ballinger urged the Smuts government to align its policies with 'the country's industrial development, the needs and aspirations of the Native population, and the principles of the Atlantic Charter'.[23] Its current policies, she argued, ran contrary to the country's economic development, and its adverse effects on the 'native population' were morally indefensible. Antagonism between the races would only increase if the country refused to face up to the reality of a permanent African presence in 'white' areas.[24]

Smuts appreciated the task entrusted to Ballinger and her colleagues and valued their attempts to keep his administration's feet to the fire on 'native policy'. But, ever the pragmatist, his heart was never allowed to rule his head. While admitting to the shortcomings of the government, he pleaded in exoneration the immensity and speed of the required social changes and the impossibility of dealing with them all at once – and in wartime. As he confessed in the House:

> In the meantime we have to resort to these makeshifts, we have had to use these dodges – that is all they are – and I know that on the benches of the Native Representatives there is a great deal of impatience which is almost becoming intolerance, but the goodwill is there. The difficulty is in a very short time to meet situations which have come upon us all of a heap within a couple of years owing to conditions over which we have not had control.[25]

The departure of the minister of native affairs, Deneys Reitz, to London as high commissioner in 1943 brought Major Piet van der Byl into the post for the remaining years of the Smuts administration. Not the most far-sighted of politicians, and goaded by the Nationalists, the new minister took a firm stand on his party's racial policy, declaring time and again in response to Ballinger and company's challenges that segregation was still the official policy of the United Party and he was doing his best to apply it.

Squatting

The temporary lifting of influx controls during the early war years so as to meet industry's growing demand for labour led to a new social phenomenon that gave headaches to urban authorities – land occupation, or uncontrolled 'squatting'. The thousands of Africans who had abandoned the reserves in search of work were flooding into the cities, especially Johannesburg and its surrounds. As housing pressures mounted, squatter settlements began to spring up on the fringes of every township, defying any attempts by the authorities to regulate or permanently remove them.

Of the four large municipal housing schemes on the Witwatersrand, Orlando – the forerunner of modern-day Soweto – had been considered a 'model' of its kind. Since very few houses could be built during the war, the rapid population increase soon resulted in Orlando and the other three townships becoming hopelessly overcrowded. AW Stadler estimates that a two-roomed Orlando house could be home to at least eight inhabitants.[26]

It did not take long for one James Mpanza, a convicted murderer from Natal turned fundamentalist Christian, to lead an exodus of several hundred migrant families from Orlando into the neighbouring veld to build shacks for themselves out of hessian, bits of wood and corrugated iron. Mpanza, a member of the Orlando Advisory Board, was able to instigate the squatter exodus by first persuading householders in the township to expel their sub-tenants and then offering these desperate people an alternative form of housing. The camp he founded, known as Masakeng, grew to 20 000 inhabitants at its height, and is the site of Orlando West today.

Equating himself to the Messiah, Mpanza drew hundreds of followers into a political party named Sofasonke (We shall die together). A charismatic though unscrupulous character, whose personal assets were said to include a string of racehorses, Mpanza ruled the informal settlement with an iron hand, deciding who might and might not enter, administering and dispensing justice, levying duties on traders, and providing a limited supply of water while deriving revenues from membership dues and other fees.[27] The main attraction of Masakeng – where living conditions were dire throughout the rainy season and in winter – was the protection it afforded to vulnerable residents.

Mpanza's initiative was directed at the Johannesburg City Council, which he hoped to pressure into undertaking a housing programme to accommodate his followers. But the council refused point-blank to expand Orlando's housing programme. Mpanza found no help either from the CPSA or ANC, which distrusted his politics and deplored his methods. He reacted to both with threats of violence. To meet the growing squatter problem, instead of building more houses in Orlando, the municipality decided to develop its own site-and-service scheme at nearby Moroka, whose water points soon attracted hundreds of home-seekers.[28]

The emergence of Moroka and other similar schemes put a temporary end to uncontrolled squatting as migrants were absorbed, from the mid-1940s onwards, into the massive basic housing complexes that grew up in and around southwestern Johannesburg. But the true significance of the squatter movement, like the Alexandra bus boycotts, lay in the manner in which it forced the state into greater intervention in the provision of basic housing and other facilities required by the huge urban African workforce.[29] Today, James Mpanza, the 'King of Orlando', is remembered by history as 'the man who founded Soweto'.[30]

Elsewhere in the World

In 1943

14–24 January	Churchill and Roosevelt meet in Casablanca
31 January–2 February	German Sixth Army surrenders at Stalingrad
1 February	Formation of 6th South African Armoured Division
9 February	US forces defeat Japanese on Guadalcanal
19 April	Start of Warsaw Ghetto uprising
13 May	German and Italian troops in North Africa surrender
10 July	Operation Husky: Allied forces invade Sicily
17 July	Death of Sir Patrick Duncan; succeeded as governor-general by NJ De Wet
5 July–23 August	Operation Citadel (Battle of Kursk), southwest of Moscow
24 July	Operation Gomorrah: Hamburg virtually destroyed by Allied bombing
3 September	Italy surrenders to the Allies
28 November–1 December	Roosevelt, Churchill and Stalin meet at Teheran Conference
1943–1944	Famine in Bengal kills up to 3 million people

CHAPTER 13

Year of Tumult

The year 1943 proved to be a seminal one for South Africa's liberation movements. Energised by the social turbulence of the war years, a new and radicalised generation of youthful activists in the major cities began to bump heads with their elders over the most effective way to bring an end to whites-only rule.[1] Organisations such as the ANC, AAC and NEUM were riven internally between an 'old guard', who had collaborated with the authorities within existing structures, and younger 'radicals', who viewed non-cooperation with racially segregated institutions as a rallying cry with which to mobilise the masses. The collaborationist-boycott argument over whether to operate within segregated structures in order to combat institutionalised racism was to plague liberation politics for decades.

Not all ANC members had been favour of AB Xuma's patient and measured approach to politics, nor of his willingness to befriend left-leaning whites; some younger supporters were pleading for more militant opposition to the wartime government's policies. In late 1943, two young ANC members, Paul Mosaka, a sitting NRC councillor, and Self Mampuru – urged on by the maverick communist and Native Representative in the Senate, Hyman Basner – broke away from the ANC to form the African Democratic Party (ADP).

The new party's manifesto was critical of the ANC for its 'political stagnation and general inaction'[2] and endorsed the use of strikes and boycotts to press home black demands. 'Our times,' the manifesto declared, 'call for unity, organisation and action.'³ Fearful of a potential split within the ANC, Xuma scornfully dismissed the ADP as a divisive force, inspired by non-Africans, and took pre-emptive steps to ensure that the Transvaal ANC did not fall into the new party's hands.⁴

A far more substantial challenge to Xuma's authority arose from within the body of the kirk, from young idealists who regarded the ANC leadership as being 'too middle-aged, too middle-class and too ensnared in the mindset of pseudo-liberalism, appeasement and compromise'.⁵ Frustrated by the founding of the ADP under their very noses, these youthful militants demanded action of the kind employed so successfully in the Alexandra bus boycotts of 1940 and 1942. Mostly Christian in orientation and strongly anti-communist, instead of joining the ADP, these Young Turks opted to try to reform the ANC from within – by establishing a Youth League to further their strategy.

These activists were all talented professionals in their twenties and thirties, the products of mission schools and colleges such as Adams and Fort Hare. They drew much of their inspiration from a deeply devout and intellectually precocious young Zulu, Anton Lembede, the architect of South Africa's first fully fledged ideology of African nationalism.⁶

Lembede

Anton Muziwakhe Lembede was born in 1914 on a farm in the Eston district of Natal, not far from Durban. His father was a poor sharecropper and his mother a teacher, who schooled her son so well at home that he was able to secure a bursary to Adams College, outside Durban, where he qualified as an elementary-school teacher in 1935. Among the young Anton's teachers at Adams was the future ANC president and Nobel laureate Albert Luthuli. Two years later, the young student passed the matriculation examination by correspondence, with a distinction in Latin.

Fascinated by the solidarity of Afrikaners, Lembede moved to Heilbron in the Free State to study their cultural pride and cohesion at first hand.⁷

During six years as a teacher in the province, he took correspondence courses through the University of South Africa (Unisa) for the BA and LLB degrees. A practising Roman Catholic, Lembede went on to enrol for a master's degree in philosophy at Unisa, the daunting title of his dissertation being 'The Conception of God as Expounded by, and as It Emerges from, the Writings of Descartes to the Present Day'.

Lembede's time in the Free State made him a fluent Afrikaans-speaker, while his first-hand experience of rising Afrikaner nationalism and European fascism in the 1930s heightened his own sense of race consciousness.[8] By the time of his death, he was proficient in at least seven languages: Zulu, Sotho, English, Afrikaans, High Dutch, German and Latin.[9]

Early in 1943, Lembede abandoned teaching in favour of a legal career and moved to Johannesburg to serve articles under the veteran ex-ANC leader, Pixley ka Seme, eventually becoming Seme's law partner. While in the Transvaal, he renewed his friendship with two other young Catholic activists, AP Mda and Jordan Ngubane, who immediately initiated him into the ANC fold.[10]

During regular intellectual discussions with Mda and Ngubane over a new political credo for black people, Lembede's thoughts began to crystallise into 'Africanism', a strand of racial nationalism that held that Africa belonged to blacks, and Africans had to stand up and reclaim what was rightfully theirs. He wanted blacks to be as proud of their blackness as he was. 'Look at my skin,' he was fond of saying, 'it is black like the soil of Mother Africa.'[11] He would always insist that the inclusion of Africans in South African society was a right and not a privilege.

The austere Lembede was never at ease in the overcrowded and turbulent Johannesburg townships, whose lawlessness filled him with dismay. In his eyes, urban-slum conditions were symptomatic of the plight of Africans, 'caught in a vicious cycle of degradation'.[12] An antidote was required, and he was determined to provide it. What Africans lacked, he would argue, was an ideology that would give them a sense of self-worth, a new pride in their blackness, and a love of Africa and a confidence in her future. 'Civilisation was the heritage of all mankind,' he would assert, 'and not the exclusive attribute of any one race or nation.'[13]

The greatest barrier to black liberation, Lembede believed, was the 'crippling complexes of inferiority and dependence imposed on Africans by their treatment at the hands of whites'. Only a policy of bold self-assertion would enable black people to correct this debasing self-image.[14] A new ideology of 'Africanism' was essential if blacks were to mount an effective challenge to white domination. Singly, Lembede's ideas were not new, having been championed in the 1930s by Clements Kadalie's Industrial and Commercial Workers' Union, but, as Karis and Gerhart explains, 'taken together and in the South African context, they represented an original synthesis of concepts with widespread appeal'.[15]

Lembede's youthful idealism extended well beyond his own country's borders: he dreamt of uniting the African continent's many tribes into one entity as a *sine qua non* for liberation and progress. At home, he asserted, the basis of national unity ought to be the nationalistic feeling 'of being African, irrespective of tribal connection, social status, educational attainment or economic class'.[16]

While his colleagues debated among themselves the pros and cons of forming a youthful think tank to invigorate the ANC, Lembede emerged as the chief advocate of the 'Africanist' philosophy, 'the more abstract notions of which were his own intellectual creations'.[17] As a devout Catholic, his spiritual beliefs made him profoundly suspicious of Marxist dogma, which he associated with the white-directed CPSA – a force as likely as any other to perpetuate the evil of 'white paternalism'.[18]

Youth League

It was at Walter Sisulu's house in Orlando that Lembede, then 29, first met Nelson Mandela, the 25-year-old son of a nobleman in the Thembu royal line. As new recruits to ANC politics, Lembede, Mandela, Sisulu, Oliver Tambo, Mda, Ngubane and others were members of a group of young black activists invited by Xuma to bring fresh thinking into the ANC. Mandela was immediately impressed with the ideas of his new acquaintance. Although he thought Lembede at times verbose, Mandela admired the vigour of his rhetoric and fully agreed with his 'Africanist' vision.[19]

As Meredith records, Mandela and his friends were dismissive of the polite methods of protest employed by their ANC elders to such little effect, and spoiled for a confrontation with white officialdom. While having little political experience and no clear idea of how to proceed, they were united in their belief that a youth movement within the ANC was urgently needed to put pressure on the 'old guard' to move in a more radical direction.[20] It was AP Mda who convened a lengthy indaba at which it was agreed to form a body to be tentatively called the Congress Youth League (CYL). But first it was necessary to obtain the approval of the cautious ANC leadership, many of whose members felt threatened by the impatience of youth.[21] 'We do not want to anger or alienate Dr Xuma,' Mda cautioned, 'because without his blessing we will be unable to influence Congress.'[22]

Over the next few months, Mda, Lembede and Ngubane met regularly to draft a manifesto for the proposed Youth League. When it was ready, Mandela joined a delegation led by Lembede to put the concept to Xuma in the library of his house in Sophiatown. As Anthony Sampson records, Mandela shared in the general admiration of Xuma for having revitalised the ANC, but was less impressed by the president's 'English' manners and demagogic style.[23] While Xuma professed his support for a Youth League at the meeting, he argued that the ANC was not adequately prepared for a successful programme of mass action. For Xuma, organisation remained paramount; for the young militants, the future was about ideology and tactics.[24]

As it turned out, Lembede's idealism – embodied by the CYL – was to leave an indelible impression on ANC methods and strategy. From it, the organisation would distil the tactics of boycotts, strikes and mass action. During the war years, the Youth Leaguers' 'Africanist' inclinations – and

Anton Lembede
ARCHIVE PL/ALAMY STOCK PHOTO

Nelson R Mandela
DRUM SOCIAL HISTORIES/BAHA/
AFRICA MEDIA ONLINE

Oliver R Tambo
DRUM SOCIAL HISTORIES/BAHA/
AFRICA MEDIA ONLINE

Walter M Sisulu
GETTY IMAGES

reservations about alien creeds such as communism – were no different from the parent body's core philosophy as articulated by Xuma. Where the militants parted company from the 'old guard' was in believing that vigorous activism was the best way to attract mass support.[25] Confrontation and mass action, however, were not methods that appealed to Xuma and the conservative faction in control of the ANC.

The NEUM

A more threatening challenge to both the ANC and its embryonic Youth League was the growing influence of the rival Non-European Unity Movement, led by radical coloured and African activists who had forced the pace by embarking on a nationwide campaign aimed at uniting all non-white South Africans.[26] Comprised mainly of teachers and other professionals, the NEUM emerged out of a union between elements of the AAC and the former Trotskyite Non-European United Front. Intellectually influential, the new movement was handicapped by its over-scholarly elitism, making the cardinal error of couching its propaganda, supposedly aimed at the working class, in arcane language suitable only for 'converts and activists' that went well over the heads of its target audience.[27]

Although small in size, the NEUM posed an ideological threat to exclusivist African nationalism. Despite being confined mainly to the Cape, its ideas had begun to influence the thinking of militants in all liberation movements.[28] Impressed by the NEUM's non-collaborationist philosophy, Lembede's Africanists nonetheless rejected any cooperation with the organisation on the grounds that (Trotskyite) communism and African nationalism were fundamentally incompatible. Xuma, too, refused to engage directly with the NEUM, but began to consider seriously for the first time the merits of formal cooperation with coloureds and Indians.[29]

If most Youth Leaguers were determined to keep their distance from the CPSA, this was not true of the entire ANC. By degrees, members of the two movements drew closer to one another. Influenced by the dynamism of the CYL, the communists now realised that the only path to socialist revolution lay through the promotion of African nationalism.[30] And not all Youth Leaguers were as vehemently anti-communist as Lembede. Mandela, for one, was impressed with the CPSA's multiracialism. Years later he wrote:

> It was only the communists who were prepared to treat Africans as human beings and their equals, who were prepared to eat with us, talk with us, live with us and work with us. They were the only political group prepared to work with Africans for the attainment of political rights and a stake in society.[31]

For Mandela and his colleagues, action was far more important than splitting hairs over doctrinal differences between nationalism and communism.

Bus boycott

In August 1943, there was a boycott of buses from the overcrowded Johannesburg township of Alexandra, some ten kilometres north of the city centre. The township lay outside the municipal boundary, and as one of the few areas in greater Johannesburg in which Africans could hold freehold title to property, it was a sanctuary for migrants lacking the necessary permission to live in an urban area. The absence of effective building regulations in Alexandra meant that landlords could build shacks on properties and offer accommodation to poor people who could not afford to live in a municipal township.[32]

Transport was of primary concern to the people of Alexandra. There were no trains, so a cheap and efficient bus service to take workers into the city and beyond was essential to survival. A rise in the bus fare from four pence to five pence, which made labour from the township less attractive to employers than workers who lived closer to the city centre,[33] meant more hardship and sparked off the third and biggest boycott since the war began. Mandela was one of 20 000 people who walked the 20 kilometres to work and back for nine days until the bus company relented and lowered the fare to four pence again. Rich records that the campaign became increasingly militant, reflecting a hardening of attitudes in the township as more moderate voices were drowned out by radicals.[34] The success of the boycott was a potent demonstration of the power of mass action, a lesson taken to heart by the ANC, especially the Youth League.

New constitutions

In December 1943, the ANC's Atlantic Charter committee, still under the influence of moderates, met in Bloemfontein to finalise the *African Claims* document, which was to form the basis of a new constitution for the organisation. The prominent Afrikaner lawyer, Bram Fischer, was among those who assisted Xuma in drawing up the constitution, which mandated the ANC to 'attain the freedom of the African people from all discriminatory laws' and to 'strive and work for full participation of the African in the Government of South Africa'.[35] Rich records that although the document was aimed more at influencing the Smuts government than at serving as the basis for African political mobilisation, it was nonetheless a landmark in the history of African politics in South Africa, because it marked a clear rejection of the 'trusteeship' principle that Africans were the wards of white colonial trustees.[36]

In his presidential address to the ANC's annual conference, Xuma had some harsh words for the government, which was leading South Africa into a 'blind alley' and whose real intentions were now apparent. In drawing up *African Claims*, Xuma declared, 'the Charter committee had bestowed a "legacy of freedom" on future generations and established a national ideal for all South Africans, drawn up by Africans themselves'.[37]

The ANC's new constitution was formally adopted by the conference on 16 December, Afrikanerdom's most sacred day of remembrance. The next day, also in Bloemfontein, the NEUM held its first national conference, under the chairmanship of DDT Jabavu. African, coloured and Indian delegates put their names to a 'Draft Declaration of Unity', which stated the NEUM's aims to be, among other things, 'the acquisition by Non-Europeans of all those rights which are at present enjoyed by the European population'. A ten-point programme spelt out the NEUM's democratic demands, chief of which was full equality of rights for all citizens without distinction of race, sex or colour. Notable by its absence, however, was any detailed plan of action.

CHAPTER 14

Indian Winter

'Colour queers my poor pitch everywhere. But South Africans cannot understand. Colour bars are to them the divine order of things,' Jan Smuts once lamented in a letter to a friend.[1] That may have been true of most whites during the war, if not of the country's other races. For no sooner had the United Party triumphed in the 1943 election than the 'Indian question' reasserted itself with a vengeance. Once again, the prime minister found himself trying – and failing – to reconcile his universal ideals with his own situation[2] and South Africa's racial complexities.

Smuts was caught in a contradiction created by history.[3] Since his days as a Transvaal politician, he had locked horns with leaders of the Indian community, and in particular their spiritual leader, Mohandas K Gandhi. Half a century earlier, indentured Indians, desperate to escape a series of famines in parts of British-run India, had been shipped across the ocean to work in the sugar-cane fields of colonial Natal. Despite harsh working conditions, most had no option but to stay and put down roots there. A second wave of 'passenger Indians', who had paid their own way and were mostly Muslim traders and shopkeepers from Gujarat, arrived in the 1870s. Thirty years later, Indians in Natal were as numerous as whites. Those with 'passenger' origins generally considered themselves of a better pedigree than their indentured compatriots.[4] Many of the wealthier, ambitious and more adventurous among them had migrated to the Transvaal, where their residential and business activities were confined to designated areas.

Few questions vexed Smuts more than how to deal with these immigrant Indians, whose religious beliefs and centuries-old culture he respected, but whose rapid proliferation was the cause of much concern to the white electorate. As the Transvaal's colonial secretary, and the Union's minister of the interior, it had fallen to Smuts to regulate the 'Asiatics' and to proscribe their movements. The measures he employed – including the carrying of passes and the imposition of a poll tax – had brought him face to face with the enigmatic Gandhi, whose tactic of *satyagraha* (passive resistance) he found difficult to comprehend or respond to effectively. In an exchange with Gandhi, Smuts once said, 'Your civilisation is different from ours. Ours must not be overwhelmed by yours. That is why we must go in for legislation which must in effect put disabilities on you.'[5] In 1913, after he and Gandhi had reached agreement on easing some restrictions on Indians, the future Mahatma left South Africa for home, and soon after the world's attention was diverted by WWI. After the war, as the Union's prime minister, Smuts found himself again fending off awkward questions about South Africa's racial policies from Indians at Imperial Conferences, the last of which he attended in 1923.

Sixteen years later, shortly before Smuts found himself prime minister again, the Fusion government had passed the Asiatic (Transvaal) Land and Trading Act, which limited Indian commercial activities in the province. In Natal, where a small number of Indians had spilled over into white residential areas and business districts, the Dominion Party – self-appointed custodian of Empire – was demanding an extension of the Transvaal legislation. Aware that further restrictions on Indians' rights in South Africa would reopen a quarrel with the Indian government that had plagued him for 25 years,[6] Smuts prevaricated, declaring a moratorium on the Transvaal legislation and 'pegging' all Indian land acquisitions until 1943. In the meantime, to quieten the clamour from Dominion MPs within his wartime coalition, he appointed Justice FN Broome to head a commission to determine 'to what extent Indians had penetrated into white areas in Natal and the Transvaal between 1917 and 1940'.⁷

At this time, Durban alone was home to more than two-thirds as many Indians as there were in the Transvaal.⁸ In the province of Natal, unlike the Transvaal, Indians were free to reside, work and buy land without legal restrictions. Preferring to live in their own communities, however, they had created 'islands' in parts of the Durban city centre and on its periphery. As their numbers increased, they outgrew these 'islands' and some wealthier Indians began to regard land acquisition as an investment opportunity.

Divided loyalties

Separated by religious, class and caste differences, Natal's Indians were further divided into rival political camps: the Natal Indian Congress (NIC), founded by Gandhi in 1894 and supported by wealthier members of the community; and the Natal Indian Association (NIA), broadly representative of the poorer classes. Despite their differences, each organisation gave its unconditional support to the war effort. In the north, pro-war moderates in control of the Transvaal Indian Congress (TIC) were under assault from within by a militant nationalist group led by a disciple of Gandhian 'passive resistance', Dr Yusuf Dadoo, a member of the Communist Party and an advocate of political alliances between Africans, coloureds and Indians. Both the Natal and Transvaal congresses were also members of the South African Indian Congress (SAIC), founded 20 years earlier.

For many years, the NIC had been headed by AI Kajee, an energetic and well-to-do Muslim businessman of politically pragmatic views. To avoid giving offence to Durban's white community, the influential Kajee had been able, informally, to discourage Indian infiltration into white residential and business areas. As long as the NIC did so, the Smuts government did not have to spend time looking over its shoulder at Natal. The rival NIA was also compliant, giving the incoming minister of the interior, Harry Lawrence, an assurance that it too would do its best to prevent the purchase of property by Indians in predominantly white areas.⁹

The differences between the NIC and NIA were personal rather than substantive. According to Surendra Bhana, both organisations opposed segregation but stopped short of challenging white authority: 'They hoped to achieve broader freedoms for Indians without alienating the white power structure.'[10] Despite persistent rumours that the restrictions on Transvaal Indians would soon be made applicable to Natal, by 1941 no fewer than 1 200 Indians, mostly from Durban, had joined up to serve in the UDF's transport corps.[11]

Ominous sign

The appointment of the Broome Commission was taken by most Indians as a sign that the Union government was determined to act firmly against them, war or no war, and despite its call for patriotic solidarity in the face of a common enemy. Indians were incensed at being singled out 'for investigation with a view to segregation',[12] pointing out that the country was fighting for democracy on one front, but practising an undemocratic policy on another. Younger, more militant politicians in the NIA and TIC, who were eventually to take over the leadership of both organisations, demanded a boycott of the Broome Commission and appealed to the government of India for help. The Union government responded by prosecuting some of the dissidents, including Yusuf Dadoo, under the War Measures Act.

In its report, the Broome Commission concluded that although there was some congestion in the Transvaal and Natal, the facts did not reveal a situation 'which can by any stretch of imagination be described as critical'.[13] In Natal, the 'penetration' of white areas by Indians was not serious, amounting to 'little more than a trickle'.[14] Broome's findings failed to satisfy the Natal Municipal Association, however, which called for legislation to rectify 'a very serious menace'. The Dominion Party went further, calling for the repatriation of Indians. An unsympathetic minister, with one eye on the war and likely Commonwealth reaction, responded that such legislation would be 'most inappropriate and inadvisable'.[15]

Smuts believed that the Broome Commission had given him the answer he wanted, but the white politicians of Natal thought otherwise, insisting that Indians had been aggressively penetrating white areas since September 1940, the cut-off date of the Broome inquiry.[16] With an election looming – and hoping to 'kick the can down the road', in the traditional South African manner – Smuts reappointed Justice Broome, as sole commissioner this time, to investigate the acquisition of land by Indians in the municipal area of Durban since September 1940. The setting up of a second commission gave further offence to the Indian communities of South Africa, as well as to the government of India.[17]

Unpalatable choice

The second Broome report vindicated the Durban City Council's assertion that there had been significant Indian penetration since September 1940 (ie 326 instances) of a small section of the Durban Berea, for investment rather than residential purposes. The report failed to make clear, however, that Indians owned a mere four per cent of land on the Berea or that building societies regarded this area of Durban as suitable for Indian settlement (as there was no law against it) and had advanced loans for that purpose.[18]

On the eve of the 1943 election, Smuts weighed up his unpalatable alternatives and decided he could not risk losing the white electorate in Natal in the midst of the war against Hitler. Instead, he temporised once again, introducing a Trading and Land Bill, applicable to both Indians and 'Europeans', but only to be implemented three years later, in 1946. In a letter to a friend in the UK, he explained:

> There is nothing for it but to peg the position and forbid property transfers [in Durban] for three years so that the whole position can be judicially inquired into. But this again has created commotion among the Indians here and in India and moved the Indian government to do its bit in the general hue and cry ... I can never get away from the Indian tangle and the troubles of East and West.[19]

The 1943 law, subsequently known as the 'Pegging Act', became notorious in India and well beyond. Shortly before submitting it to Parliament, Smuts had to deal with the threatened resignation of JH Hofmeyr from his cabinet. Hofmeyr objected in principle to the legislation, not because he was opposed to separate residential areas – of which he approved – but because the law applied to both whites and Indians in Natal, but in the Transvaal to Indians only, and was thus 'discriminatory'. As Hancock comments drily, Hofmeyr was 'straining at the Witwatersrand gnat, but he swallowed the Durban camel'. It did not take much persuasion from Smuts for the finance minister – having made his point – to agree to withdraw his resignation and soldier on in government.[20] (According to Jeremy Lawrence's memoir of his father, Harry, Smuts once said of Hofmeyr: 'A good man, but he has principles – I discarded mine twenty years ago! Not only does Hoffie have principles, he invariably chooses the wrong ones to stand on.'[21])

Agent-General

Since 1927, the rights of Indians in South Africa had been recognised by the Cape Town Agreement, a treaty negotiated between the governments of South Africa and India, which made provision for the voluntary repatriation of Indians through a subsidy scheme, as well as the 'upliftment' of those Indians who chose to remain in South Africa.[22] Under the agreement, local Indians were to be represented in negotiations with the authorities by an agent-general from India. From 1935, the agent-general had been the outspoken Sir Syed Raza Ali, who had not hesitated to criticise the Union government when necessary, or to demand an extension of the franchise for Indians. Not surprisingly, his strictures and those of his successors had not made the agent-general's office popular in the eyes of most white South African politicians.

Not long into the war, the status of the agent-general was raised to that of high commissioner. The change was significant, since the agent-general's role had been to speak out on behalf of South Africa's Indians, whereas the high commissioner represented the government of India, and was thus debarred by convention from publicly criticising his hosts. The Union government, which had generally regarded the agent-general's strictures as an unwarranted interference in the country's domestic affairs, talked up the change as an indication of the growing importance of Indian affairs. South African Indians, on the other hand, saw it as an attempt to silence dissent.[23]

Another 'Indian' issue to cause much head-scratching among officialdom during the war was the treatment of visiting dignitaries and troops from India passing through South African ports en route elsewhere. Smuts was alert to the situation and appointed liaison officers in Durban and Cape Town to ensure that important Indians received the necessary courtesies. But the consideration extended to officers only: other ranks and visiting civilians felt the full effect of local discrimination. In late 1942, a letter from members of the Indian intelligentsia in London to the Durban newspaper *The Leader* complained that the colour bar in South Africa had confronted them on all sides. The signatories declared themselves amazed that such a situation could exist at a time 'when we are supposed to be fighting for democracy ... What hope is there for mankind if fascist forces are destroyed in Europe only to preserve them in South Africa?'[24]

Reciprocity

The passage of the Pegging Act through Parliament aroused heated protest from Indians in both South Africa and India. (The Act proved to be the forerunner of the National Party's post-war policy of apartheid in urban residential areas.) In Natal, the NIC and the NIA presented memoranda to cabinet ministers and held meetings with MPs, to no avail. The Act also attracted attention further afield, being gleefully denounced by Axis radio stations in Berlin, Rome and Tokyo, which pointed out that the Allies had no right to condemn the domestic behaviour of other nations while claiming the right to regulate their own internal affairs.[25]

In New Delhi, the Indian government retaliated against the Pegging

Act by passing a Reciprocity Act, which provided for the imposition of economic sanctions on South Africa. Although the new viceroy, Lord Wavell, was initially reluctant to approve the Act because of his close friendship with Smuts, he soon had to give way to public opinion, which was outspokenly critical of the British government for failing to protect the interests of Indians in South Africa. Troubled by the mounting criticism from India, which he blamed on the agitation of local Indians, Smuts refused to meet a delegation from the SAIC.[26]

Despite its postponement for three years, the Pegging Act caused severe ructions within the local Indian community. Within three months, the NIC and the NIA had amalgamated to fight the law under the banner of the Natal Indian Congress. The new NIC's inaugural meeting was presided over by the Indian high commissioner in South Africa himself, Sir Shafa'at Ahmad Khan, who had been instrumental in bringing the two bodies together to oppose the legislation.

Startled by the range of opposition to the Pegging Act, the Smuts government scrambled to counter the unfavourable publicity its legislation had attracted. In a speech to municipal officials, Lawrence's successor as minister of the interior, the 'tolerant and level-headed'[27] senator from Natal, CF Clarkson, conceded that Natal and the Transvaal would have to consider some form of the franchise for Indians. 'We cannot expect the Indian population, which now equals the European population in Natal, to be voiceless in the control of municipal and state affairs,' the new minister declared.[28] Soon thereafter, the appointment of a third and enlarged Broome Commission was announced – to enquire into all matters affecting the Indians of Natal. This time, however, the commission would include two Indian representatives – AI Kajee and SR Naidoo – both of whom accepted nomination only on condition they remained free to campaign for the repeal or withdrawal of the objectionable Pegging Act.[29]

CHAPTER 15

In the Middle

The run-up to the wartime election of 1943 brought long-standing differences in the coloured community to a head – between pragmatists, who sought reform through existing channels, and militants, who advocated non-collaboration and boycotts in response to the threat of tighter segregation. South Africa's mixed-race population, located mainly in the Cape Province, had become despairing at its treatment by successive Union governments, which had gone back on past promises of special consideration for coloured people.[1]

Coloureds had always considered themselves closer to whites than Africans, but found themselves steadily pushed further away. The gradual radicalisation of coloured politics, which began in the mid-1930s, was a consequence of Hertzog's segregationist legislation of 1936. Regularly assured that their destiny lay with whites, with whom many had blood relationships, coloured people began to lose faith in the empty promises of politicians.

When the war broke out, coloured people made up approximately eight per cent of South Africa's population, and were exceptionally diverse when measured by ethnic, cultural and economic criteria.[2] Their political leaders were drawn from a thin layer of Christian and Muslim professionals – mainly teachers, small-businessmen and artisans – atop a large pyramid of unskilled urban and rural working poor, who were often treated with patronising disdain.[3] Many of the underclass were illiterate farm workers, who shared white prejudices and fears about other races – especially Africans,[4] with whom they vied for living space and jobs.

Prior to Union, there had been limited legal discrimination against coloureds in the Cape Colony, but after 1910 the barriers that went up in the northern provinces began filtering down to the Cape, where local restrictions and administrative action made it difficult for coloureds to compete effectively for jobs with whites. Many lighter-skinned and sophisticated coloureds, conscious of their deteriorating status, were more intent on retaining their privileges – and keeping their distance from the African underclass – than creating a common society regardless of skin colour. And those hoping to bring about such a society were mainly young intellectuals prone to over-theorising and sermonising in a manner that left their potential allies in other races confused and sometimes bitterly angry.[5]

Radical protests

An upsurge in coloured radicalism had led, in 1935, to the formation of the National Liberation League (NLL), headed by Marxist intellectuals such as the Muslim physician Dr Goolam Gool, a disciple of Leon Trotsky, his outspoken sister-in-law, Zainunissa (Cissie) Gool, and James (Jimmy) La Guma. In 1938, the NLL became the Non-European Forum (NEUF), which attempted – without much success – to forge working-class solidarity with Africans. From then until 1943, the NEUF focused instead on opposing the growth of European fascism in South Africa and resisting attempts by municipal authorities to tighten racial discrimination against coloured men and women.[6]

In 1939, the Cape Provincial Council had introduced an ordinance empowering town councils to segregate residential areas, some public places and city buses. On 27 March, an NEUF campaign against the measure culminated in a huge public demonstration, which degenerated into a riot. The Council withdrew the offending ordinance.[7]

At the outbreak of war, the UDF's call to citizens to rally to the flag revived intense debate within the coloured community. To allay white fears, only white soldiers were to be permitted to bear arms, so those coloureds, Indians and Africans who volunteered for war service would have to take on a variety of non-combatant roles. However, as Van der Ross points out, the aversion to colour discrimination was quite insufficient 'to quench the Coloured people's eagerness to enlist'.[8] The former Cape Corps was resuscitated by a recruitment campaign headed by the mayor of Cape Town himself. Its commanding officer, Lieutenant Colonel Charles Hoy DSO, was given the responsibility of training drivers for the UDF's motorised units. As with other non-white recruits, these volunteers received small-arms training in case they were needed for service with combat units outside the borders of the Union.[9]

An unusual volunteer

An unusual recruit to the UDF's ranks was the 46-year-old trade unionist and lapsed communist Jimmy La Guma, who regarded the war as a continuation of the Spanish Civil War (1936–1939) and the struggle of the working class against fascism. Unlike most of his contemporaries, who opposed black participation in the war because of racially segregated enlistment, La Guma argued that socialists had a duty to volunteer: 'After victory, when we ask for a better deal, it cannot be said of us that we did not help our country in her hour of need.'[10] Lying about his age in order to join the Indian & Malay Corps, La Guma spent seven years in the ranks, fighting in East and North Africa and rising to the rank of staff sergeant. Upon demobilisation in 1947, he immediately rejoined the Communist Party, and was elected to its executive.

During the war, La Guma published the following lament for those who served with him:

> *Those Brown African Sons*
>
> Fettered and oppressed, they wearily drag their load,
> Praying for bread – they pitifully champ on stone.

Comes the clarion call, and like man Unit'd
Struggle they cease and struggle commence –
Brown Sons of Africa.

They're hated and spurned 'neath oppressor's heel
But 'tis Esprit de Corps they still preserve.
Emotions bitter they so willingly suppress
For Brotherhood common to Man to express –
Great Sons of Africa.[11]

Fears raised

Shortly before the 1943 election, however, coloured apprehension grew stronger when the minister of the interior, Harry Lawrence, announced the government's intention of reviving plans for a separate section within his ministry to deal with coloured affairs. Officials would be assisted by a permanent advisory body of coloured representatives from all four provinces. Despite official assurances that the aim was to improve the residential, social and economic circumstances of the coloured people, and was not a step towards a separate coloured-affairs department (CAD), similar to the department of native affairs, non-collaborationists and many others smelt a rat. A radical movement, spearheaded by a group of Trotskyites, sprang up in opposition to the proposed new Coloured Advisory Council (CAC).

The ensuing brouhaha between supporters and opponents of the Advisory Council split the coloured political class down the middle.[12] Members of the CAC – some of the most respected individuals in the community – were branded by the radicals as Judases and Quislings (a Norwegian politician who collaborated with the Germans during WWII), and there were excited claims that the coloured people were about to be 'enslaved',[13] as Africans had been by Hertzog's 1936 legislation. When the matter was debated in Parliament, an indignant Lawrence protested that the government had no such intention: 'To suggest that a government with General Smuts at the head – a government composed of many persons who are tried friends of the Coloured community – is about to embark on a swindle on the Coloured people would be just about as true as to suggest that my honourable friend here, the minister of finance [the strait-laced JH Hofmeyr], was a passionate protagonist of polygamy.'

How do you know he isn't? interjected the minister of labour, Walter Madeley.[14]

Abdullah Abdurahman

Since the turn of the century, coloured politics in South Africa had been dominated by a singular man, Dr Abdullah Abdurahman, a Scottish-trained medical practitioner turned politician. Born in Wellington in 1872, he was the grandson of freed slaves and schooled at the South African College, alma mater of JH Hofmeyr and other notables. After qualifying as a doctor at the University of Glasgow, Abdurahman returned to Cape Town, where he developed a lucrative non-racial practice. In 1904, he was the first coloured to be elected to the Cape Town City Council. Gaining a reputation as a powerful orator, efficient administrator and adroit politician, he retained his seat on the Council (except for two years in 1913–1914) until his death in 1940, at the age of 69. His 14-year chairmanship of the Council's important streets and drainage committee gave him considerable clout in city affairs.

A believer in education for all and a qualified, non-racial franchise as two essential steps towards an inclusive society, Abdurahman was also elected to the Cape Provincial Council in 1914, as a supporter of the Unionist Party and its successors. A true assimilationist, he preferred to support those white politicians who promised to promote coloured advancement in return for coloured votes.[15] Remaining a member of the Provincial Council for the rest of his life, Abdurahman was able to influence many aspects of provincial policy, especially in health and education.

In his study of coloured politics, Gavin Lewis describes Abdurahman as 'looming so large in the history of organised politics in the first half of the last century that he threatened to blot out all other features of the political landscape'.[16] Because of his exceptional organisational skills, easy manner with all sections of the community and apparently inexhaustible stamina, he is still regarded by many coloureds as the most outstanding leader yet produced by his people. Not that he was universally popular: non-admirers claimed he was intolerant of opposition, jealous of rivals and blind to the shortcomings of his own middle-of-the-road political outlook.[17]

Abdurahman's political activities were not confined to the Cape alone. In 1905, he became president of the African People's Organisation (APO), the most significant non-white national body of its time. In 1906 and 1909, he travelled to Britain in deputations to appeal for the entrenchment of the Cape's non-racial franchise, and to protest at the colour-bar clauses in the draft Act of Union. He was the prime mover in early attempts to achieve a united front with Indians and Africans, travelling to India in 1925 to urge the government to intervene on behalf of South African Indians, before organising the first mass conference of coloured, Indian and African political organisations in Kimberley in 1927. He convened three subsequent conferences in the early 1930s.

As Lewis records, Abdurahman epitomised the urban coloured elite, with a flourishing medical practice, a healthy income, a car, a yacht, a holiday cottage and a comfortable house in the middle-class section of District Six.[18] In his bearing, lifestyle and many personal achievements, he embodied the highest social aspirations of a people wanting, for the most part, and with notable exceptions, as Mohamed Adhikari writes, 'little more than to be judged on merit, exercise their citizenship rights and win social acceptance within middle-class white society'.[19]

Inevitably, like most political moderates, Abdurahman found himself trapped between competing fires in the simmering cauldron of South African politics. His close connections with white politicians and desire to incorporate coloured people into white-dominated society led to accusations by radicals that he was a sell-out who blinded his people to their oppression. Communists wrote him off as the captive of capitalist interests, intent on protecting the coloured petit bourgeoisie. Not that his constituents seemed to mind, re-electing him to his various positions year after year.

When Abdurahman died early in the war, his funeral procession attracted one of the largest crowds ever seen on the streets of the Mother City.[20] In 1999, in one of Nelson Mandela's last acts as president, he bestowed the Order for Meritorious Service (gold) upon Abdurahman posthumously for his lifelong contribution to a democratic South Africa.[21]

By the time of Abdurahman's death, the APO's tactics of collaborating with white politicians and failure to protect coloured rights effectively, or to ward off encroaching segregation, had been widely discredited.[22] To growing numbers of young and politically aware coloureds, excited by the wave of anti-colonial and anti-war sentiment unleashed throughout Africa in the early 1940s, the APO's policies served merely to reinforce white supremacy at the expense of the wider community.

Support for the CAC

Abdurahman's successor as APO president in 1943 was Dr FH Gow, a former cleric and fellow political moderate. After meeting privately with interior minister Lawrence, Gow and several members of the APO executive agreed to give the Coloured Advisory Council their support. At the CAC's inaugural meeting on 28 April 1942, members laid down the conditions under which they had accepted appointment: no segregation; no CAD; no tampering with the franchise; and no new measures affecting coloureds without prior consultation. The Council's main aims would be better nutrition, health services and housing, improved educational facilities, wider employment opportunities and the extension of franchise rights to all coloureds.[23] Implicit in the trade-off was the promise of protection for coloured workers against cheaper African labour.

The establishment of the Coloured Advisory Council provoked an immediate response in the formation of what became known as the 'Anti-CAD movement'. The Council was roundly denounced by its critics as being a CAD in another guise and an alternative to the granting of further franchise rights; its individual members were excoriated for accepting that coloureds were a separate group with special problems of their own.[24] Representatives of 25 organisations banded together to launch a campaign against the Council and form an Anti-CAD committee, made up mainly of young teachers, lawyers and doctors under the chairmanship of Goolam Gool, brother-in-law of Abdurahman's daughter, Cissie. The committee's intellectual mainspring was the schoolteacher Ben Kies, another Trotskyite activist, who advocated working-class solidarity with all racial groups, and rejected any kind of accommodation with 'the European ruling class'.[25] The Anti-CAD movement focused narrowly on issues affecting the coloured community, however, and failed to broaden its scope to include Africans.[26]

Strikes and demonstrations being illegal in wartime, the Anti-CAD movement's main thrust was instigating a social and political boycott of the Advisory Council and its members. As its propaganda organ, *The Bulletin*, commanded: 'Don't have any social or personal intercourse with them. Don't visit them, and don't invite them to your home. Don't meet them even if it is necessary to cross over to the other side of the street. Don't see them, even if you do come face to face with them.'[27] Rancour ran deepest within the ranks of the Teachers' League of South Africa (TLSA), where many older teachers were ostracised by their colleagues and some pupils.

On 29 May 1943, the Anti-CAD movement held its first national conference in Cape Town: more than 300 delegates from 70 affiliated branches included representatives from as far afield as Port Elizabeth and Kimberley. The highlight of the conference was an address by Kies, who tore into the government's '*herrenvolk*' (master race) ideology of 'divide and rule' which had percolated down to the coloured, Indian and African communities, so that each felt superior to the other, and whose representatives had created sectional organisations confined to their own group.[28] The solution, Kies declared, was to break down these specious feelings of superiority, forge a mass alliance among black people, and launch a united struggle against segregation.[29]

As Lewis observes, the dynamic Kies shaped the ideological views of his many youthful contemporaries, as well as a generation of radical coloured leaders, which endured until the 1970s. But his arguments – and tactics – failed to inspire most of his middle-of-the-road, non-socialist kinsmen, unimpressed with Marxist (and Trotskyist) rhetoric and without any strong ideological convictions of their own.[30]

Boycott ignored

In the 1943 election, the Anti-CAD movement called on voters not to support the United Party – advice rejected even by communists because it might lead to a Nationalist victory and hamper the war effort.[31] This did not dissuade the movement from supporting communist candidates in Cape Peninsula constituencies, who made the Advisory Council a central target in the election.[32] The election result was a severe setback to those opposed to a separate department of coloured affairs, however: their boycott call had been ignored because most coloured voters, even those opposed to the Council, were more concerned about the potential threat of HNP-imposed segregation once the war ended.

Having failed to use the CAC as a bogey to stir up the masses, the radicals refocused their efforts on driving out 'segregationist' leaders from professional organisations, most notably the hitherto apolitical TLSA, within whose ranks there was bitter infighting. Not all teachers wished to follow Kies's advice and put their jobs at risk by defying the authorities in the interests of working-class solidarity.

Agitation from within the community did not prevent the Advisory Council, which had grown to 25 members, from successfully implementing some limited social-welfare reforms and redressing local grievances in rural towns and villages. Progress in three key areas – improved education, equal economic opportunities and extension of the franchise – was much slower, as it became apparent that the authorities would only support reforms that reinforced rather than reduced segregation.[33]

To counter the Council's activities, and to broaden their movement's appeal, supporters of the Anti-CAD movement set about forging a common front with other non-white organisations[34] and revived their efforts to forge a united front against segregation, turning once again to the All African Convention, which it had earlier failed to radicalise. At the AAC's triennial conference in Bloemfontein in December 1943, Dr Gool and others successfully persuaded the Convention to end its collaboration with segregated political structures such as the Native Representative Council and the CAC, and lend its support to organisations promoting black unity.

As the AAC conference came to its end, the delegates convened a Unity Conference, which agreed to launch the Non-European Unity Movement (see Chapter 13), under the chairmanship of DDT Jabavu. Dominated by teachers, the NEUM programme may have been more radical than that of the Anti-CAD movement, but it also failed to grow beyond the tactics of non-collaboration.[35] The communist activists Jack and Ray Simons's crushing verdict on Anti-CAD was that 'its main achievement was to immobilise a generation of coloured intellectuals, immunise them against Marxist theory, and isolate them from the liberation movement'.[36]

Among the absentees from the Unity conference was the ANC, which was suspicious of radical Marxists and resentful of the potential challenge to its leadership among Africans. The South African Indian Congress, still in the hands of moderates, also stayed away, pleading its preoccupation with opposing the Pegging legislation and sending a message of support instead. Midway through the war, black unity among South Africans seemed as distant a prospect as ever. Despite the exertions and exhortations of politicians, it was colour rather than class that continued to define relations between the country's racial groups.

CHAPTER 16

Smuts Wins

Despite the United Party's difficulties with issues of race, Smuts was able to appeal to the white electorate with confidence in the 'khaki' election of 1943. By now, the fortunes of war had turned in the Allies' favour. The Axis defeat in North Africa and Hitler's travails in Russia had put an end to the Afrikaner Nationalist wartime republican dream.[1] A confident Smuts prolonged his coalition arrangements with the Labour Party, allowing it to keep its four seats, and the Dominion Party its seven Natal seats, without opposition from UP candidates. The electoral law had been amended to allow soldiers serving outside the Union to vote, and the 1st South African Infantry Division had returned from North Africa for service at home.[2] The votes of servicemen were to make a difference in several constituencies. The UP could also count on the support of some 12 000 coloured voters on the Cape's common roll.[3]

The central issue in the election, inevitably, was South Africa's continued involvement in the war, which DF Malan continued steadfastly to oppose, an attitude that many considered treasonable. With Smuts commanding the overwhelming support of English-speaking whites, the election was essentially a contest for the allegiance of uncommitted – or half-committed – Afrikaners.[4] Now firmly on the back foot, the HNP was obliged to modify its electoral platform, playing down demands for an Afrikaner-led republic, offering equal treatment to English-speaking whites, and highlighting the dangers of communism, as well as making capital out of the rising cost of living and wartime inconveniences and austerities.[5]

The election, held on 17 July, was peaceful and won easily by the United Party-led coalition, which garnered 105 seats (plus the support of the three Native Representatives and two independents). The Nationalists were reduced from 63 to 43 seats, giving the government a comfortable parliamentary majority of 67. Some 650 000 voters had come out in support of the war, with 350 000 voting against. Significantly, however, all 43 opposition seats had fallen to Malan's HNP, which wiped out both Oswald Pirow's New Order and Klasie Havenga's Afrikaner Party.[6] The former Cape dominee was now *die Volksleier*, the undisputed leader of Nationalist Afrikanerdom. To quote Paton, the Ossewabrandwag and the Afrikaner Party had been forced to realise that anti-war Nationalists preferred Malan 'to both Hitler and the ghost of Hertzog'.[7]

Smuts wrote to his friend Margaret Gillett in England, saying the election result vindicated 'what I have stood for and suffered for. I feel that at last I have been repaid with more than compound interest … it is indeed a famous victory! The political front is now secure, with a parliamentary majority which is now an embarrassment. And we can go on with the job.'[8]

The prime minister was not to know it, but he had reached the peak of his political influence in South Africa. From here on, his United Party began its political decline at the hands of the Nationalists, who had polled 36 per cent of the vote and had grown under Malan from being a rump party into one that threatened the ruling government.[9] Once again, it had taken a general election to throw into sharp relief the fault line running through the politics of white South Africa.[10]

The Cape sea route

Fortune had once again dealt Smuts a poor hand. As if to coincide with his election triumph, the Mediterranean had been reopened to Allied shipping following the defeat of Axis forces in North Africa, reducing at a stroke the importance of the Cape sea route for shipping to and from the Commonwealth and Far East. In Hancock's words,

> Without the Cape route, the Commonwealth could hardly have survived the war; without the Commonwealth, the Russians and Americans could hardly have won it ... It was an irony of fate that Smuts and his country should find themselves so much diminished by victories they had done so much to win ... What South Africa now did or failed to do, no longer made much difference to the Allied cause.[11]

Not that this reduced the prime minister's stellar international reputation by much. At Churchill's special request, Smuts made his second wartime visit to London in September 1943, leaving an overworked Hofmeyr in charge of the government. In speeches at London's Guildhall and to the Empire Parliamentary Association, South Africa's war leader dazzled large audiences with his analysis of the conflict and his plea for a new world organisation, with effective peacekeeping powers this time, vested in a post-war 'trinity' of Great Britain, the United States and the Soviet Union.[12]

Dissatisfaction rises

At home, the less the anxiety about the war's outcome, the more the tendency to find fault with the ruling party. There was grumbling that the government was overreaching itself, with even certain pro-Smuts newspapers suggesting the cabinet had too much power and that Parliament was becoming a rubber stamp. Afrikaner Nationalists complained bitterly that the security forces and civil service had become partisan and turned into instruments of war policy. Within the UP-led coalition, Labour began to voice criticism of the government for not doing more to protect white workers, notably in the building trades. The Dominion Party, as strongly anti-Indian as it was pro-British, was openly critical of the 'appeasement' of Natal Indians. And with more than sufficient statutory powers at its disposal, the government was failing to meet its promises to improve public health services and housing. In August 1943, it responded to the social problems caused by returning soldiers and airmen not involved in the fighting in Italy by setting up a Directorate of Demobilisation, under Major-General George Brink. Although the demobilisation process was carried out relatively efficiently, many ex-soldiers found it difficult to readjust to civilian life and their complaints added to the general atmosphere of dissatisfaction with the ruling wartime coalition.

Education issues

The government's temporary ascendancy over the opposition was confirmed in the provincial elections held separately in October 1943, which the UP won by large majorities in three of the four provinces. The central issue was which of three education models to adopt for white children: mother-tongue, dual-medium or parallel-medium. Encouraged by the success of bilingualism in the armed forces, the government favoured dual-medium for high schools (some subjects taught in English, some in Afrikaans) over parallel-medium schools in which both language groups were taught in separate classrooms but came together in residences and on sports fields.

The Nationalists were vigorously opposed to dual-medium schooling, fearing the 'anglicisation' of their offspring, and insisted on mother-tongue education from kindergarten to university.[13] In early 1944, the opposition introduced a motion in Parliament demanding single-medium education, which was defeated by an amendment in favour of a dual-medium system. Strong opposition in the Free State and Transvaal, however, ensured that the dual-medium policy was never successfully implemented. As Paton notes, dual-medium education was one of the oddest issues in South African history: politically, it further divided the white population, but educationally, it never got off the ground.[14]

Anti-pass campaign

An indication of the re-elected UP government's self-confidence was its renewed crackdown on pass-law offenders, in a direct response to Nationalist taunts that its softness on law enforcement in urban areas was giving rise to crime. Seizing the opportunity to put itself in the vanguard of African protest,[15] the Communist Party now sprang into action, announcing its intention of mounting a nationwide protest against the pass laws. In November 1943, a committee comprising the Transvaal physician and CPSA executive member Dr Yusuf Dadoo, as well as JB Marks, Moses Kotane and other communists, decided, in collaboration with the ANC, to call an anti-pass conference. At its annual congress in December, the ANC formally endorsed the proposal and resolved to actively support the campaign.

The resolution presented the ANC president-general, AB Xuma, with a dilemma. Though ideologically opposed to Marxism himself, he realised the CPSA was not only a potential ally but also a rival for the allegiance of African workers. Having kept the ANC independent of other organisations – especially the AAC and NEUM – in order to strengthen its Africanist credentials, Xuma began to see the merits of a wider coalition of the disenfranchised, provided the ANC's separate identity remained intact and any alliance was multiracial rather than non-racial. Suppressing his misgivings, he reluctantly agreed to chair the anti-pass campaign's working committee, with Dadoo as his deputy.[16] While detesting the pass laws as much as anyone, the anti-populist ANC leader was not prepared to countenance the burning of passes or any other form of civil disorder.

A national anti-pass conference took place in Johannesburg's Gandhi Hall on 20–21 May 1944. It resolved, among other things, that the pass laws were in conflict with the country's war aims, held the African people in abject poverty and subjugation, retarded the economic and industrial development of South Africa, weakened the labour movement, and filled the jails with innocent people. In support of their call for the immediate repeal of the pass laws, the anti-pass campaigners announced their intention to collect one million signatures by August 1943 for a petition to the government. Xuma agreed to chair the national campaign and for the next few months, he, Dadoo, Kotane and others spoke at peaceful protest meetings up and down the country. The Native Representative Council also passed a resolution in support of the campaign.[17]

Pretoria Agreement

Before the third Broome Commission into matters affecting the Indians of Natal could get under way, the Natal Indian Congress proposed a compromise to ameliorate the far-reaching provisions of the Pegging Act of 1943. It was proposed by the ever-pragmatic AI Kajee, whose lifelong aim was to cultivate harmonious relations between whites and Indians:[18] 'Kajee accepted the Cape Town Agreement as a basis from which to secure the best possible advantage for the Indians; and if this meant compromises, he was willing to make them.'[19] He was supported in his endeavours by a well-to-do estate agent and businessman, PR Pather, at one time secretary of both the NIC and the SAIC.

Kajee wished to keep ill-disposed white politicians and militant Indians out of discussions with the government, so he approached Smuts with a proposal that when the Pegging Act expired, an independent board comprising three whites and two Indians, with a lawyer as chairman, would be appointed to review all interracial property transactions and decide whether or not a transaction constituted 'penetration' – in essence, the maintenance of residential segregation on the basis of consensus.[20] Smuts agreed, and at a high-level meeting attended by members of the SAIC and the prime minister himself, the so-called Pretoria Agreement was signed on 18 April 1944.

A much-relieved Smuts sent a message to Wavell in India, informing the viceroy of an accord that provided 'a fair solution of the trouble which has arisen in connection with the Pegging Act and will, I trust, be as welcome to Your Excellency as it has been to me'.[21] With that, Smuts left South Africa for a Commonwealth Conference in London and the founding conference of the United Nations Organisation (UNO, later UN) in San Francisco.

No sooner was his back turned than the Pretoria Agreement began to fall apart. Some Indians objected to it for being a voluntary acceptance of segregation; others denounced it as having been negotiated by 'wealthy Indians' who only had their own interests in mind. The Dominion Party claimed it had not been consulted, and the Natal Provincial Council drew up three ordinances that the NIC complained were in conflict with the agreement. The atmosphere became so acrid the Broome Commission decided not to resume its public sittings.

Within the Indian community itself, many old animosities were aroused. The Kajee-Pather group, accused of only being interested in promoting Indian business interests, were outflanked by younger rebels who formed themselves into a new protest group, the Anti-Segregation Council (ASC), which set about ousting moderates from the NIC. At a mass meeting following a conference of 29 organisations on 6 May 1944, the ASC rallied several thousand supporters against the Pretoria Agreement.[22] In November, the ASC announced a manifesto for a non-racial South Africa that was to serve as the basis of NIC policy for the next 16 years. Kajee was ousted as NIC president and replaced by Dr GM (Monty) Naicker, who was to hold the position until 1961. The Kajee-Pather group retained control of the SAIC.

The ASC's ten-point programme of action, based on the provisions of the Atlantic Charter, could be summed up in the slogan 'Equality Now', which became the battle cry of a campaign supported from afar by nationalists in the government of India, who launched their own campaign against racism in South Africa.[23] Symbolically, a notice outside the Taj Mahal Hotel in Bombay declared: 'South African Europeans Not Allowed.'

Realising the Pretoria Agreement was now unworkable, Smuts wrote to Wavell to explain that the Indians of Natal had moved more forcefully to the left, while the 'Europeans' were 'panicky' about their future.

The Natal Indian Congress had become more uncompromising, while the growing tension within the wartime coalition had made the position more difficult, as the Labour and Dominion parties were exploiting the Indian question for their own interests.[24]

He was planning to introduce legislation, Smuts said, to give Indians representation in both Houses of Parliament and in provincial councils in Natal and the Transvaal, as well as administrative measures to make it possible for Indians to become involved in municipal affairs. He hoped to make a fresh start 'along the path of co-operation'.

It was a forlorn hope. The idea of giving the vote to anyone other than whites raised a storm of protest in Parliament. Colonel Stallard, leader of the Dominion Party, said it was wrong 'in principle'[25] to give Indians representation in the House, and Labour leader Madeley declared it wrong to have Indians represented in the House, the Senate or anywhere else. Malan roundly denounced the idea too, promising to repeal any such legislation if and when the HNP came to power. With Smuts stymied, militant Indians began planning a new 'passive resistance' campaign.

CHAPTER 17

Congress Youth League

In hindsight, the most significant political development of the war years was the birth of the Congress Youth League, later the ANC Youth League. Most of its founding members were to play leading roles in South Africa's freedom struggle over the next 50 years, culminating in the transition to majority rule in 1994. The parent body had expected subservience from its new youth wing; instead the ANC was given a shot in the arm that helped it become the pre-eminent black political movement in the country.[1]

The CYL was formally launched on Easter Sunday 1944, at a meeting of 200 activists in the Bantu Men's Social Centre, Eloff Street, Johannesburg.[2] The only woman present was Albertina Sisulu, wife of Walter. Most of its founders – William Nkomo, Jordan Ngubane, Nelson Mandela, Oliver Tambo and others – were in their twenties; Anton Lembede was 30, and Walter Sisulu and AP Mda into their thirties. Nkomo was elected as the initial leader of the CYL, but his ideas were too far to the left for most members, and Lembede soon succeeded him as president, with Mandela, Tambo and Sisulu as members of the executive committee.[3] Membership of the CYL was open to all Africans between the ages of 12 and 40, and anyone older than 17 automatically became an ANC member too.

The CYL's founding manifesto, drafted by Lembede, Mda and Ngubane, expressed withering criticisms of the parent body, claiming that the ANC had habitually yielded to oppression, was weakly organised, represented only the most privileged Africans, and was concerned mainly with preserving the rights of an elite.[4] Its tactics, furthermore, were outdated and its strategy reactive.

The manifesto went on to set out the CYL's more militant philosophy. The most pressing need was the rooting out of any sense of African inferiority among members and the inculcation of a creed based on 'the primary, inherent and inalienable right of the African to his homeland and his continent'.[5] The CYL foresaw 'a long, bitter and unrelenting struggle' against 'European' domination, which might only be shortened through a compromise in which whites would be admitted to 'a share of the fruits of Africa' on three conditions: the abandonment of racial domination, the proportional redistribution of land, and assistance in establishing a free people's democracy – in South Africa in particular and Africa generally.

Coloureds, the manifesto declared, were of Hottentot, African and Bushman stock and thus among the 'children of Africa', who should cooperate in the freedom struggle. Indians were another oppressed group, and should not be regarded as 'intruders or enemies' as long as they did not undermine the African fight for liberation.[6] The CYL was not opposed to Europeans as such, but 'totally and irrevocably opposed to white domination'.[7]

With reference to the war with Nazi Germany, 'it would be the highest folly', the manifesto declared, 'to believe that after the war, South Africa will treat the African as a citizen with the right to live free. South African blood, of Africans and whites alike, was being shed to free the white peoples of Europe, while Africans within the Union remained in bondage.'

Early days

In its early stages, the CYL confined its activities to the Transvaal, but over time, branches were established in Natal and elsewhere. Its membership attached much importance to sport, believing that it promoted health and the team spirit essential in all areas of life. In Europe at that time, a belief in the value of outdoor activities crossed ideological lines, from German

Nazis to British socialists. Open-air camping in the countryside, athletics and team sports such as football were widely regarded as an antidote to idleness and urban degeneration. The CYL also organised youth labour camps in tandem with the Young Communists, but when invited by Ruth First, of the communist-dominated Progressive Youth Council, to affiliate, firmly declined to do so.[8]

Committed to working within the ANC but restrained by the caution of the parent body, the CYL began circumspectly, giving itself three to five years to grow and in the meantime to study 'all those forces working for or against African progress'.[9] Though there was general agreement on promoting an assertive African nationalism, there was also vigorous internal debate between the few pro-Marxists, such as Nkomo, and a larger group who were deeply suspicious of the CPSA's Stalinism, regarding it as an alien European (and non-African) ideology, antithetic to the black nationalist struggle.[10]

In its formative years, the CYL was thus extremely wary of 'the left'. Since the 1920s, there had been an overlap between ANC and CPSA membership, and Youth Leaguers suspected that communist ideology not only cloaked a white paternalism but was also divisive. In their view, Africans were not victims of a class struggle, but were discriminated against on the basis of race – as an ethnic group and as a nation.[11] Yet even within the anti-communist faction of the Youth League itself, there were differences in outlook – between 'nationalists' such as Tambo, Ngubane and Mda, who laid more emphasis on black self-assertion but worried also about black racialism, and 'Africanists' such as Lembede, Mandela and Sisulu, who were determined to develop an ideology 'dynamic enough to rouse the masses to political awareness and action'.[12]

Independent mind
Jordan Ngubane, a friend of Anton Lembede's and fellow student at Adams College, was a fiercely independent thinker, hostile to the influence of communists within the ANC. His bleak observation that to reach

the top, 'the Communist has to fight the Afrikaner-Nationalist, seek to destroy the capitalist within the United Party, undermine the liberal and sabotage the African Nationalist', did not endear him to those members of the ANC who sought to gloss over the communists' role in the formation of a popular front.[13]

After graduating from Adams in 1937, Ngubane was offered the assistant editorship of John L Dube's newspaper, *Ilanga lase Natal*, from where he launched a distinguished career as a journalist and political commentator. Moving to Johannesburg to work with Selope Thema on *Bantu World*, Ngubane renewed his friendship with Lembede and was introduced to AP Mda, already a seasoned politician. The trio became 'the principal architects of the Youth League's emerging ideology',[14] as well as of the CYL's 1944 manifesto.

Returning to Natal in 1944 to take over the editorship of *Inkundla ya Bantu*, the only newspaper wholly owned by Africans, Ngubane made the newspaper the country's leading voice of African political opinion from 1944 to 1951.[15] He used *Inkundla*'s influence to unseat the ANC's conservative 'old guard' in Natal, led by AW Champion, and to promote Albert Luthuli as a political leader and, subsequently, the ANC's president-general.

Ngubane was one of the few critics of the ruling government 'to attempt a non-vindictive and even compassionate view of whites in his future society'.[16] His views, as Munger observes, were too radical for most whites, but not nearly radical enough for black and white opponents of the government.[17] In sympathy with neither the left nor the extreme nationalist wing of the ANC, he was drawn – in the 1950s – into the Liberal Party, of which he was to become national vice-chairman.

Smuts in London

In May 1944, Smuts left for a two-week visit to London to attend the Commonwealth Prime Ministers' Conference, seek support from Britain on the Indian question, and, more importantly, obtain approval for the incorporation of neighbouring South West Africa into the Union. Since

1919, South West Africa had been administered by Pretoria as a Class C mandate of the League of Nations, and was virtually a fifth province of South Africa. On more than one occasion during the war, Winston Churchill had hinted to Smuts that South Africa should go ahead and annex the territory while no one was looking, as the Soviets had done with the Baltic States, but Smuts's respect for international law had always kept him from doing so.[18]

While in Britain, South Africa's prime minister was given the Freedom of the City of Birmingham and used the occasion to plead that the war be brought swiftly to an end. Expressing grave misgivings about the Soviet Union's post-war intentions, he urged his largely working-class audience 'to follow the Russia of Tolstoy, not of Karl Marx'.[19] Smuts's international stature was such that he was able to say publicly what Stalin's other Western allies felt but did not dare to utter.[20]

Soon afterwards, on 6 June 1944, came the start of Operation Overlord, the Allied troop landings on the beaches of Normandy. A few days after the invasion, Smuts was invited to accompany Churchill on a visit to General Bernard Montgomery's headquarters at Bayeux, the only Commonwealth leader in the party. The accompanying journalists were asked not to report his presence because of the offence it would cause General De Gaulle, the ever-prickly – and uninvited – leader of the Free French.

Smuts startles

Caught up in the heady atmosphere of wartime London, Smuts sent Hofmeyr a cable announcing that he had agreed 'in principle' to the formation of a coloured brigade to help the UDF's 6th Armoured Division, which was heavily engaged (as was the SAAF) in the campaign to liberate Italy. His message read in part: '[It] will largely solve our manpower problem in case war is unduly prolonged. Matter is being examined by Defence Department and I hope my political colleagues will give sympathetic consideration.'[21]

From a more sober-minded Cape Town, a startled Hofmeyr, speaking for a unanimous cabinet, poured cold water on the proposal, pointing out that the government was bound by its assurance that 'non-Europeans' would be armed only as a last resort. To go back on that undertaking would require the approval of Parliament. 'Apart from that, we feel that long-range consequences of Coloured men being asked to do fighting job for which we have been unable to find white men would be considerable,' wrote Hofmeyr.[22] The UP cabinet feared exactly what Malan had warned about – if one wanted non-white men and women to fight for their country, they would have to be given the vote. And to give more votes to coloureds would play directly into the hands of the HNP.[23]

Tempting target

In effective charge of the country in Smuts's absence, the diligent and devout Hofmeyr continually found himself conflicted between what his conscience demanded of him and what was acceptable to his colleagues and political constituents. Widely regarded as the most liberal member of the government on racial matters, Hofmeyr was an inviting target for Nationalist resentment – and withering scorn. The HNP's Transvaal leader, JG Strijdom, was his most venomous critic, despising Hofmeyr for his apparent abandonment of the Afrikaner cause, for his 'English mind', and particularly for espousing the dangerous ideal of racial equality, which threatened to destroy white civilisation in Africa.[24]

As he had demonstrated in 1936, however, Hofmeyr was more of a defender of the status quo than a visionary or radical reformer. Although aware that the time for whites to negotiate change was short, he was driven not by that knowledge but rather by what he believed was 'right'.[25] He accepted that there were wide cultural, educational, religious and other differences between the races in South Africa, but wanted no one to think he either hoped, or believed, it would always be so.[26] Speaking at a Fort Hare graduation ceremony shortly before the war, Hofmeyr had asserted that South Africa did not have a 'native' problem but a problem of 'race relations', which could only be solved by recognising that 'the white man and black man are possessors of a common humanity'.[27] Unlike most whites, he understood that South Africa's future lay eventually in a common society. The HNP would never let him forget it.

As South Africa's minister of finance throughout the war, 'Jan Tax', as he was dubbed, became known for his careful stewardship of the economy and, to some more liberal critics, his parsimony. Thanks primarily to gold, the country was coming through the war without the severe economic difficulties and privations experienced in most of the other belligerent nations.[28] Able to find enough money to fund the war effort and contain inflation to a reasonable level without mortgaging the country's future, Hofmeyr was set on extending social-security benefits to South Africans of all races.

Enlightened planning

Early in 1944, the final report of the Social and Economic Planning Council (SEPC), set up two years earlier by Smuts 'to plan for a national economy offering security and well-being for all',[29] was put before Parliament. Described by Nattrass as 'a bastion of reformism', the SEPC, under the chairmanship of Dr Hendrik van Eck (an industrial chemist recruited by Hendrik van der Bijl to help him establish Escom and Iscor, later managing director and chairman of the Industrial Development Corporation, and a pivotal figure in the growth of industrial South Africa), had recognised the problems brought about by racism but complained that discussing solutions all too often degenerated into the emotional response from whites: 'But would *you* allow your daughter to marry a black man?'[30]

In response to these fears, the SEPC declared the following:

> Rising social and economic standards and increasing opportunities need not threaten the economic security of the European groups; on the contrary, the ill-health, ignorance and poverty of the non-Europeans constitute a drag of immense proportions on the whole economy of the country, to the detriment of all races. Poor social

conditions produce inefficiency, disease and crime, which affect the whole community.[31]

The SEPC's remedies for these ills included an enlargement of the reserves, proper urban township planning, the vigorous expansion of industry, more opportunities for non-whites in the public service, compulsory education for all, and a comprehensive social-security system. Its final recommendation was that 'every effort be made to promote the growth of a sense of interdependence and economic unity'.[32] The bill for implementing these far-reaching reforms, however, would amount to an eye-watering £35 000 000 – far too much for the South African economy to afford, especially in wartime.

Steps forward

It fell to Hofmeyr, in his national budget of 1944, to react to the SEPC's ambitious recommendations, and to do this without increasing the tax burden on whites (taxes had risen by over 70 per cent since 1939).[33] Shortly before budget day, he had to fend off criticism from an unexpected quarter – the redoubtable Dr Hendrik van der Bijl, who mounted a fierce attack on the finance minister's taxation policies.

Alarmed by the cost of the SEPC's proposals, the director-general of war supplies warned that there could be no social security without employment, claiming that excessive taxation was hindering job creation. The gold mines could not go on paying higher taxes while being expected to employ more people, he argued. The country's current tax regime was stifling enterprise and giving no incentive to entrepreneurs.[34]

Hofmeyr understood Van der Bijl's arguments but did not agree with them, and was angered by their timing.[35] As minister of finance, he had been given the task of funding the war effort while simultaneously steering a middle course between the claims of the present and those of the future. And he intended to do exactly that, within the limited fiscal scope available.

In his budget speech, Hofmeyr announced the first steps towards across-the-board social-welfare payments for all South Africans. While he conceded that social security had to be funded by increased industrialisation rather than higher taxes, this could not absolve the government from its current responsibilities. He had therefore set aside funds for old-age and disability pensions for Africans, Indians and coloureds (albeit at widely discriminatory levels). Unemployment benefits were introduced and a modest amount allocated to African education. The charge levied on the mines for the disposal of their gold was lifted, so that the wages of African miners could be increased.[36]

By comparison with defence spending, the amounts allocated to social welfare were derisory, yet they indicated a timely change of heart on the government's part and set a precedent for the future. Critics such as the independent MP JR Sullivan, whose election platform was 'Social Security', claimed the new allocations were not nearly enough, but the forthright Donald Molteno, one of the three Native Representatives, while critical of the small size of the grants, declared that the people he represented would be grateful for benefits to which they had never before been entitled.[37]

Nationalist reaction to Hofmeyr's proposals came from JG Strijdom, who wanted to know why whites should have to fund the pensions of other races: 'I ask again whether we can afford, in view of the poverty prevailing among the white population in South Africa, to put a tax on the white man which is going to cost millions of pounds in order to help old natives to get old-age pensions?' To which Hofmeyr responded: 'Which country in the world would tolerate a position under which the money for social services for the poorest section of the population had to come from that section of the population only?'[38]

Campaign flounders

While white politicians argued over the extension of welfare benefits to the poorest sections of the population, the joint ANC/CPSA-led anti-pass campaign had not gone well. Intended to culminate in the collection of a million signatures by August 1944, followed by demonstrations and the burning of passes, the initiative was proving to be little more than 'a premature gesture'.[39] Apart from a few dedicated activists in their ranks, neither the ANC nor the CPSA could arouse much enthusiasm among their followers, and Xuma's leadership of the campaign was rhetorical and half-hearted.[40] Always more at home in committee rooms than out on the hustings, the ANC president found it difficult to work with a committee dominated by communists.[41]

Africanists in the ANC were hostile to the campaign, fearing they were being 'used' by Indian militants such as Yusuf Dadoo. And there was friction among the anti-pass organisers themselves, with allegations flying around that the communists were not prepared to accept anything but token ANC leadership.[42]

By the August target date, the anti-pass campaign had lost momentum because of an inability to arouse popular interest and a shortage of money, so the deadline was moved to January 1945, and then to March of that year. After an emergency meeting chaired by Xuma and attended by Dadoo, Kotane, Marks, Mosaka and others, it was agreed to launch a last-ditch signature drive, the results of which would be presented to the government. But when Dadoo and others travelled to Cape Town in mid-year to hand over the petition, Smuts was out of the country and Hofmeyr was 'too busy' to see them. The ill-fated venture was allowed to fizzle to an end, to be revived several years later in the form of the Defiance Campaign.[43]

By-election pointer

The impending defeat of the Axis Powers failed to inhibit the Nationalists from censuring the government at every opportunity for keeping South Africa involved in the war. While Smuts, at the UP congress in 1944, gave high praise to his countrymen and women for their patriotism and for having 'set a high standard in this the greatest crisis of our lives and of world history', the HNP simply changed the thrust of their attacks on the prime minister by charging him with aiding and abetting an American and Russian victory in the war. America was an uncertain friend, while Russian communism was a dangerous enemy of South Africa, the Nationalists alleged.

The first indication since the 1943 election that these tactics might be having an effect came at a by-election in Wakkerstroom in late 1944, when the seat vacated upon the death of UP cabinet minister Colonel Collins was won decisively by the HNP. Now free of the stigma of support for the Ossewabrandwag and the New Order, and proclaiming themselves the upholders of parliamentary democracy, Malan and his party were given a huge psychological boost at Wakkerstroom and began to appear more like an alternative to the increasingly divided and dispirited UP coalition.

Noël Coward

Among the diversions of 1944 was a visit to South Africa by the celebrated British composer and playwright Noël Coward, who gave a series of concerts in aid of Isie (Ouma) Smuts's Gifts and Comforts Fund for service personnel in the UDF. As during WWI, the prime minister's wife had set up networks of women volunteers around the country to knit or assemble small luxuries (scarves, socks, chocolates, books and cigarettes) for the 'boys up north'. Work parties were held at the prime ministerial residences of Groote Schuur and Libertas, and at the Smuts home at Doornkloof, outside Pretoria, in support of the Fund.

As Jeremy Lawrence recounts in the biography of his father, Harry, Coward was treated with the deference usually shown to royalty: he was given a ministerial railway coach and driven through crowded streets in an open-topped car flanked by motorcycle outriders. Royalty itself was present at Coward's premiere at the Alhambra Theatre in Cape Town, in the form of the pretty young Princess Frederica of Greece – in temporary refuge from the war in Europe – flanked by the entire cabinet and their wives as well as the cream of Cape Town society. Neither of the Smutses appeared to enjoy the performance much: Ouma Smuts spent her time doggedly knitting, while her husband was visibly irritated when Coward launched into his witty new hit song, 'Don't Let's Be Beastly to the Germans'. No one appears to have told the maestro that Frederica, sitting beside the prime minister as the guest of honour, was German by birth and a granddaughter of Kaiser Wilhelm II.[44]

Elsewhere in the World

In 1944

17 January–19 May	Battle of Monte Cassino
27 January	Siege of Leningrad ends after 872 days
April	6th SA Armoured Division, under Major-General WH Evered Poole, arrives in Italy
4 April–22 June	Battle of Kohima, in northeast India, ends Japanese U-Go offensive
4 June	Allied troops enter Rome
6 June	D-Day: US, British and Canadian troops land in Normandy
15 June–9 July	Battle of Saipan in the Marianas Islands
22 June–19 August	Red Army launches Operation Bagration to clear Byelorussia (Belarus)
1 July	Bretton Woods Conference on post-war financial system opens
4 August	South African troops enter Florence
24 August	Liberation of Paris
September	RAF and SAAF aircraft drop supplies to Polish Home Army during Warsaw Uprising
8 September	First V2 rockets hit London
19 October	Death of Deneys Reitz, soldier, author, politician and diplomat
23–26 October	Battle of Leyte Gulf breaks Japanese naval power in the Pacific
7 November	Franklin Roosevelt wins fourth term as US president

CHAPTER 18

Victory

With the end of the war in sight, Smuts viewed with mounting concern the power vacuum developing in Europe. He could foresee only one clear victor in the war – Stalin's Soviet Union.[1] Month by month, communism was being imposed upon every country occupied by Soviet forces. What would become of Africa – and South Africa – in the post-war world, he wondered. Europe might still be in effective control of sub-Saharan Africa, but for how long? In the Far East, newly liberated colonies, urged on by the Soviets, were challenging the power of their European masters, while the Americans were caught between their strategic ambitions and their anti-colonial impulses.[2] The new arena of great-power conflict, Smuts predicted, would be the new United Nations Organisation. Writing to Hofmeyr from San Francisco, where he (Smuts) was attending the new body's founding conference, he observed that 'a strong humanitarian tendency' was expressing itself in 'a demand for equal human rights all round, and other somewhat embarrassing proposals. Trusteeships have become a bone of contention and mandates are involved in this bigger issue.'[3]

For this tendency, as he well knew, Malan and the HNP would blame him too. No longer able to defend Hitler, the Nationalists had switched to condemnation of America and Britain for destroying Germany and abetting the advance of communism. *Die rooi gevaar* (the red peril) was now the theme of every HNP speech. It was not only Alan Paton who wondered why Afrikaner Nationalism should react so violently to communism and so unconcernedly to Nazism; why it should be so revolted by Russia's godlessness yet unmoved by Hitler's?[4]

In his heart of hearts, Smuts shared Malan's fears about Russia. To a friend, he declared pessimistically: '[M]y faith in man does not extend to faith in Russia, with no check upon her in Europe and Asia, and [as] mistress of the continent of Europe. Such a position is too much of a temptation even to the wisest, let alone an upstart power such as Russia.'[5] And from America, he commented to Hofmeyr: 'Everywhere I find people in an anxious mood over the doings of the Great Bear. There is no doubt that Russia now occupies a position in the world which will give us all more thought and more headaches.'[6]

Inflation

At home, dissatisfaction with Smuts and his government went much further than the ranks of the HNP. The cost of food had risen steadily throughout the war, despite efforts to control it. Price controls – and the export of produce such as maize and citrus at a loss in order to prop up prices to farmers – were not helping either. Eggs, poultry, dairy products and especially meat were in short supply, for which the new minister of agriculture, JGN Strauss, had to shoulder much of the blame. Despite the overall rise in purchasing power, brought about by higher wartime wages, too much money chasing too little food was a home-made recipe for inflation.[7]

Adding to the government's woes were the high expectations of returning UDF servicemen, who had put their lives on the line for their country. Not enough thought had been given to the political, social and economic implications of the promises made to them. During the parliamentary debate on demobilisation, the Labour MP the Reverend CF Miles Cadman suggested to Smuts that in making promises to soldiers, he had been carried away by his own eloquence. To which Smuts replied that optimism and faith were the basis of most ambitious plans. 'I should like to remind the honourable member that unless he had a certain amount of faith, his profession would go out of business in a week or two.'[8]

The Directorate of Demobilisation had been set up to repatriate, demobilise and compensate the thousands of volunteers, now anxious to return to civilian life, and the responsible minister, Harry Lawrence, had promised 'there would be no forgotten men'. But, writes Ian van der Waag, for many ex-soldiers 'ideas of a post-war Utopia were dashed by seemingly inexplicable delays and apparent unfairness, all exacerbated by [their] poor socio-economic conditions'.[9] Some Nationalist-controlled town councils even refused to offer municipal employment to the returnees.[10] Earlier, Smuts had been forced to admit that 'for many the help we shall be able to offer may be incommensurate with their sacrifices. There are some things incapable of compensation. And patriotism is above nicely calculated monetary evaluations.'[11]

No amount of UP mockery of the opposition for their misguided support of Hitler could deflect justified criticism that bureaucracy had become rife in wartime South Africa, where the solution to every problem seemed to be one more commission, advisory body or committee.[12] (The malaise is still rife today.) By July 1945, the (white) housing situation had become scandalous. Because of red tape, fewer than 4 000 of the 12 000 houses promised by the July deadline had been built. A Housing (Emergency Powers) Bill had to be rushed through Parliament, giving the state drastic powers for three years to find the necessary land, material and labour, and to limit builders' profits to a maximum of cost plus six per cent. With no sense of irony, the HNP's JH Conradie accused Smuts in Parliament of being 'a little Hitler'.[13]

Bolshevist bogey

As the end of the war drew closer, Malan was also turning his mind to its implications for South Africa. However one viewed Nazi Germany, it had been a bulwark against the spread of Bolshevist communism. Back in 1941, Malan had warned:

> Bolshevism is a destroyer of the foundations of civilisation and of everything the Christian nations deem to be holy ... It wants to initiate a Bolshevist revolution here and therefore seeks its support mostly with the non-white elements. Under the leadership of Communist Jews, it has nestled itself into a number of our trade unions. It does not acknowledge the colour bar in any sphere and where it is legally possible, it agitates tirelessly – with the vehement incitement of the non-whites – to remove it ... Bolshevism is the negation of everything Afrikanerdom has stood for and fought for, suffered for and died for, for generations.[14]

Malan felt sure that a new and potentially more devastating war, between the US and Britain on one side and Soviet Russia on the other, was inevitable. In his view, the world was still caught up in a battle between nationalism and imperialism, in which one of the battlegrounds was race relations. 'Imperialism,' he warned, 'in tandem with capitalism, had always used political rights for Coloureds and Africans as a weapon against Afrikaner nationalism, and in so doing had opened the door for communist agitators to instigate the removal of all colour distinctions.'[15]

Apartheid

According to Lindie Koorts, it was Malan who first introduced the word 'apartheid' into parliamentary debate in South Africa. Speaking in the House of Assembly in January 1944, he declared that the country's future lay in a republic that was anti-capitalist and anti-communist and should be safeguarded for the white race and Christian civilisation by adhering 'to the principles of apartheid and trusteeship, as well as the development of the non-white population according to their nature and their abilities'.[16] The HNP leader was determined to translate principle into policy in his native Cape Province, where he and his supporters regarded the coloured vote as an ever-present threat, believing it had cost them at least six seats in the 1943 election.[17] In late 1944, he appointed a commission under

Paul Sauer to formulate a 'positive and constructive Coloured policy for the HNP'.[18]

The Sauer Commission duly reported a year later that the tensions resulting from whites and non-whites living, working and voting together could only be relieved by a policy of separation, or apartheid. Fears among whites were being aggravated by a new development – the 'communist exploitation' of coloured voters. Coloureds occupied 'the middle ground between whites and Africans and their privileged position had to be preserved'. This required, among other measures, race classification and the establishment of a population register. As for the vote, coloureds should be removed from the common roll and given three coloured representatives in Parliament – similar to the Native Representatives. At a municipal level, there should be separate coloured residential areas and 'autonomous' councils.[19]

Released shortly after the end of the war, the Sauer report was well received by the HNP leader and his party[20] – but by almost no one else. While bewailing the hostility that Nationalist Afrikaners had to endure from other sections of the community, Malan continued to warn that South Africa's future as a white-led country was in the balance. Like Hertzog of old, he maintained that the only solution was for Afrikaners to look inwards and close ranks in support of the HNP.

At the UN

Smuts, in the meantime, had left South Africa again, bound for London and San Francisco, carrying with him the baggage of the suspended Pegging Act and the enmity of the government of India. He was determined that the UNO should not fail as the League of Nations had done. In London, he took it upon himself to propose amendments to the wording of the proposed UN Charter to include references to the protection of fundamental human rights, equality between the sexes, the practice of tolerance and security from attack for all nations big and small. His amended version of the Preamble to the Charter was approved by the Commonwealth prime ministers and put forward at the founding conference in San

Francisco, where the Charter was adopted with minor amendments. The Indians were to seize upon it gleefully as a rod with which to beat Smuts and post-war South Africa.

At the conference, Smuts was given formal notice that South Africa and the other mandatory powers would be invited to bring their mandates, including South West Africa, into the proposed UN trusteeship system. Expressing objections to the proposal, he reserved South Africa's right to submit a response to the UN General Assembly when it was duly constituted.[21] Ever the philosopher, he viewed the drawn-out proceedings in San Francisco with mounting scepticism, noting privately, 'My reflections and experience of life have led me to question the adequacy of the Marxian view that human conflicts arise solely from material and economic causes, and can be dealt with on that level merely by economic and social reform. There is something else the human spirit wants and craves for its satisfaction.'[22]

Germany capitulates

In late April, while Smuts was still in San Francisco, Hitler committed suicide in his Berlin bunker, to be succeeded briefly by Admiral Dönitz as head of state. On 7 May, Germany surrendered unconditionally to the Allies, and the war in Europe (though not in the Far East) was over. At 3 pm the next day, called Victory in Europe (or VE) Day, Winston Churchill's dramatic announcement in the House of Commons that 'the German war is at an end' came crackling across the airwaves, sparking off joyous celebrations throughout the UK, US, France and the Commonwealth.

In Johannesburg, where guns boomed, sirens blared and mine hooters blasted in triumph, ticker tape and scraps of paper fluttered down from office towers in Commissioner Street onto a celebrating crowd below. More than 10 000 people, among them returned soldiers and airmen, gathered in the city square to listen to Churchill's solemn pronouncement, at the end of which trumpets sounded and the assembled crowd sang 'God Save the King'. On the mines, work was halted, offices in the city closed, and even in the jails prisoners were able to rejoice at a three-month remission of sentence.

'It was a mad, merry, unforgettable moment,' *The Star* newspaper reported, 'into which the people tried to compress all the relief they felt from the suspense, anxiety and strain of five years of terrible war.'[23] Not to be outdone, the ANC and the SACP also celebrated VE Day by staging an impromptu march through the streets to the City Hall, where Dr Yusuf Dadoo and JB Marks were among those who addressed a jubilant audience.

Similar scenes played out in Cape Town, where flags flew and a huge crowd thronged Adderley Street amid a cacophony of hooting ships and tugs in Table Bay, and in Pretoria, where the city was 'a riot of red, white and blue'. In Durban harbour, returning soldiers had been welcomed as always at the quayside by the megaphone of the city's most famous citizen, the 'Lady in White', Perla Siedle Gibson, a trained soprano who had sung her way into the hearts of thousands of Allied servicemen aboard troopships entering and leaving Durban from 1940 to 1945. On one occasion, her rendition of 'Waltzing Matilda' had brought so many Australians rushing to the side of their ship that the vessel listed and its mast crashed into a grain elevator.[24]

Most South African newspapers carried banner headlines proclaiming the end of the war in Europe and announcing details of thanksgiving services. Nationalist newspapers recorded the news with a notable lack of enthusiasm, a sourly worded editorial in *Die Vaderland* of 8 May expressing gladness that the guns in Europe had fallen silent after five years but expressing no satisfaction at the defeat of Hitler's Germany. In an overview of the war, the newspaper managed to avoid any reference whatsoever to South Africa's participation in the Allied victory.

After adjourning for two days, Parliament reconvened on 11 May to discuss three resolutions moved by Hofmeyr, acting in the absent Smuts's stead. To the first, which congratulated King George VI, Malan moved an amendment thanking God instead; to the second, which expressed gratitude to the men and women of the armed forces, Malan moved another amendment thanking those whose bravery and endurance had brought honour to South Africa. Both amendments were defeated. To the third resolution, which paid homage to the dead, no amendment was proposed. The procedure was repeated in the Senate, where the HNP's PW le Roux van Niekerk used his moment to assert bitterly that 'the fame of the prime minister at "San Fiasco" was not worth the lives of fifty young South Africans'.[25] To which Hofmeyr reacted strongly, saying that anti-Semitism, racism and colour prejudice had increased over the preceding few years because of the growing tendency of people to 'think with their blood', as had happened in Nazi Germany.[26]

On the evening of 8 May, Hofmeyr made a victory broadcast to the nation. After giving thanks to God and all those – especially the deceased, prisoners of war and the missing – who had contributed to the victory, the acting prime minister declared, 'We have made a much larger contribution to the cause to which we pledged ourselves than at first we dared to hope … This has been a great period in our history. Viewed aright, it could become a mighty force for the building up of a great, a truly united South Africa.'[27]

Winston Churchill also sent a special message to the people of South Africa that read: 'History will record the heroic achievements of South Africa's fighting men who once again on land and now in the air and at sea have proved themselves second to none.'[28]

Smuts returns

More than a month later, on 16 July, Smuts returned to South Africa to a tumultuous reception. Speaking a few days later to a cheering crowd at the Union Buildings, he said that in honour of the 9 000 servicemen who would never return home, 'we should strive to make South Africa a land of honour, freedom and justice'. From the Union Buildings, he went to Pretoria's Market Square, where a large multiracial crowd welcomed him with a roar of 'Pula' ('rain' in Sesotho).[29]

In August, the Native Representative Council passed a motion of appreciation for Smuts's leadership of the country's war effort. Dr Moroka, the chairman, commended the prime minister for his courage in going to war with the white population so divided, while the African people had always been 'unanimous'. Councillor Selope Thema explained that 'the Natives [had] participated in the war because they felt they must be on the side of democracy ... Recently the Prime Minister said that there is room enough for both races in South Africa. We want to know in what way there is room for us both?'[30] Only days later, the Native (Urban Areas) Consolidation Act, which regulated the movement of Africans, was passed by Parliament. The NRC had not even been consulted.

Atom bombs

On 6 and 9 August, the United States dropped atomic bombs on the Japanese cities of Hiroshima and Nagasaki, respectively, causing hundreds of thousands of civilian deaths and casualties. On 2 September, the Japanese sued for peace and formally surrendered to General Douglas MacArthur aboard the battleship the USS *Missouri* in Tokyo Bay. South Africa was represented at the ceremony by Commander AP Cartwright of the South African Naval Forces, the senior South African officer on the staff of Admiral Chester Nimitz, the Allied commander-in-chief in the Pacific Ocean.

At long last, WWII was over.

Elsewhere in the World

In 1945

25 January	End of German counteroffensive in the Ardennes (Battle of the Bulge)
30 January	Hitler makes his last public speech
4–11 February	Yalta Conference: Churchill, Roosevelt and Stalin agree post-war European settlement

19 February	US Marines land on Iwo Jima
2 April	Death of Franklin Roosevelt; Harry S Truman becomes US president
16 April	Red Army launches offensive to take Berlin
4 May	Surrender of German forces in Netherlands, Denmark and northern Germany
8 May	VE Day
26 June	UN Charter signed by 50 countries in San Francisco
14 July	6th SA Armoured Division holds victory parade at Monza racing circuit outside Milan
17 July–2 August	Potsdam Conference held to discuss post-war settlement
26 July	Winston Churchill succeeded as prime minister by Clement Atlee following Labour election victory
2 September	Japan surrenders following atomic bombing of Hiroshima and Nagasaki
2 September	Ho Chi Minh declares Vietnam independent from France
20 November	Start of Nuremberg War Crimes Tribunal

PART THREE

Post War

CHAPTER 19

Taking Stock

South Africa emerged from the war as a quasi-developmental state, the product of an alliance between mining capital, a few large state-owned entities such as Iscor and Escom, and the ruling United Party. The UP's declared intention was to further the interests of all racial groups – under the banner of 'white trusteeship'. As Bill Freund observes, South Africa's industrial development during and after the war was marked by increased government intervention. Every Allied belligerent nation had been obliged to suspend free-market policies in favour of state intervention in key areas, and South Africa was no exception: 'The imperatives of mobilisation strongly favoured breakneck economic development,' and South Africa moved sharply in the direction of a developmental state.[1]

Smuts was a Keynesian, a proponent of the state-directed industrial development that had resulted in a significant reshaping of the economy. War-related production demands and the need for import substitution had made manufacturing rather than mining the dominant growth sector of the economy, while the expansion of international trade from 1945 carried both mining and manufacturing even 'further along the path of industrial diversification'.[2] And, as Nattrass points out, the consequent entry of black workers into industry in large numbers, and the growth of the secondary sector in general, helped reduce income inequality between the races.[3] Throughout the war, Smuts had held out a vision of a better post-war future for all South Africans, promising in 1943 to combat want, poverty and unemployment 'to the best of our ability'.[4]

Franchise reform was never in prospect, of course, but the official discourse had switched irreversibly from social exclusion to inclusion, provision having been made for the first time for the poorest African men and women, albeit at racially determined and deeply unequal rates.[5] South Africa had entered the 1940s with a fragmented and racialised public-welfare system from which Africans and Indians had been excluded. During the war, that had changed for the better: unemployment insurance was now available to all; there were grants for the blind and disabled; spending on black education was three times higher than ten years before; and non-contributory old-age pensions had been introduced. As Seekings points out, today, in the 21st century, the old-age pension is still at the core of South Africa's public-welfare system.[6]

Break-up

Within a month of VE Day, the United Party suffered another debilitating loss in the parliamentary constituency of Kimberley, which the HNP won with a swing of some 750 votes. The UP's taxation policies received most of the blame, but other factors were soldier dissatisfaction, the housing shortage and the high cost of living.[7] Business was particularly resentful of the extra duties on excess and trade profits imposed by the finance minister. Defending his policy, Hofmeyr warned there could be no return to pre-war levels of taxation or expenditure: the public now demanded better health services and improved social-security measures.[8]

Towards the end of the year, the long-threatened break-up of the UP-led wartime coalition finally occurred when first Walter Madeley, the Labour leader, and then Colonel Stallard, leader of the Dominion Party, resigned from the cabinet, after which they led their MPs across the floor of the House to join the HNP on the opposition benches.[9] On the racial question – now the litmus test in white politics – these white conservatives no longer felt at home in the party of Smuts, and more especially of Hofmeyr, and regarded themselves as better attuned to the Nationalists.

No mixing

The year 1945 was the one in which the HNP formally adopted apartheid as its official racial policy. In an unpublished but revealing manuscript, DF Malan laid bare his instinctive belief that whites and non-whites were not of the same kind and no good could be found in miscegenation – physical or political.[10] It was the Voortrekkers' deep Christianity that had prevented such mixing. Afrikaner 'trusteeship' not only entailed white rule but 'also white protection of the Africans, which gave them the opportunity to develop themselves in their own reserves'.[11] Yet the white race was threatened by the erosion of its boundaries and the agitation of communist rabble-rousers, who were infiltrating the trade unions and all other non-white organisations. Acknowledging, for the first time in years, that whites and non-whites shared the same fatherland, Malan asserted that the implementation of apartheid 'would eradicate whites' fears of Africans and Africans would soon realise they had nothing to fear'.[12]

So much for the theory, in the Cape at least. In the minds of apartheid's cruder advocates to the north, such as JG Strijdom, it meant the application of *baasskap* (white supremacy) at every turn, as well as implacable opposition to the Commonwealth (notably India), the UN and its subversive Declaration of Human Rights, the communists and of course any liberal sentiments within South Africa itself. Once again, the wagons were circling and another migration of Afrikaners – this time inwards – was about to begin. Now that the war was over, there was no let-up in the hostility and ugly political rhetoric that continued to disfigure white politics.

Growing in confidence

The momentum generated by the ANC under AB Xuma during the war years quickened with the coming of peace.[13] Inspired by the Atlantic

Charter, the organisation no longer looked to Britain for support but instead began to pin its hopes on the United Nations, where two issues – South West Africa and the treatment of South Africa's Indian population – offered opportunities to both oppose and embarrass the Smuts government. In response to Pretoria's protestations that both matters fell within South Africa's jurisdiction and not that of the UN, the ANC was able to claim that South West Africa was now effectively a UN rather than a League of Nations mandate and the Indian question a dispute between member states that could well become a threat to world peace. As Barber points out, these were effective hooks on which to hang any attack on South Africa's racial policies.[14]

The ANC's growing self-confidence was given a further boost by an invitation to participate in the 5th Pan African Congress, held in Manchester in October 1945, where the two ANC representatives, London-based Mark Hlubi and the novelist Peter Abrahams, rubbed shoulders with leading African nationalists, including Kwame Nkrumah from the Gold Coast, Jomo Kenyatta from Kenya and Hastings Kamuzu Banda from Nyasaland. The congress, attended by 90 delegates from Africa, Britain, the US, Europe and the Caribbean, is seen today as marking a turning point in the decolonisation of Africa.[15]

Among the many topics under discussion was 'Oppression in South Africa'. Although the ANC representatives failed to use the opportunity to present a fully developed case to the conference,[16] the assembled delegates pledged to work unceasingly until 'our "non-European brothers" in South Africa had achieved the status of freedom and dignity'. They also addressed a formal protest to the UN over South Africa's wish to terminate the South West Africa mandate, and over the treatment of its Indian population. International links forged by the ANC in Manchester were renewed in Dakar two years later, and proved useful in the long-drawn-out liberation struggle that lay ahead.[17]

Broeders curbed

Shortly before the end of the war, Smuts had been forced to take a step he had hitherto resisted – curbing the activities of the secretive Afrikaner Broederbond. Believing that the more attention paid to organisations such as the Bond and its soulmate, the Ossewabrandwag, the stronger they would become, the prime minister had deliberately ignored both of them for most of the war, but was eventually persuaded to take action by members of his own party as well as by a report compiled by military intelligence.[18] The confidential report detailed the extent of the Bond's infiltration of the civil service, and of the teaching profession in particular. Almost 40 per cent of Broeders, the report claimed, were teachers, lecturers, *predikante* (ministers) or members of school governing bodies. Drawing attention to the Bond's 'all-pervasive grip' and 'octopus-like tendencies', its long-range revolutionary plans for the establishment of a republic, as well as its undercover links with Nazism, the report summarised the organisation's key role in fomenting internal opposition to the war effort and pleaded for speedy government intervention.[19]

Announcing that civil servants and teachers would no longer be permitted to be members of the Broederbond, Smuts had this to say:

> I warn the people that there is something in their midst which conflicts with our better feelings and customs, affects the ethical character of our society and in the long run is going to pollute our society. A small secret minority, or oligarchy, is working itself into a position of power. It is clear that the Broederbond is a dangerous, cunning, political, fascist organisation of which no civil servant, if he is to retain his loyalty to the state, can be allowed to become a member.[20]

No action was taken against the Broederbond itself, but the ban significantly reduced its membership – and greatly increased the level of anti-government resentment among Nationalists. In the parliamentary session of 1945, Malan denounced the measure and accused Smuts of persecuting Afrikaners. The Broederbond, he declared, was a cultural organisation similar to the Freemasons or the Sons of England; its only aim was to promote the cultural and economic interests of the Afrikaner. *Die Transvaler*'s editor, HF Verwoerd, warned Smuts that the Nationalists would retaliate once they were in government.[21]

Ghetto Act

Three months before the expiry of the Pegging Act in March 1946, Smuts set the cat among the pigeons by announcing his intention of introducing new legislation to regulate the acquisition of land by Indians in Natal. The Natal Indian Congress was furious, sending a telegram to Delhi that read in part: 'Honour of India at stake. The situation demands immediate action to uphold the honour and dignity of Indians abroad. Urge Government of India should raise the question at the General Assembly of UNO.'[22] The Transvaal Indian Congress sent a similar message to the viceroy of India, Lord Wavell, and world leaders. A deputation of some 50 members of the SAIC, headed by AI Kajee and Sorabjee Rustomjee, met around a table in Cape Town with Smuts, who listened mostly in silence. The delegation reported to the SAIC that their appeal had been 'in vain'.[23]

The Asiatic Land Tenure and Indian Representation Bill, which became known as the Ghetto Act, was tabled in Parliament on 15 March 1946 and consisted of two parts. The first regulated the acquisition of urban and rural property and divided the province of Natal into Controlled and Uncontrolled areas. There would be no restrictions on property purchases in Uncontrolled or 'free' areas, which were mostly dwellings already owned or occupied by Indians. In Controlled Areas, however, property transactions between 'Europeans and Asiatics' were prohibited, unless authorised by permit.

The second part of the Bill provided for the political representation of Indians. Three Europeans would represent the Indian population in the House of Assembly, and two in the Senate. Two representatives, who could be Indian, would sit in the Natal Provincial Council. Not surprisingly, the proposal caused an immediate outcry from Indians in South Africa and India, with Delhi announcing its intention of imposing economic sanctions on South Africa.

AI Kajee, who had tried so hard to find a compromise over the land issue, declared despairingly: 'General Smuts might gain the support of British people in Natal, but [he] would lose his international soul.'[24] However, as Alan Paton observed bluntly, it was hardly possible to be prime minister of white South Africa and possess an 'international soul'. The Indians were asking Smuts to do something that no leading white politician in South Africa could do – unless, that is, he wished to cease being a leading white politician in South Africa.[25]

On his own

Typically, Smuts insisted on piloting the Ghetto Act through the House himself, not wishing to pass the buck to the minister of the interior. Once more, he found himself assailed from all sides. If he ever thought that breaking precedent and giving Indians representation in Parliament for the first time was a suitable quid pro quo for the loss of property rights, he was mistaken. Yet within white ranks, not only the Nationalists but also members of his own caucus were strongly opposed to the notion of granting any vote to 'non-Europeans'. They regarded Smuts's land tenure and franchise proposals as far too liberal and resented any 'interference' in South Africa's domestic politics, particularly as Indians were now generally accepted as members of the country's permanent population. Malan declared that his party would repeal the franchise legislation as soon as it came to power.[26]

Longest-ever debate

On 31 March, 6 000 demonstrators marched down West Street in Durban to protest against the impending Ghetto Act, and to listen to addresses by Monty Naicker of the NIC and representatives of the ANC and the APO. The gathering endorsed the decision taken earlier by the NIC 'to launch a concerted passive resistance struggle for the defeat of this measure'.[27]

Posters calling on Natal Indians to resist segregationist legislation.
NAT FARBMAN/THE LIFE PICTURE COLLECTION VIA GETTY IMAGES

The Ghetto Act became law on 3 June 1946, after the longest-ever debate in the House of Assembly and five days of argument in the Senate. Ten days later, a group of Indians occupied a vacant site in Gale Street, Durban, setting off a campaign in which people from all walks of life – including doctors and lawyers – deliberately courted arrest over a period of several months and were imprisoned. Nearly 2 000 men and women, Naicker among them, went to jail, causing grave embarrassment for Smuts and making useful propaganda for the Indian nationalists in Delhi.

White South Africa could hardly have chosen a less propitious time to advertise its racial prejudices. As DW Krüger reflected, since the end of the war irreversible changes had taken place in the field of race relations worldwide, from which a geographically isolated South Africa was not immune.[28] In Asia, Japan's military successes in the early phases of the war had 'pricked the bubble' of Western imperialism and aroused the dormant political consciousness of subjected peoples, who refused to bow the knee any longer to their former colonial masters, whether British, Dutch or French. Their reawakened national pride would have a galvanising effect on the colonised masses in Africa.[29]

Symbolic campaign

In India, Mahatma Gandhi and Jawaharlal Nehru, the prime minister in waiting, had thrown their considerable moral weight behind a South African campaign that, in their view, had a much wider context and symbolised the struggle of oppressed people around the world. Nehru urged 'UNO and the rest of the British Empire' to 'dissociate themselves from South Africa and cut her away from the family of nations if she follows the Nazi doctrine'.[30] He advised the Indians of South Africa to make common cause with the African people, for if Indians thought themselves superior to Africans, 'then others [ie Europeans] will consider themselves your superiors'.[31]

As soon as the Ghetto Act became law, the provisional government in Delhi imposed an economic boycott of South Africa. As Ahmed Kathrada recalls, India was the world's primary producer of jute, the raw material from which grain sacks were made. The Indian embargo on jute sales hit farmers in South Africa's maize belt particularly hard, causing mountains of harvested maize to pile up and rot, and putting many small farmers out of business.[32]

In addition to the economic boycott, India recalled its high commissioner from the Union. And on 22 June, India formally requested the UN secretary-general to put the treatment of Indians in South Africa on the agenda of the forthcoming session of the UN General Assembly. In this tense atmosphere, and with denunciations of South Africa's racial policies echoing in his ears, Smuts took the speaker's podium in San Francisco for the second time in 1946, deliberately putting himself, rather than any of his colleagues, in the eye of the gathering storm.

Postscript

A curious episode in mid-1946, which led to heated scenes in Parliament, was the enquiry into a report that the leader of the opposition, DF Malan, had been in direct contact with German agents during the war. The allegation, if proven, would amount to treason. Notes had turned up in the ruins of the German Foreign Ministry in Berlin of a meeting in Cape Town between Malan and the wife of Hans Denk, a man known to the Allies as a Nazi spy. Mrs Denk had been given a meeting with Malan at his house in Sea Point in January 1940, at which the Cape leader of the HNP, Karl Bremer, had acted as interpreter. At the meeting, Mrs Denk had allegedly presented Malan with a message about relations between Nazi Germany and South Africa in the event of a separate peace between the two countries.[33] According to an 'embellished' account of the meeting sent by Hans Denk to the German authorities,[34] Malan had expressed his thanks for the message, which he promised to pass on to Hertzog and other leading Nationalists. The Denk report was duly passed on to the Smuts government after the war.

The matter surfaced in Parliament when the minister of justice, Harry Lawrence, suggested that the Denk-Malan encounter might have inspired the HNP's proposal for peace with Germany, put before the House in January 1940, only three days after the meeting. Predictably, Lawrence's suggestion caused an uproar, leading to the appointment of a select committee to investigate the matter.

Appearing before the committee, Malan explained that he had listened politely to Mrs Denk but had offered no response, and had sent his visitor on her way. He did not report the conversation to the government because he regarded the meeting as inconsequential and possibly an attempt at entrapment, as Germans would often ask to see him. (Shortly after the war, Malan was approached to be patron of an organisation aimed at facilitating the adoption of German war orphans. Despite knowing it would not be viewed as a neutral act, he and his wife chose to set an example by adopting a ten-year-old girl, renamed Marietjie, in 1947.) Since it was not an offence to be approached by the enemy, the select committee accepted Malan's explanation and found his reasons for failing to report the incident 'in view of all the circumstances at the time adequate'.[35] Lawrence was angered by the finding, and offered his resignation, but Smuts would not hear of it.[36]

When the committee's report was tabled in the House, there were furious exchanges between Lawrence and leading Nationalist MPs, notably the voluble Strijdom and the equally excitable Eric Louw, who accused the minister of impugning Malan's integrity. To this Lawrence replied that he had a responsibility to the country to disclose the contents of the documents he had been sent. In a scathing comment on an affair that excited newspaper leader writers and cartoonists on both sides of the political divide, the *Cape Times* drew a sharp distinction between Malan's legal duty, which he had observed, and his moral duty as the citizen of a country at war with another.[37] According to Koorts, rumours of Malan's complicity with the Germans did the rounds for many years after the end of the war.[38]

CHAPTER 20

Miners' Strike

In the early dawn of a chilly Monday morning in August 1946, more than 70 000 workers on 12 Witwatersrand gold mines downed tools, sparking off a confrontation with the authorities that became a landmark in South African politics, the repercussions of which may still be felt today. The strike was the culmination of years of simmering resentment among miners over dangerous working conditions, inadequate accommodation, poor food rations and, above all, low wages. With pay rates virtually stagnant during the war and the cost of living rising inexorably, the fledgling African Mine Workers' Union made repeated pleas to the Chamber of Mines to raise the minimum shift wage. Looking to the interests of shareholders rather than those of its miners, the Chamber turned the deafest of ears to the union.

Not for the first time, the Smuts government found itself trapped between the Chamber of Mines and militant workers. Thanks to lessons absorbed during the early war years, officials of the department of labour were supportive in principle of trade unions, realising that they were essential to maintaining social order and industrial peace, and hoping to exchange recognition for control by bringing black unions under special industrial conciliation laws.[1] But the department of native affairs would not accept unionisation on the mines – a strategic industry – and neither would the department of mines nor a resolute Chamber. Senior civil

Mineworkers on strike, 1946.
MAYIBUYE CENTRE, UWC

servants were of the view that the wartime wave of strikes had not been spontaneous, but had been orchestrated by the CPSA.[2]

The mineworkers were caught in a double bind: if they did not demonstrate, they were deemed to be satisfied with their working conditions; if they did protest, they were accused of pushing the government into the arms of the Chamber, ever quick to point out that its profitability was of vital importance to the nation's fiscal well-being. In 1943, a threatened strike on two mines had prompted the government to set up the Lansdown Commission to investigate working conditions in the industry. Reporting some months later, the commission recommended a 17 per cent increase in wages, allowances and leave pay, which the miners regarded as hopelessly inadequate. Lansdown also advised against the recognition of the AMWU on the grounds that the trade union had not originated from within the body of mineworkers itself, but was the outcome of communist manipulation.[3]

As noted earlier, the war had created an acute shortage of labour on the mines because secondary industry offered better-paid jobs to Africans. A consequent decline in gold output on the one hand, and a sharp rise in working costs (including labour) on the other, meant that by the mid-1940s the profitability of mining had decreased considerably. Reluctant to invest in costly mechanisation, the Chamber stubbornly defended its 'cheap labour' policy, arguing that it could not afford wage increases because of declining profit margins. It looked to the state to make possible the implementation of the Lansdown Commission's recommendation on wages, which the government was unable to do fully.[4]

Discontent was fuelled by both low wages and a reduction in food rations following a nationwide drought in 1945 and a poor maize harvest.[5] At the urging of the Chamber, and in order to counter alleged communist agitation, the government had already taken drastic measures to curb the unionisation of miners by passing War Measure 1425, which prohibited gatherings of more than 20 people on mine property. More than a year later, the AMWU once again approached the Chamber with a demand, this time for a basic wage of ten shillings a day (more than three times the prevailing rate) as well as the repeal of War Measure 1425. The Chamber ignored the wage claim on the grounds that the AMWU was not a recognised trade union, and hid behind the wartime ban on meetings on mine property – still in force although the war had ended. The Chamber's attitude to unionisation and collective bargaining was soon to be revealed in an extraordinarily patronising statement issued shortly after the strike ended: 'A trade union organisation would be outside the comprehension of all but a few educated Natives of the urban type; it would not only be useless, but detrimental to the ordinary mine Native at his present stage of development.'[6]

Without any other means of pressing its demands, the AMWU took its members and other miners out on strike on 12 August 1946. The next day, the Council of Non-European Trade Unions called for a general strike in sympathy with the miners. Faced with the threat to law and order and the need to reassure the mining houses, as well as the frightened citizens of Johannesburg, that it had matters under control, the government sent in large contingents of policemen to quell the unrest. On 13 August, six strikers were shot dead at the Sub Nigel mine, and three to six more (reports vary) were trampled to death in the ensuing stampede.[7] On the following day, an underground sit-down at the rock face was broken up 'with great brutality' by the police.[8] Stope by stope, level by level, the miners were forced up to the surface – and back into their compound.

Hundreds more workers were injured when police, wielding bayonets and batons, intervened to break up a march from East Rand mine compounds to the chief native commissioner's offices in downtown Johannesburg. An attempt to hold a protest meeting in the city was banned by the chief magistrate, and a massive police presence at railway stations and bus terminals outside townships prevented the CNETU from bringing all workers out on strike in sympathy with the miners.[9]

It took a week before the strikers were forced back to work. Leading communists, among them JB Marks (president of the AMWU), Bill Andrews (national president of the CPSA) and Moses Kotane, were arrested and their offices raided. Not one of the AMWU's demands was met. Wilmot James concludes that while the individual miner and the AMWU might have won a moral victory, in terms of actual gains the strike was an abject failure and seriously weakened both the AMWU and the CNETU.[10] Within a year, 22 African affiliates had resigned from the CNETU because of dissatisfaction with both its communist leadership and the strike weapon.[11] According to Paul Rich, AB Xuma opposed using the ANC to promote trade unions. He was suspicious of the CPSA's control over the CNETU and wanted the unions rather to accept ANC leadership – in the same way that British trade unions accepted the political leadership of the Labour Party.[12] The Chamber's tough 'no-concessions' approach had paid off, because its refusal to concede wage increases had prevented a (short-term) profitability crisis in the gold industry.[13] Moreover, its intransigent attitude had handed the Smuts government – and the cause of law and order – yet another pyrrhic victory.

The NRC protests

Two days after the strike began, while thousands of mineworkers were marching on central Johannesburg, a sitting of the Native Representative Council opened in Pretoria. Some weeks earlier, AB Xuma had called on ANC councillors – in the majority on the NRC – to adjourn the forthcoming session in protest at the government's dismissive response to the anti-pass campaign. Because of his appeal, and the situation on the mines, the atmosphere in the council chamber was tense. In the absence of the minister, and of WG Mears, the secretary of native affairs – both attending to the strike – the meeting was chaired by a deputy secretary, one Fred Rodseth, who made no reference to the grave situation on the mines and could give no details when pressed for information. When a councillor demanded a full statement, Rodseth said he would first have to refer to the minister.[14]

The councillors reacted furiously to the brush-off, with the Free State physician James Moroka accusing the government of treating them like children. The real cause of the trouble, Moroka said, was the 'Native' policy of the government; he declared defiantly, 'You can do what you like, you can shoot us, arrest us, imprison us, but you are not going to break our spirit.'[15] Councillors asked to go to Johannesburg to see at first hand what was happening on the mines. Rodseth refused. As Alan Paton noted bleakly, the councillors stood revealed in all their impotence: 'They may have represented 8 000 000 people, but they had less power than this young under-secretary for Native Affairs.' Councillor Paul Mosaka described the NRC, memorably, as 'a toy telephone'.[16]

The next day, Dr Moroka used the outbreak of the strike to justify the proposal – decided beforehand – to adjourn the council sitting. His motion also called on the government 'to abolish all discriminatory legislation affecting non-Europeans in this country' and was supported by the 12 elected councillors and three government-appointed chiefs, all of whom voted in favour. Copies of the resolution made their way to the minister of native affairs and to JH Hofmeyr, the acting prime minister.[17]

Credibility test

The suspension of the NRC's activities, and its challenge to the government, was widely viewed as a test of both sides' political credibility. DL Smit, who had been opposed to any major reform of the NRC during the war, thought it would be impossible for the government to parley with the NRC without diminishing the authority of the department of native affairs.[18] Hofmeyr, acting on behalf of the absent Smuts, met with Professor ZK Matthews of Fort Hare, a senior member of the NRC (and of the ANC), and declared afterwards that the government could not be seen to submit publicly to NRC demands because it would be accused by the Nationalists of 'surrender'.[19]

To the white public, most of whom regarded the government's crackdown on the miners as a justifiable response to communist incitement, the NRC had become a bunch of extremists – 'it was proof, was it not, that if you gave a black man your finger, he would take your whole hand? … it was proof, was it not, of the folly of liberals who argued in favour of a common society'.[20]

Realising the significance of the standoff, the white Native Representatives in Parliament tried to bring the two sides together. Edgar Brookes urged the government to undertake a meaningful programme of reform, to include the pass laws, recognition of trade unions and respect for the status of the NRC. Against his better instincts, Hofmeyr temporised, writing to Smuts in Paris that 'we can't allow [moderate intellectuals of the Matthews type] to be swept into the extremist camp, but I don't see what we can do to satisfy them which would be tolerated by European public opinion'.[21] Smuts responded by asking for Brookes's proposal to be presented to the cabinet, agreeing that 'our native policy will have to be liberalised at modest pace, but public opinion has to be carried with us'.[22]

Hoping to accord the NRC its due respect, Brookes persuaded Hofmeyr – instead of the minister of native affairs, Piet van der Byl – to respond to the council personally when its session resumed on

20 November. Hofmeyr's demeanour during the discussion was conciliatory, but his address dwelt more on how much the government had done for the African people, and failed to reveal any of the government's future intentions.[23] The removal of all discriminatory legislation was simply impracticable, he declared, and not in the interests of the African people themselves – giving as an example the Native Trust and Land Act, which had set aside land for African occupation that might be lost if there were open competition for it.

The NRC adjourns

The NRC took a few days to consider its response before reconvening on 26 November. It rejected Hofmeyr's defence of the government's actions because he had made no attempt to deal with the pass laws, the industrial colour bar or the political rights of 'Non-Europeans', nor would recognition be given to the miners' union. Councillors now demanded direct African representation at all levels of government, from municipal councils to Parliament.[24] Until then, they felt unable to cooperate further with the authorities.[25]

ZK Matthews moved another resolution to adjourn the council, this time so that councillors could go to the country to make the government's attitude 'fully known to the African people'. Moroka remarked that the real reason Hofmeyr had rejected the NRC's demands was his fear of the Nationalists, who were threatening to fight the 1948 election on the colour issue.[26]

The proposal to adjourn indefinitely was unanimously agreed to by the councillors present. The (white) chairman of the NRC recorded his regret at the decision: 'I think you have not acted in the best interests of the "Native" people, but you have taken this decision deliberately. I did not rush you into it, and it is your affair.'[27] As Paton records, the NRC meeting marked a turning point in South Africa's politics: 'After that, the demand of non-white people was for equality, not alleviation or improvement.'

That day, 26 November 1946, also marked the virtual end of the NRC. The council was not to meet again until January 1949, when it was informed by the new Nationalist government that it was to be abolished, which duly came to pass in 1951.[28]

Boycott call

A month earlier, Xuma had responded to the NRC's decision to suspend its activities by convening a special meeting of the ANC in Bloemfontein. Disparaged by members of the Youth League for failing to support the call for a general strike, and privately critical of the communists for 'provoking a premature test of strength' with the government,[29] Xuma hoped to use the opportunity to reassert his authority over the ANC and recover some of the prestige he had lost through the failure of the anti-pass campaign.[30] The NRC's defiance of government had aroused such interest among Africans that more than 500 people attended the special meeting – more than four times the number at the ANC's annual congress that December.

Two motions were put before the special meeting: one proposed that the functions of the Native Affairs Commission, an ineffectual body set up by statute to liaise between white politicians and Africans, be transferred to the NRC; the other, moved by Moses Kotane and Anton Lembede, proposed a total boycott of all elections held under the 1936 Representation of Natives Act. After much deliberation, the second proposal was adopted, although no one other than Lembede and a few members of the CYL were in favour of an unconditional boycott, while the Youth League itself was split over the issue. What made this form of resistance so appealing to some CYL radicals was the opportunity it offered the ANC to join the Indian community's defiance of the Ghetto Act. If a boycott of elections were to grow, they argued, it might develop into 'a vast civil disobedience movement'.[31]

No passive example

What the boycott proponents had overlooked, however, had to be pointed out to them by Paul Mosaka, who described the 'passive resistance' campaign of the Indians in Natal as being anything but 'passive'. It was not simply a protest, but an active demonstration to the world that the Indian people were prepared to undergo hardship in order to show their hatred of segregation. The anti-pass campaign, Mosaka explained, had failed because of the absence of the very factors that were making the Indian campaign so successful – good organisation, strength of will and the determination to suffer for one's principles. As Xuma, Mosaka and the ANC 'old guard' on the NRC understood, without these essential ingredients there was no reason to believe an African boycott movement would be any more successful than the anti-pass campaign had been.[32]

The ANC's boycott resolution thus had little effect on the members of the NRC. None of them, ANC elders included, contemplated resigning from the council, even after the climactic meeting of 26 November. This was an indication, Roth concludes, not only of the ANC's lack of influence on grassroots African opinion at this time, but also of the importance that NRC members still attached to the Council[33] – for all its shortcomings still the only direct political link between whites and blacks in South Africa.[34]

Xuma did not attend the ANC's December conference. He was away in New York to lend support to the international protest against the government's attempts to incorporate South West Africa into the Union. In his absence, the conference 'impetuously' accepted the boycott decision of October 1944, a resolution it soon had to back away from when the time came for fresh elections under the Representation of Natives Act.[35]

The CNETU stalls

Despite the wartime boost to trade unionism, and the rise in wages produced by several successful strikes, membership of the CNETU peaked at around 158 000 workers in 119 trade unions, but tailed off after the war. By 1950, for a variety of reasons besides state repression, the CNETU had virtually collapsed. As Philip Bonner explains, by the war's end the great majority of urban African workers were still migrant or transient, and the turnover of labour was 'massive', making it difficult for union organisers to consolidate membership. And only a small number of African workers were semi-skilled, giving their unions little bargaining power. The CNETU itself, 'riven with political divisions over the extent to which strike action should be encouraged during the war', had split irretrievably in 1944.[36] The final straw, however, was the violent crushing of the mineworkers' strike in 1946. According to Bonner, the CNETU's inability to organise a general strike in sympathy with the AMWU – its largest affiliate – laid bare its deep internal divisions and lack of self-belief, and was a failure from which black trade unionism in the country took a long time to recover.

Communists hard hit

For the Communist Party, the miners' strike of 1946 also had far-reaching consequences. Fifty-two members, including the entire Johannesburg district committee, were charged with conspiracy to commit sedition, later changed to assisting an illegal strike. All the accused pleaded guilty, among them Yusuf Dadoo, still in prison in Durban, and the advocate Bram Fischer, neither of whom had had anything to do with the strike. The court proceedings were to drag on for two years, with some accused being fined and others eventually having their charges withdrawn. The popular support the CPSA had built up during the war quickly evaporated. Many fringe members deserted the party, leaving behind a hard core of committed activists to carry on the anti-imperialist, anti-capitalist, non-racial struggle.[37]

Elsewhere in the World

In 1946

7 January	Allies divide Austria into four occupation zones
10 January	First meeting of United Nations Organisation, in London
20 January	Charles de Gaulle resigns as head of provisional government of France
5 March	Churchill warns of 'Iron Curtain' descending over Europe, in a speech at Fulton, Missouri

10 May	Jawaharlal Nehru elected as Congress Party leader in India
25 June	World Bank begins operations
15 October	Hermann Goering commits suicide during Nuremberg trials
19 December	Viet Minh begin war against French occupying forces in Vietnam
	Civil war between Nationalists and Communists intensifies in China

CHAPTER 21

Prejudices Rearranged

The 1946 miners' strike may have ended in failure, but it had one significant political consequence: it brought Indian and African activists much closer together. Nelson Mandela was one of several members of the Congress Youth League who had been struck by the solidarity and selflessness of the Indians in their opposition to the Ghetto Act.[1] As he later wrote in *Long Walk to Freedom*: 'The Indian campaign became a model for the type of protest that we in the Youth League were calling for ... it instilled a spirit of defiance and radicalism among the people, broke the fear of prison ... reminded us that the freedom struggle was not merely a question of making speeches, holding meetings, passing resolutions and sending deputations, but of meticulous organisation, militant mass action and, above all, the willingness to suffer and sacrifice.'[2]

Although Gandhi had never concerned himself with the rights of Africans while in South Africa – though once volunteering for ambulance work to assist the colonial authorities during the Bambatha Rebellion (1906) – his success in having the pass laws and poll taxes affecting Indians rescinded through the tactics of passive resistance was well remembered by non-Indians. To the consternation of Africanists, in the aftermath of the miners' strike it was Indians and communists who once again led the way.

The strike had brought Mandela, whose first job in Johannesburg was guarding a mine compound, and who had several relatives working on the mines, into close contact with JB Marks, the avuncular AMWU president, a former schoolteacher of mixed parentage, whose dignified leadership during the crisis, leavened by a sense of humour, made a deep impression on the younger man. Mandela would accompany Marks from mine to mine, talking to workers and discussing tactics. After the strike, he would spend many hours in discussion with the AMWU president, arguing in favour of nationalism over communism. The older, more experienced Marks never took Mandela's objections personally, saying it was natural for a young man to embrace nationalism and that his views would broaden when he grew older.[3]

Although the gregarious Mandela had many friends and acquaintances among the radicals of all races who frequented the International Club in downtown Johannesburg, he identified strongly with the Lembede group within the CYL, which remained hostile to any suggestion of collaboration with whites, Indians or communists.[4] He still believed that the mainly white-led CPSA was intent on taking over the ANC for its own purposes, and the emphasis the communists placed on class struggle rather than racial oppression only strengthened his conviction.

Despite, or perhaps because of, his friendship with the young Indian law students Ismail Meer and Jaydew Singh, Mandela feared that Indians, with their better education and training, would dominate African political initiatives. He also believed that the goals of the two races differed: Africans were intent on fighting the pass laws, which did not apply to Indians, while Indians were resisting the Ghetto legislation, which did not affect Africans. The most he was prepared to concede was that Indians were not 'intruders or enemies', as long as they did not get in the way of the struggle for African liberation.[5]

Breach widens

The election of at least three veteran communists – JB Marks, Moses Kotane and Dan Tloome – to the ANC's executive committee widened the breach between the Youth League and the parent body. Communist members of the ANC objected to the exclusivist ideology of the young Africanists, such as Lembede, Sisulu, Tambo and Mandela, who had gone so far as to propose, a year earlier, that members of the ANC with dual affiliation to other organisations should be expelled from the party. The proposal had attracted significant support in the Transvaal but was voted down by the national ANC.[6]

The two seminal events of 1946 – the miners' strike and the Ghetto Act – caused Mandela, if not his fellow Africanists, to re-examine his prejudices and reconsider his approach to cooperation with other races. It was not only Marks who had made an impression on him, but also outspoken Indian leaders such as Yusuf Dadoo, who argued persuasively that communism should be adapted to the African situation rather than vice versa.

The inspirational Dr Dadoo had already brought a much younger Indian activist into his orbit, with whom Mandela was to become closely identified. In his memoirs, Ahmed (Kathy) Kathrada describes how for the first time since Gandhi had left South Africa, an Indian leader who advocated non-violent defiance had captured the imagination of his people, especially the youth.[7] Even in sleepy Schweizer-Reneke, where Kathrada grew up, young volunteers, including his eldest brother, Solly, were preparing themselves to follow Dadoo's example by sleeping on mattresses on the floor and eating maize-meal porridge in preparation for time to be spent in prison in protest at the Ghetto Act.[8]

Yusuf Dadoo

Who was this man who played such a pivotal, though largely forgotten, role in South Africa's liberation struggle for more than half a century, and served as a role model for so many young radicals?

Yusuf Mohamed Dawood was born in Krugersdorp on 5 September 1909, the son of a politically aware Indian shopkeeper who had arrived in South Africa in the 1880s. Schooled initially in Krugersdorp and Johannesburg, where he fell under the influence of a militant nationalist teacher, the young Dadoo was sent to Aligarh Muslim University in India in 1927 to matriculate. Returning to Krugersdorp, he gave early evidence of his political precocity when, at the age of only 18, he was asked to move a vote of thanks to the first Indian agent-general to South Africa and used the opportunity to deliver a long speech in which he accused the guest of honour of betraying the Indian community.

Worried about his son's activism, Dadoo senior sent Yusuf to London to study medicine – instead of the law, which Yusuf would have preferred. In Britain, the young student joined the Independent Labour Party and was soon arrested for demonstrating in favour of Indian independence. A firm admirer of Jawaharlal Nehru, he was to read the Indian nationalist leader's autobiography three times. He also studied Russian in order to learn more about the Soviet Union.

In an attempt to curb his son's political activities, Yusuf's father sent him from London to Edinburgh, where he completed his medical studies and steeped himself in Marxist literature. There, he befriended another young student from South Africa, GM (Monty) Naicker, also to become prominent in the liberation movement.

Returning to South Africa to open a medical practice in 1936, Dadoo immersed himself immediately in politics, becoming a founding member and first secretary of the countrywide but short-lived Non-European United Front, which advocated closer cooperation between Africans, Indians and coloureds in opposing segregation. Invited to join the Communist Party, he became a signed-up (and lifelong) member in early 1939.

As recorded earlier, the additional restrictions on Indian land ownership and occupation in the Transvaal imposed by the wartime government had brought to a head the divisions within the conservatively inclined Transvaal Indian Congress. A group of radicals under Dadoo's leadership, known as the 'nationalist bloc', decided to challenge the new legislation by proposing a campaign of passive resistance, which would mean defiance of the law and the prospect of imprisonment – tactics last employed by Gandhi in his day.

PREJUDICES REARRANGED

Dr Yusuf Dadoo, the fiery president of the Transvaal Indian Congress.
NAT FARBMAN/THE LIFE PICTURE COLLECTION VIA GETTY IMAGES

On 7 May 1939, the nationalist bloc in the TIC organised a mass meeting that resulted in a vote in favour of a passive resistance campaign and chose a Council of 25 under the leadership of Dadoo's friend, Ebrahim Asvat, to conduct the campaign. The South African Indian Congress, however, refused to recognise the validity of the decision on the grounds that it could only be made by the national body. This led to a further mass meeting at Osrin's Picture Palace in Johannesburg on 4 June, during which the proceedings turned ugly.

As Kathrada recounts, support for the proposed action posed a threat to the incumbent TIC leadership, which resorted to violence in their efforts to halt the campaign. Thugs armed with clubs, bottles and bicycle chains assaulted members of the nationalist bloc; one man died and several suffered severe injuries. Their particular target was Dadoo, who was attending to victims before being forced to take refuge in a private home until the danger was over.[9]

Far from intimidating the supporters of passive resistance, however, the

TIC's thuggish tactics swung Indian sentiment towards Dadoo and his nationalists. But, to their dismay, the resistance campaign had to be put on hold because of the intervention of Gandhi, of all people, who had engaged in talks with Smuts and the British government and asked for the campaign to be postponed because he expected Smuts to withdraw the Pegging legislation. Dadoo masked his disappointment and respectfully complied, issuing the following statement:

> Mahatma Gandhi has been our guide and mentor in all the passive resistance council has been doing in this matter, and we shall wholeheartedly await his advice; for we realise that his interest in the cause of the Indians in South Africa has not abated one whit, even though many years have elapsed since he left South Africa.[10]

With his campaign against the Pegging Act in abeyance, Dadoo turned his attention to South Africa's involvement in an 'unjust war' that was not intended 'to free the people but to maintain and extend imperialist domination'.[11] He tried unavailingly to persuade DDT Jabavu and the All African Convention not to support the recruitment of Africans, 'because the government had not made the slightest effort to lighten the burden of oppression which weighs so heavily on the shoulders of the people'.[12] Dadoo's outspoken anti-participation stance and distribution of anti-war pamphlets led to his arrest under the emergency regulations. Sentenced to a fine of £25 or imprisonment for a month, as well as an additional two months' hard labour suspended for two years, a defiant Dadoo refused to pay the fine, but was bailed out of prison by a fellow nationalist on the TIC.

Volte-face

When Hitler invaded the Soviet Union in 1941 and the CPSA decided to launch its 'Defend South Africa' campaign, Dadoo had to perform a rapid about-turn, which many of his African supporters in the party found difficult to understand or explain. At a conference convened by Dadoo himself to discuss an appropriate 'non-European' response to the war, opinion was split between those who hoped that Japan, the third member of the Axis, might liberate non-white South Africa, and those who thought that fascism had to be defeated whatever the cost. Dadoo sided with those who favoured support for the UDF, but demanded the provision of arms to all volunteers and the lifting of restrictions on non-whites so they could 'go all out to win the war'.[13] The authorities took no notice.

A Stalinist rather than a Trotskyite, who believed – despite the ample evidence in Soviet Russia to the contrary – that communism imposed by a centralised state was the only social system in which all people would be treated with respect and dignity, Dadoo was elected to the central committee of the CPSA in early 1941, and was to remain a member for the next 42 years. Before long he was in court again for contravening the emergency regulations, and was sentenced this time to four months' imprisonment with hard labour and a fine of £40. In his speech from the dock, published by both *The Star* and the *Rand Daily Mail*, he declared: 'The government may imprison me, it can fling hundreds and thousands into jail and concentration camps, but it cannot and it will not suppress the demand for freedom which arises from the crying hearts of the Non-Europeans and other oppressed peoples.'[14] In Boksburg's notorious 'Blue Sky' prison, Dadoo insisted – Gandhi-like – on carrying out the menial tasks performed by other prisoners.

For the rest of the 1940s, Dadoo played a leading role in most CPSA-inspired or -directed political campaigns, among them the Alexandra bus boycott, the national anti-pass campaign, the miners' strike of 1946, and especially the upheavals within Indian politics in Natal and the Transvaal, which resulted in a takeover of the NIC by radicals led by his old friend Monty Naicker, and by his own nationalist bloc within the TIC. The indefatigable Gandhian, now chairman of the TIC and Transvaal leader of the Indian Passive Resistance Council, became known as 'Mota' (meaning 'big' or 'sturdy' in Hindi), a term of affection for someone who is widely respected in the Indian community.

Of all the Indian leaders, Yusuf Dadoo most clearly exemplified how 'the construction of Indianness went hand in hand with a sense of South African belonging'.[15] He and Naicker would spearhead a new alliance 'that would transform the face of resistance politics and further reshape identities over the next two decades'.[16]

Dividing line

Another direct outcome of the miners' strike and other labour protests was their effect on white politics. In advance of the approaching 1948 election, both the UP and HNP realised that the time had come to refurbish their respective 'native policies', now the dividing line between them. The steady influx of African migrants into urban areas was by then a fact of life, and although the UP government responded to the concerns of its supporters (and its Nationalist opponents) with promises of swift and decisive action against migrants, there was little it could do to stem the tide.

For the Smuts government, there were no easy options. On the one hand, to repatriate thousands of 'illegals' to the reserves – even if it were possible – would seriously hamper the booming industrial sector, yet allowing the migrants to stay was alienating Afrikaner blue-collar workers and arousing protests from the influential farming lobby. Recognising the permanence of workers from the impoverished reserves, on the other hand, would mean scrapping the migrant-labour system on which the profits of the mines, and indeed the entire economy, depended. As the election drew near, the UP's temporising over its 'native policy' became critical – and a potential vote-catcher for Malan's HNP.[17] Both parties reacted by doing what politicians usually do when short of answers – set up a commission to propose the way forward.

Shortly before Smuts left to attend the UN General Assembly in 1946, he appointed Justice Henry Fagan to examine the issue of African urbanisation and make policy recommendations. Fagan, a former cabinet minister in the Hertzog government who had voted for neutrality, assembled a panel of non-parliamentarians, who consulted with organised business and agriculture. Malan responded by appointing his closest ally, Paul Sauer, to head a commission to 'turn apartheid into a comprehensive racial policy'.[18] The Sauer Commission comprised three HNP parliamentarians (two from the northern provinces) and a prominent Stellenbosch theologian and protagonist of apartheid, GBA Gerdener, to keep the Dutch Reformed Church on side. Representations were invited from ministers of religion, academics, professional men and journalists rather than farmers or businessmen, in the belief that 'the need to secure Afrikaner survival outweighed the accommodation of other Afrikaner interest groups'.[19]

As we shall see, except in one fundamental respect, the reports of the two commissions were to differ in degree rather than substance in their proposals for a solution to the 'native problem' that was so troubling to the white electorate. Hindsight suggests that the problem was not as much a 'native' as a 'white' one.

CHAPTER 22

Pandit Attacks

Shortly before the UN General Assembly resumed its first session, at its temporary home at Lake Success on Long Island, New York, in October 1946, Jawaharlal Nehru became the de facto prime minister of India. Concerned that Smuts's international prestige would give him an advantage at the UN, the South African Indian Congress begged India to appoint either Nehru or Gandhi to head its delegation to the General Assembly, and to include the Muslim leader MA Jinnah as well. Gandhi could not leave Delhi, where he was trying in vain to stop the spread of communal violence between Hindus and Muslims in anticipation of partition, while Nehru had more important matters on his plate. Both Gandhi and the viceroy, Lord Wavell, thought that Nehru's sister, Vijaya Lakshmi Pandit, might be an effective advocate for India – as she certainly proved to be. Before leaving for New York, Pandit was told by Gandhi that Smuts was 'his friend and a man of God, even though we were often on opposite sides … I would not like to lose [Smuts's] friendship and respect for the sake of gaining majority. I have chosen you because I know you understand what I'm saying and will do what I ask.'[1]

The government of India's objection to the treatment of South African Indians was the first dispute taken to the UN General Assembly and resulted in the UN's opening attack on South Africa. From the perspective of 1946, Lorna Lloyd observes, it was remarkable that the UN should 'even have discussed South Africa's treatment of its Indian citizens'.[2] And it put Smuts in an unenviable position. As perhaps the staunchest supporter of the Commonwealth, which he hoped would serve as both a role model for a devastated Europe and a potential mediator between the US and the Soviet Union in the incipient Cold War, he now found himself being blamed for the first rupture in the imperial structure he had championed as a positive force for stability and world peace.[3] And, as the author of the Preamble to the United Nations Charter, acclaimed for inserting the protection of fundamental human rights into the Charter, he was the first to be arraigned for violating its principles.[4]

His purpose in attending the General Assembly session in person was to win UN approval for the incorporation of South West Africa into the Union, but in New York he found himself having to defend his government against sustained attacks by Mrs Pandit and her delegation over the treatment of Indians in South Africa. He also had to face concerted opposition from India and other unaligned countries to his plans for South West Africa.

Members of the South African delegation at Lake Success included Senator DG Shepstone from Natal, Smuts's adviser on Indian affairs, Dr Colin Steyn, the legal expert who had drafted the Ghetto Act, and South Africa's high commissioner in London, the long-serving Natal politician Heaton Nicholls. Also in New York, at the invitation of the Indians, to lend support to the anti-Smuts faction, were the ANC leader, AB Xuma, and, at his own expense, the new Native Representative in Parliament, the CPSA's Hyman Basner.

Reflecting the internal differences and personal rivalries among South African Indians, two other deputations had made their way on the same plane to New York to make their views known to Mrs Pandit's delegation. The SAIC was represented by two conservatives, PR Pather and Albert Christopher, both from Natal, while the Joint Passive Resistance Council (JPRC) of the Transvaal and Natal sent Sorabjee Rustomjee, who had recently fallen out with Pather and resigned from the SAIC. Worried by the prospect of Indian disunity weakening his government's case, Nehru intervened to declare that the decisions of the SAIC would only be recognised if they were endorsed by the Joint Passive Resistance Council.

Fifty-one member countries were present at the resumption of the UN General Assembly session. As Friedman points out, of these, no fewer than 27 were ex-colonies of one or other of the Western powers – an early indication that the 'non-white countries' had achieved a status of equality and that 'the epoch of white supremacy was over ... The newly emancipated powers, who constituted the African-Asian group, could no longer be treated as a negligible factor in world affairs.'[5]

First round

Smuts's concerns about India's international ambitions once it became independent were revealed in an article he wrote shortly before the General Assembly meeting:

> South Africa is a little epic of European civilisation on a dark continent. India is threatening this noble experiment with her vast millions who have frustrated themselves and now threaten to frustrate us. All along the coast of Africa from Mombasa to Durban and ultimately to Cape Town, they are invading, infiltrating in all sorts of devious ways to reverse the role which we have thought our destiny. East and West meet at this moment of history and I frankly am a Westerner, though I love and respect the whole human family, irrespective of colour and race.[6]

In advance of the Assembly debate, India and South Africa both submitted draft resolutions for the consideration of UN members. The Indian resolution called on the Union government 'to revise their general policy and their legislative and administrative measures affecting Asiatics in South Africa so as to bring them into conformity with the principles and purposes of the Charter'.[7] In reply, Smuts asserted that how

South Africa dealt with its Indian citizens was a domestic matter, which fell outside the ambit of the Charter, and proposed that the recently established International Court of Justice in The Hague be asked for an advisory opinion.

After a preliminary skirmish in the legal subcommittee of the General Assembly, in which Britain took South Africa's side and the Soviet Union and the United States (with its Asian concerns) that of India, the committee voted by five to three, with two abstentions, to bring the dispute to a joint session of the political and legal committees of the General Assembly. Round one to India.

In the first of six long speeches to the joint committee, Mrs Pandit argued forcefully that South Africa's indigenous Indians were not alien 'birds of passage' but citizens contributing to the economy of the country and entitled to the protection of the UN Charter and its Preamble. The question before the committee, she said, was political rather than legal. India's case against South Africa was based on a violation of the fundamental principles of the Charter, the repercussions of which extended beyond the two countries concerned and were an international issue deserving of the attention of the United Nations.[8]

In reply, Smuts began by agreeing with Mrs Pandit that the issue was of much wider relevance than the relationship between India and South Africa, and one that 'affects the functions of all governments, if not indeed the very future of this organisation and ultimately the prospects of peace in the world'.[9] The real question was whether the UN was entitled to interfere in the domestic affairs of member states. If international peace were to be maintained, Article 2(7) of the Charter had to be observed, that is, there should be no infringement of the domestic jurisdiction of any state.[10]

If South Africa's race policies were indefensible, Smuts continued, by the same standard India's caste system and the massacre of fleeing Muslims by Hindus were indefensible too. 'South Africa is still a peaceful, well behaved and well-ordered country, free from these violent international antagonisms,' he declared, 'and it is the policy of the Union government to keep it so. It is to prevent such conditions of social clash arising in South Africa, where so many races, cultures and colours come together, that the Union is doing its best on fair, decent and wise lines to keep the different elements apart and away from unnecessary intermixture, and so prevent bloody affrays like those in India or pogroms such as we read of in other countries.'[11]

Smuts went on to assert that South Africa had violated no fundamental human rights laid down in the Charter, as there was not yet any internationally recognised formulation of human rights, nor had the framers of the Charter ever intended to give political equality the status of a fundamental human right.[12] (According to Lloyd, Article 2[7] had been included in the Charter at the behest of Commonwealth countries anxious to prevent discussion of their racially discriminatory internal policies.[13]) The human rights envisaged by the framers of the Charter, he said, included the right to exist, to freedom of conscience, to freedom of religion, to freedom of speech and to access to the courts. In the absence of any internationally recognised formulation of such rights, member states did not have any specific obligations under the Charter.[14]

As Hancock notes, Smuts's arguments might have been cogent, but the rules of diplomatic practice had been altered by the new world order.[15] Diplomats now had a new mantra: if you have a good political argument, use it; if you do not, use a legal one. Smuts had pinned almost his entire case upon a legal argument, and it got him nowhere.[16] The mood of the General Assembly was such 'that appeals to cold reason were of no avail whatsoever'.[17] (In a BBC interview in 1969, Mrs Pandit admitted that she had made an emotional case out of her country's indictment of South Africa in 1946–1947. Smuts and his delegation had erred, she said, in seeking to answer her arguments with logic and points of law. 'And pure logic bores the United Nations to death.'[18])

Smuts was not without support for his argument, however. There were several countries in Europe and Latin America that feared the consequences of undermining the principle of domestic jurisdiction and agreed that the interpretation of Article 2(7) was a proper matter for the International Court of Justice.[19] As Britain's lead prosecutor at the Nuremberg war-crimes tribunal, Sir Hartley Shawcross asked the Assembly what would happen if the UN enquired into India's domestic caste system.[20] But despite Smuts's plea that many UN member countries still practised racial discrimination, he could not get around the awkward fact that South Africa was the only Western-allied country to discriminate as a matter of official policy.[21]

At the end of proceedings in the joint committee, a resolution sponsored by France and Mexico was adopted that called on South Africa 'to take heed of its international obligations in respect to Indian citizens and ensure that the latter's treatment was in accordance with the terms of the UN Charter'. An amendment proposing that the issue be referred to the International Court of Justice for an advisory opinion was rejected.[22]

Final straw

The dispute then moved to the floor of the General Assembly, which voted to affirm the Franco-Mexican resolution and brushed aside South Africa's request that the matter be sent for adjudication to the International Court of Justice. At this critical juncture, as Vineet Thakur notes, South Africa needed a speech of political maturity to reassure its diminishing band of allies, instead of which Heaton Nicholls delivered a 90-minute diatribe for which he felt obliged to apologise the next day.[23]

Chiding the joint committee for having swallowed India's 'propaganda', Nicholls treated his audience to his blinkered observations on the 'barbarism' of black Africans in central and southern Africa, who were in need of the guiding hand of Christian whites. The African population, he asserted, had never produced, constructed or discovered anything worthwhile until white rule had guided them towards the benefits of civilisation. This had been a difficult task, but it was a burden that South Africa was willing to bear in order to advance white civilisation. 'What is on trial here,' he added, 'is not only South Africa but also Western civilisation and the methods it has used, and is still using, to banish barbarism from the face of the earth.'[24] Even South Africa's dwindling band of friends at the UN were embarrassed.

On the question of human rights, Nicholls claimed that the only definition the UN could consider was that contained in the Atlantic Charter – freedom of speech, freedom of religion, freedom from want and freedom from fear. This contradicted Smuts's earlier argument that the UN could not enforce or defend human rights that had never been properly defined. Except for political rights, Nicholls argued, Indians in South Africa enjoyed all other basic freedoms. To argue that political rights were fundamental human rights was 'tantamount to saying that the progressive races should be retarded by the less progressive, if in fact they constitute a majority'. Equal rights for all races, he asserted, 'was a reversion to barbarism'.[25]

Describing Nicholls's strictures as 'frivolous and offensive', Mrs Pandit declared it was up to members to decide whether Western civilisation was founded on racial supremacy or on justice and equality. During a lengthy discourse on the history of India, she observed that Western civilisation had, 'in one generation, witnessed two world wars ... and had much to learn in the art of human relationships from Asia'.[26]

Most speakers who followed Pandit in the debate came down on the side of India. Even those countries, such as Britain, who believed the interpretation of Article 2(7) should be referred to the International Court of Justice agreed that human rights had to be upheld by the UN. Not a single country uttered a word in justification of South Africa's treatment of its Indians.[27] Even Britain, anxious to avoid a defeat for Smuts because such an outcome would strengthen Malan's Nationalists, failed to express any sympathy for South Africa's racial policies.[28] Five days later, the matter was put to a vote in the General Assembly. Countries that had supported South Africa in the joint committee abstained this time, instead of voting against the Franco-Mexican resolution. By a narrow two-thirds majority, the Assembly called on South Africa to ensure that its treatment of its Indian citizens was in accordance with the UN Charter and enjoined the two disputants to report on measures taken to the next session of the Assembly.

Apology to Smuts

In her memoirs, Mrs Pandit recalled that at one point in the proceedings she walked across to Smuts and – as Gandhi had requested – asked for forgiveness if she had overstepped the mark during their exchanges. Smuts took her hand in both of his and said: 'My child, you have won a hollow victory. This vote will put me out of power in our next elections, but you will have gained nothing.'[29]

As Lloyd records, Smuts explained to India's legal representative at the UN, Mr Justice MC Chagla, that he could only push his country to a certain point, and given the extreme racist positions within South Africa (to be confirmed by the 1948 elections), he felt himself unable to push it further. 'A time will come,' Smuts warned, 'when you realise that what I have done is nothing compared to what will be done and what will happen in the future.'[30]

Smuts was right that South Africa's Indians would have little reason to celebrate. As the Natal newspaper *The Leader* observed, the United Nations did not have the power to enforce compliance of its resolutions by member states. At most, its decision was a grave moral censure, and 'moral censures have been disregarded with impunity by Christian South Africa'.[31]

India, nonetheless, had emerged as a key factor in widening the struggle against racism in South Africa.[32] In Lloyd's judgement, India had 'succeeded brilliantly' in throwing the spotlight on South Africa and putting racism squarely on the international agenda. The Indians had also provided the UN with its most enduring and time-consuming topic thus far.[33]

In a broadcast to the nation on 18 December 1946, Smuts expressed his disappointment with the UN's decision, asserting that the General

Assembly had denied South Africa the fundamental right of access to the International Court of Justice, and usurped the authority of the court by assuming implicitly 'the guilt of the Union'.[34]

Defeat over the mandate

Smuts and South Africa fared no better in the UN debate on the future of the former League of Nations mandates, during which India took up the cudgels on behalf of the people of South West Africa. In San Francisco a year earlier, South Africa and the other mandatory powers had been invited to bring their mandates into the proposed UN trusteeship system.[35] Smuts had immediately served notice that South Africa would not comply with the request as it wished to terminate the mandate, and would submit its reasons to the first meeting of the UN General Assembly.

Besides the geographic, ethnic and economic links between South Africa and South West Africa, Smuts contended, incorporation into the Union was desired by the people of the territory themselves. The white Legislative Assembly was unanimously in favour, while the non-European population, voting in blocs via tribal chiefs, had also given incorporation overwhelming approval. The government of India believed otherwise, and launched yet another vigorous counterattack on Smuts and South Africa.

Led by Mrs Pandit, whose withering denunciation of South Africa's racial policies was proving so effective, the Indian delegation opposed the incorporation of South West Africa into the Union not only on the legal ground that it infringed the principle of non-annexation established at Versailles, but also because the Union's racial policies meant the non-European inhabitants of South West Africa would not benefit from incorporation.[36] Implying that the Union was not fit to administer South West Africa, she demanded that the territory be brought under UN trusteeship, and found strong support from China, Egypt and the Soviet Union and its satellites.[37]

By 37 votes to none, and with nine abstentions, the General Assembly adopted a compromise resolution, rejecting South West Africa's incorporation into the Union but not insisting on UN trusteeship either. Pending a definitive legal determination of the territory's status, the Assembly requested the Union to administer South West Africa 'in the spirit of the principles laid down in the mandate'.[38] For Smuts, the international statesman, the vote was a stinging setback, which he took personally. He was nonetheless able to see the Indian point of view. 'I am suspected of being a hypocrite,' he admitted after his verbal battering at the UN, 'because I can be quoted on both sides. The Preamble of the Charter is my own work, and I also mean to protect the European position in a world which is tending the other way.'[39]

New ANC strategy

Two other African leaders had been instrumental in lobbying UN delegates behind the scenes and bolstering the case against Smuts and South Africa. One was AB Xuma, who had cabled a terse but widely circulated protest at the country's racial policies to the General Assembly's chairman, Peter Fraser, in early 1946. Part of Xuma's message read: 'In short, Africans underfed, underpaid, undereducated, underemployed, poorly housed and indirectly represented. The eight million Africans have no direct representation. Therefore no direct influence in the policy of the country.' With the sending of that cable, Gish observes, a 'new strategy of appealing to the UN had been born'.[40]

With his leadership under threat from Youth League militants, Xuma had accepted Indian financial assistance to fly to New York in person. Obtaining a passport was not easy; the ANC leader had to state that he was travelling to the US for specialised medical treatment, which was quite legitimate given his various health problems. But the secretary of native affairs, Mears, feared that Xuma had ulterior motives and tried without success to persuade him not to criticise the South African government while abroad. In the end, Xuma was granted a passport, but was told that he would not be given another if he used his visit to the US to attack government policy.[41]

In New York, Xuma was warmly welcomed 'as a visiting dignitary' by the Council on African Affairs, chaired by the famed singer and actor Paul Robeson.[42] The opportunity to forge links with Pan African leaders not only strengthened his resolve but also 'gave him a sense of belonging to the anti-colonial movement whose parameters stretched far beyond South Africa'.[43] From his base at the YMCA in Harlem, he embarked on six weeks of feverish political activity.

Xuma was at the UN partly to bolster the case against South Africa's treatment of its Indian population but primarily to lobby members of the General Assembly, in particular the UN secretary-general, Trygve Lie (whom he met), against supporting Smuts's case for incorporating South West Africa into the Union. Helped by his former African Democratic Party rival, Hyman Basner, he circulated a pamphlet entitled 'South West Africa: Annexation or United Nations Trusteeship?', which cast doubt on the legitimacy of the survey of indigenous opinion in the mandated territory and declared: 'We oppose the incorporation of South West Africa and the British Protectorates of Bechuanaland, Swaziland and Basutoland into the Union of South Africa because such incorporation would facilitate the extension of South Africa's colour and race disruption and domination. It would bring under this policy hundreds of thousands of innocent victims.'[44] The document also highlighted the restraints imposed on black South Africans wishing to travel overseas.

Support from a neighbour

Xuma found strong support for his arguments from Tshekedi Khama, regent of the ruling Bamangwato tribe in neighbouring Bechuanaland (now Botswana), who had taken it upon himself to conduct a well-publicised campaign on behalf of the indigenous people of South West Africa. Khama had been prevented from travelling to London and New York to present his case by Britain's Labour government, which was anxious not to alienate Smuts or undermine South Africa's attempt to terminate the mandate and incorporate South West Africa into the Union, but was coming under increasing pressure from the press and within its own ranks to change its stance.[45] Well aware of Pretoria's long-held hopes of incorporating all the British protectorates in southern Africa into the Union, and a believer in the 'domino' effect, Khama was concerned that once the mandate became part of South Africa, his Bechuanaland would be surrounded by white-controlled governments, its inhabitants a permanent labour reserve for the mines, farms and industries of South Africa.[46]

By skilful lobbying of Labour politicians in Britain, interviews with newspapers in the UK and South Africa, and direct contact within the Indian delegation at the UN, Khama succeeded – together with Xuma – in bringing an international spotlight to bear on the entire southern African region. Together, the pair represented a formidable obstacle to Smuts's ambition to extend the borders of the Union.

During the proceedings of the General Assembly, the first and only recorded meeting between Smuts and Xuma took place, by accident, at a press reception in New York. Introduced by his private secretary, Smuts is said to have put his hand on the ANC leader's shoulder and said: 'Xuma, my dear man, what are you doing here?' To which Xuma replied, 'I have had to fly 10 000 miles to meet my prime minister. He talks about us, but won't talk to us.' Smuts responded by saying, 'Man alive, let's get together. You know, Xuma, I am a most misunderstood man.' Smuts was about to raise the matter of the Native Representative Council when his secretary drew him away. The two men were never to meet again.[47]

CHAPTER 23

Out of Step

Chastened by his experience in New York, Smuts slowly made his way home via London and Athens, arriving in Pretoria to find his white supporters 'dazed and amazed'[1] at South Africa's unexpected rebuff by the UN. Before going to Lake Success, the prime minister had assured Parliament that he had firm support from the US, the UK and the Commonwealth, so India's humiliation of South Africa had come as an unpleasant surprise. It fed a wave of anger against India and a (short-lived) boycott of Indian businesses in Natal and the Transvaal.

Press comment on the UN vote reflected the political affiliations of the country's mainstream newspapers. Smuts-supporting papers such as the *Rand Daily Mail* warned that South Africa was out of step with the new world, which was discarding practices of racial discrimination.[2] The *Natal Witness* wrote that it 'was absurd to think that we can snap our fingers at world opinion, walk out of the UNO in a huff, and expect to benefit from it in the long run'.[3] The *Natal Mercury* noted that the UN vote was 'the first success gained by East over West, by non-European over European in the international sphere'.[4] Radical and communist journals pronounced the outcome as an important step 'towards an alliance between the peoples of the colonial world and the progressive working class of the industrially developed Western nations',[5] while the Nationalist press exulted at Smuts's humiliation and warned again that his gradualist approach would undermine racial segregation.

The prime minister landed in Pretoria shortly before Christmas 1946. In a radio broadcast, he told his audience that there was 'a solid wall of prejudice against the colour policies in South Africa'.[6] He promised, however, that the last had not been heard of either the South West African or Indian questions. As always, Smuts found himself between Scylla and Charybdis, his old maxim of 'conservative at home and liberal abroad' no longer serviceable.[7] Should South Africa's foreign policy, he asked himself, now dictate domestic policies, or vice versa? Was racial instability less of a danger than international isolation? For Smuts, the arch-pragmatist about to face re-election, there was no real choice: he could not make any concessions to foreign opinion that South Africa's legislators and voters would not tolerate.[8]

He felt the need nonetheless to warn white South Africans of their tendency to judge people on the basis of skin colour. 'Man,' he said, 'is not necessarily the same because he has the same colour of skin. A question to be seriously considered is whether we should not give a man of a different colour who is highly educated and with outstanding qualities of leadership a chance. Why treat them all on the lowest level?'[9] Sentiments like these would be thrown back at him not only by his Nationalist opponents but by many liberals as well.

Twin targets

When Parliament reconvened in January 1947, the Nationalists were on the warpath, with twin targets in their sights: Smuts for his unwanted and futile 'internationalism', and Hofmeyr for his racial liberalism, which would lead inevitably to the downfall of 'white civilisation'.[10] For once in agreement with Smuts that the UN vote was 'an attack on our freedom as a nation and our sovereignty',[11] Malan demanded that the Union should reject any UN interference in South West Africa or over the Indian question. The mandated territory ought to become a province of South Africa and the law giving Indians parliamentary and provincial representation should be scrapped, he said. Playing party politics, the HNP leader proposed the appointment of a special committee to devise a comprehensive policy of racial segregation 'that would be constructive and equitable in respect of the specific interests of each racial group'.[12] If his motion failed to receive support, Malan warned, he would take the policy of apartheid to the voters.[13]

Another matter fuelling Nationalist anger was the steady stream of post-war emigrants from Britain and Europe (but not Germany) invited to settle in the Union and looking to exchange life in their war-torn homelands for a place in the South African sun.[14] Believing immigration to be a priority if South Africa were to alleviate the shortage of skilled manpower and remain 'a permanent home for the white man',[15] Smuts had begun implementing a scheme for extensive state-assisted immigration, which, the HNP claimed, would affect the 'composition of the nation' – meaning, of course, the language balance of the white electorate.[16] Worse still, many of the incomers were Catholics. Immigration selection committees were set up in London, The Hague and Italy,[17] attracting as many as 60 000 immigrants to the Union in 1947–1948.[18]

Warning voices

A harbinger of what lay in store for Smuts and the government came in January 1947 with the shock defeat – in a parliamentary by-election in the Cape constituency of Hottentots-Holland – of the popular young UP up-and-comer, Sir De Villiers Graaff, godson of Louis Botha, at the hands of the NP's HJ van Aarde. The result reflected voter resentment at the world's criticism of South African racial policies.[19] The Nationalists, who converted a minority of 637 at the 1943 election into a comfortable majority of 1 228, believed that Hofmeyr had also inadvertently boosted their campaign by prophesying, in a speech in the constituency, that the day would come when Africans and Indians would sit in Parliament. Not long afterwards, Smuts appointed Hofmeyr as his deputy prime minister, thereby delivering himself, in Hancock's words, 'into the hands of his enemies'.[20]

Besides racial fears, there were many other causes of voter dissatisfaction: the prospect of post-war food rationing, the resentment of immigrants taking jobs from locals, irritation at the number of control boards, the shortage of housing, and the poor treatment of white pensioners.[21] Floating voters were put off by the administrative ineptitude of the UP government, whose attempts to solve post-war problems were 'laughed to scorn' not only by the opposition in Parliament but also by many who had voted UP in 1943. 'Warning voices were heard,' says DW Krüger. 'Smuts heeded them not.'[22]

Royal diversion

A welcome diversion from politics in early 1947 was provided by the royal tour of South Africa by King George VI, Queen Elizabeth and their two daughters. It was the first overseas visit by the monarch since the war, and his first to a Commonwealth country. The two-month-long royal pageant offered a richly coloured spectacle and an opportunity for celebration to a public starved of both during six years of wartime austerity. Smuts had mooted the tour a year earlier, hoping, according to Hilary Sapire, 'to use the crown's charisma to galvanise support for the United Party in the face of an ascendant Afrikaner nationalism'.[23] The British government – and the King – had assented readily to the tour for fear that a Nationalist victory in the forthcoming 1948 election might result 'in the loss of South Africa to the Commonwealth at a delicate moment of decolonisation in Asia'.[24]

The tour took the royal family across the length and breadth of South Africa, the Rhodesias and Bechuanaland at the height of summer, in a cavalcade of banquets, civic balls, mayoral receptions, military parades, drives-past and tribal indabas. Meticulously planned and given lavish publicity at home and abroad, the tour was designed to show off South Africa to the world, as well as to reinforce ties of kith and kin, while paying due respect to Afrikaner and African traditions and culture:[25] 'The immense publicity given to the tour meant that at its culminating moment – the celebrated speech by Princess Elizabeth dedicating her life "to the service of our great Imperial Commonwealth to which we all belong" – South Africa commanded the world's attention.'[26]

In typical South African style, events were carefully segregated: official functions were all-white affairs, with separate provision for African, Indian and coloured citizens to meet the royal visitors. Wherever large crowds gathered on city streets, areas were cordoned off to prevent racial mixing.[27]

Mixed messages

The royal party arrived in Cape Town harbour on 17 February 1947, aboard the battleship HMS *Vanguard*. At the presentation of a royal address at Government House that afternoon, the King bestowed the Order of Merit on Smuts, a rare honour afforded to only 24 living recipients and a measure of the respect in which South Africa's premier was still held internationally. Opening Parliament a few days later, George VI acknowledged South Africa's steadfast support for Britain in WWII, saying, 'Thank God, victory was won and I can at last tell my South African people, in person, how deeply I honour them for the splendid contribution they made.'[28] He repeated his gratitude to the country on every official occasion.

All shades of the political spectrum seized upon the royal tour as a means of putting their own messages across to the people of the country. The government sought to play up popular enthusiasm for the visit, not only among English-speakers and Afrikaners who had fought in the war but among all races, while African, Indian and coloured intellectuals and politicians made use of the opportunity to advertise to an international audience the denial of democratic rights to the majority of South Africans. Their objections to the tour were all but drowned out, however, by the enthusiasm of the people.

Nationalist politicians had been quick to denigrate the royal tour as an unwarranted waste of public money. When Smuts had given notice, a year earlier, of his intention to invite the King, the elderly HNP warhorse, General Kemp, voiced the disapproval of the party: 'The position of the

Afrikaner and Republican is clear. Those of us who took part in the South African War, or whose forebears took part, and who have striven and are still striving for a republic in South Africa ... cannot take part in a festivity which will strengthen the monarchy in South Africa.'[29] The NP mouthpiece, *Die Transvaler*, resolutely avoided any coverage of the royal tour, but such futile gestures (and poor journalism) failed to prevent republicans in their droves from coming to take a look at their King and Queen.[30]

As royal fever engulfed the country, many Afrikaner Nationalists in platteland towns, beguiled by the warmth and common touch of the visitors (Queen Elizabeth, especially), could be seen bowing and curtseying at official functions. One of the most amusing (and perhaps apocryphal) examples of the royal charm was the Queen's reply to an elderly Afrikaner who confessed to her, 'I'm sorry, I can't help it, but I just hate the English.' 'I know how you feel,' replied the Queen; 'we feel the same way in Scotland.'[31]

The boycotters

Among the population at large, it was the Joint Indian Passive Resistance Council, still battling against the Ghetto Act, that took the lead in advocating a boycott of the tour. Yet the PRC had misread popular opinion: the divisions between rival factions within the Indian community were laid bare as large crowds at Curries Fountain in Durban – 65 000 people, more than half the Indian population of the city[32] – Pietermaritzburg and Ladysmith gave the visitors a rapturous welcome.

The PRC's lead was followed by the ANC, which, in the absence of AB Xuma, who was in the US, had resolved at its December 1946 conference to 'devise a boycott strategy' against the forthcoming royal tour 'in protest against the barbarous policy of the Union Government of denying elementary rights to Africans'.[33] Yet even the Youth League, which met in Nelson Mandela's house in Orlando and decided to urge a boycott, was a house divided. On one side were members such as the Zulu writer, poet and broadcaster HIE Dhlomo, heir to the long-standing tradition of 'black loyalism' to the British Crown; on the other were the likes of Anton Lembede, who argued passionately against paying tribute to the head of a country that had failed to do its duty to the African people. Mandela himself – with his chiefly background and long-held respect for the British monarchy – found himself 'somewhere in the middle': he could not oppose a boycott, but refused to criticise those who went to meet the King, recalling afterwards that in their circumstances he might well have done the same.[34]

Some ANC stalwarts, including Paul Mosaka and Dr James Moroka, did decline, on principle, to attend the carefully staged indabas, whereas others, among them NRC members such as Chief Albert Luthuli, DDT Jabavu and ZK Matthews, took up their invitations. Even AB Xuma, infuriated by the Youth League's (and the CPSA's) call, in his absence, for a boycott, ignored the dissenters and flew to Zululand with his American wife to pay respects to the King.

As Hilary Sapire records in her account of African responses to the royal tour,[35] the spectacular pageantry, free food and release from the tedium of work brought large numbers of township dwellers onto the streets, while in the reserves, where the inhabitants were under orders from chiefs and officials, tens of thousands – many having travelled on foot and by donkey cart for several days – flocked to take part in the colourful ceremonies.

The reason why the call for a boycott failed so dismally was simply because there was so little public appetite for it. Radical and nationalist politicians of all stripes had misjudged the mood of the people, who had made up their minds that the British monarchy was non-partisan and were not going to let politicians interfere with their enjoyment of a once-in-a-lifetime celebration. In reaffirming their loyalty to the King, a rapidly dwindling 'royalist minority of Africans felt they were renewing their claim to the rights and freedoms that citizens of the Commonwealth enjoyed'. They clung to the outdated notion that the Crown afforded a measure of protection against the vicissitudes of white-settler societies – in this case the segregationist and republican intentions of Afrikaner Nationalists.[36]

The royal tour eventually wound to a triumphant climax in Cape Town on 24 April 1947. Far from being a rest-cure after the rigours of war, the trip had been an exhausting experience for the far-from-well King and his family, who had travelled some 11 000 kilometres and spent 35 nights on the specially commissioned White Train, keeping their composure and good humour (at least in public) throughout. An indication of the tour's success was that an even greater multiracial throng lined the streets of Cape Town to bid farewell to the royals than had turned out to welcome them.[37]

Post-mortems

Predictably, post-mortems on the royal visit diverged widely. A euphoric Smuts, in his letter of thanks to the King, thought the 'effect of the visit on South Africa had been unbelievably wonderful'.[38] Mainstream British and South African newspapers commented that positive images of the tour would offset some of the adverse publicity the country had received since the end of the war. Malan dourly called on other sections of the community to 'show the same respect for Afrikaner sentiments as was shown by Nationalist and Republican Afrikaners for the sentiments of the English-speaking community'.[39] Many black, Indian and coloured newspapers expressed the hope, rather than the expectation, that the warmth and respect shown by the royals to non-Europeans might rub off on their white countrymen.

It took *The Economist* in London to put the royal tour into perspective. Observing, in its issue of 10 May 1947, that the forthcoming general election in South Africa would be fought not over the monarchy but over the colour problem, and no doubt with the post-war electoral fate of Winston Churchill in mind,[40] the journal warned that after eight years in power, an anything-but-united United Party faced a formidable challenge at the polls: '[Smuts] is too much of an international statesman not to realise how the tide is flowing in a world which is shortly to see an independent India. But his political acumen is too great for him to risk his leadership of the country by taking too pronounced a liberal line which would drive many of his supporters into the Nationalist camp.'

Concerned that public opinion might be swinging away from the UP, the administrator of Natal, Douglas Mitchell, accompanied by a senior UP senator, made a special trip to Cape Town to urge the prime minister to call an early election in order to capitalise on the favourable atmosphere engendered by the royal visit. Smuts expressed interest, until reminded by Hofmeyr that he had made a promise to Malan not to call an election for at least a year after the tour, so that the UP government could not be accused of benefiting unfairly from the royal presence.[41]

Elsewhere in the World

In 1947

31 January	Communists take power in Poland
1 March	International Monetary Fund begins operations
12 March	Truman Doctrine proclaimed, to counter the spread of communism
18 April	Skull of 'Mrs Ples' discovered by Dr Robert Broom at Sterkfontein
5 June	Marshall Plan for European reconstruction announced
6 July	Invention of AK-47 assault rifle by Mikhail Kalashnikov revealed
15 August	India and Pakistan become independent
14 October	American pilot Chuck Yeager breaks the sound barrier
20 November	Princess Elizabeth marries Philip, Duke of Edinburgh
29 November	UN votes to partition Palestine

CHAPTER 24

The Doctors' Pact

AB Xuma's disregard of the ANC's decision to boycott the royal tour stemmed partly from his enhanced self-confidence since the success of his endeavours in New York. Tributes to his leadership had poured in from all sections of the African population. James Calata wrote that people everywhere were talking about Xuma and applauding his recent achievements: 'Allow me, dear president, to congratulate you on your strategy. You fought a good fight over there. Your people in Africa admire you and are proud of your leadership. You have brought your enemies to their knees.'[1]

Even members of the Youth League, still intent on replacing Xuma and the ANC old guard, were effusive in their praise. One of its most prominent figures, AP Mda, wrote flatteringly to the ANC president, saying, 'Your monumental work over in the States will go down in history. You have once again come out not only as a nation-builder at home, but as an international diplomat of no mean adroitness and astuteness abroad.'[2] Xuma was not to know – as biographer Steven Gish records – that his triumphant homecoming from the US marked the high point of his political career. Never again would he achieve such widespread acclaim.

Reinvigorated by his Lake Success experience, Xuma had finally shed his reservations about alliances with other races, and was set upon building closer ties with the Indian community, which had helped to finance his trip to the UN. At a homecoming rally organised by Monty Naicker and the Natal Indian Congress, Xuma praised the contribution of Indian South Africans and asserted that they deserved full citizenship rights. 'If India comes of age,' he declared, 'there is hope for world peace.'[3] His sense of indebtedness drove him to seek a formal alliance with Drs Yusuf Dadoo and Monty Naicker, chairmen of the TIC and NIC, respectively. The trio agreed to work together to demand full franchise rights for all races and the removal of all discriminatory legislation affecting 'non-Europeans'. Their agreement to cooperate, which capitalised on the publicity generated by the five-month-long passive-resistance campaign,[4] heralded a significant change of heart on the part of the ANC, which consented formally, for the first time, to work together with other racial groups in the fight against discrimination.

The Joint Declaration of Cooperation, better known as the Doctors' Pact, was signed on Sunday 9 March 1947 (while the royal visit was in full swing) by the three leaders in the apartment of Mandela's close friend Ismail Meer. Three days later, Drs Dadoo and Naicker flew to India to meet Jawaharlal Nehru and attend the first Inter-Asian Conference, taking with them the good wishes of the ANC, as well as a friendly message from Anton Lembede, who had surprised his CYL colleagues by supporting the Doctors' Pact. Lembede was a warm admirer of India's anti-colonial struggle, and of Nehru, whom he described as 'one of the greatest men of modern times'.[5] He liked to quote Nehru's saying that 'nationalism was and is inevitable in the India of my day; it is a natural and healthy growth. For any subject country, national freedom must be the first and dominant urger'.[6] However, Lembede's admiration for India's independence struggle did not prevent him from regarding the Indian diaspora in Africa and the Communist Party of South Africa as genuine threats to African nationalism.[7]

Not long afterwards, a large joint meeting of Africans and Indians, presided over by Xuma, was held in Newtown's Market Square, Johannesburg, in support of the Pact and in celebration of the United Nations resolution on South West Africa.

THE DOCTORS' PACT

Drs GM Naicker, AB Xuma and Yusuf Dadoo (shown from left to right) sign the 'Doctors' Pact', 9 March 1947.
OFF/AFP VIA GETTY IMAGES

By no means everyone in the ANC shared Xuma's enthusiasm for cooperation with Indians. Many members of the Youth League harboured misgivings, notably Lembede, who expressed the view in 1945 that Africans were fighting for Africa, but Indians were essentially merchants, 'who fought only for their rights to trade and extract as much wealth as possible from Africa'[8] – overlooking the reality that most Indians in South Africa were actually industrial workers or farm labourers.[9]

Natal ANC leaders such as AW Champion and Selby Msimang, conditioned by years of mutual mistrust, were outspokenly opposed to the Pact because of the resentment among Natal Africans of their exploitation at the hands of Indian merchants and traders. Pointing to the outrage among Africans in Natal, they accused Xuma of going beyond his mandate without their consent and insisted that because of the 'strained relations' that prevailed in Natal, any statement of cooperation must 'guarantee the Africans a measure of protection from the Indians'.[10]

Xuma chose to disregard the Natal ANC's strong disapproval and stuck to his guns, urging his fellow Africans to overcome their fear of Indians and meet them as equals. By signing the Doctors' Pact, he implicitly rejected any separate solutions to the African and Indian 'questions' and helped to lay the foundations of the Afro-Indian Congress Alliance of the 1950s. Though the ANC in Natal refused to be bound by the Pact, young Indian activists, especially, were excited by it, as it reinforced their belief that Indians were above all else South Africans.[11]

NRC deadlock

Smuts was also prompted into action by his put-down at the UN, making an immediate effort on his return to mend fences with the Native Representative Council. Urged on by Margaret Ballinger and Donald Molteno, Smuts invited six members of the council, including ZK Matthews, Selope Thema and Paul Mosaka, to meet him to discuss what might be done to break the NRC-government standoff.

At talks in Cape Town in May, which both sides agreed would be merely exploratory, Smuts indicated his desire to make a fresh start in his relationship with the NRC, suggesting a possible enlargement of the council to 50 members, to be elected by Africans only, with a chairman drawn from the NRC itself.[12] In addition, he envisaged the recognition of African trade unions (except in mining) and the extension of the NRC's powers to urban townships. He did *not* visualise, however, any immediate changes to the representation of Africans in Parliament. These were tentative suggestion for discussion, he hastened to say, not firm proposals but a 'bone to chew on'.[13]

Smuts was in another no-win situation. With an election in sight, every olive branch he held out, every concession he offered to black people meant more votes for Malan. To the National Party, the NRC was an 'impudent and truculent' body that ought to be abolished.[14] As Alan Paton wrote, the prime minister's dilemma was that he was trying somehow to delegate power, and white South Africa was either deeply resistant or distinctly nervous about delegating power to other races.[15]

The six NRC councillors asked to be allowed to consult their colleagues, but even before they were able to do so, a confident Xuma, speaking on behalf of the ANC, rejected Smuts's suggestions outright, saying, 'We do not accept any proposal that does not provide for the direct representation of all sections of the community in all legislative bodies.'[16] The six councillors then met in November, by which time Smuts had not made good on a promise to reconvene the discussions. After due deliberation, they issued a carefully worded statement declaring Smuts's suggestions to be 'entirely consonant with the familiar policy of separation, a policy which engendered a spirit of hostility and racial bitterness between black and white'.[17] What was required to heal the breach between council and government, and to restore the confidence of the Native people, the councillors asserted, was a policy that 'recognised that Natives were citizens of this country'.[18]

The cautious tone of the statement was an indication of the NRC's desire to keep open its channel of communication with the authorities. Not one councillor considered resigning or not seeking re-election in 1948. Ignoring the calls for a boycott, the council called on Africans to choose representatives at the upcoming election who would pursue the policies to which the present NRC was committed.[19] Despite the indifference of the government to their advice and entreaties, councillors were well aware that the NRC represented the only formal link between black and white South Africans. The UP government realised it too: in Hancock's view, negotiations would almost certainly have resumed had Smuts not fallen from power a mere six months later.[20]

Lembede dies

It took a thunderbolt out of a clear sky – and an enforced leadership change – to shift the Youth League towards adopting a more conciliatory attitude towards other races. On 27 July, Mandela was visiting Anton Lembede at his law office during a lunch break when Lembede complained of severe stomach pain. He was rushed to Coronation Hospital, where he died that evening of causes never precisely identified. He was only 33 years old. Throughout his short life, the 'arrogant but disarming'[21] Lembede had driven himself at a frenetic pace, scarcely pausing to sleep or eat, and refusing to give in to frequent illnesses. The young CYL president had been an enigma to many – a man of unbending principle, a hater of pretension, a staunch Catholic who fiercely condemned those who disagreed with him, and one imbued with a racial pride that could sometimes obscure the virtues of someone of another colour.[22]

The CYL was stunned by the premature death of a man who had given the group its philosophy and founding creed. Walter Sisulu, who had grown particularly close to Lembede, was so grief-stricken he had to be aided at the graveside.[23] Recognised by posterity as one of the early architects of African nationalism in South Africa, Lembede is sometimes referred to today as 'the greatest future leader the Africans never had'.[24] In retrospect, however, his narrow nationalism and inflexibility on racial questions might have proved a handicap for the ANC had he lived long enough to head the organisation.

Lembede was succeeded as leader of the Youth League by AP Mda, esteemed also by his colleagues as a gifted theoretician and strategist. As Gail Gerhart records, Mda's close relationship with Lembede and the nature of their intellectual partnership made it difficult to distinguish between the two men's ideas on African nationalism. Some in the Youth League even thought that Lembede had derived much of his ideology from Mda, rather than vice versa.[25] Mandela wrote that while Lembede tended to imprecision and verbosity, Mda was specific and scientific:[26] 'In his broad-minded tolerance of different views, his own thinking was more mature and advanced than that of Lembede. It took Mda's leadership to advance Lembede's cause.'[27]

AP Mda

Ashby Peter Solomzi (AP) Mda has never received the recognition accorded to many of his more celebrated CYL colleagues. The father of Zakes Mda, the well-known novelist and poet, AP was born to devout

Anglican parents in the Herschel district of what is now the Eastern Cape and educated at Catholic schools. Qualifying as a schoolteacher, he struggled to find a teaching post in either East London or Johannesburg, to which he moved in 1937. After having to accept kitchen work and gardening in white households, he found employment at a Catholic primary school in Orlando.

As a young man, Mda had grown up believing firmly in the superiority of Western civilisation over African culture, but disillusionment with the white political establishment and its 'civilised' values set in after the Hertzog legislation of 1936. Encouraged by his father, he attended the All African Convention gathering in Bloemfontein to protest the Hertzog Bills. It was to prove a life-changing experience.

Gravitating to politics at a time when the AAC was much more popular than the weak and divided ANC,[28] Mda nevertheless pinned his colours to the mast of the smaller and more 'Africanist' organisation, becoming a party organiser in Orlando. After AB Xuma became ANC president, Mda's energy and enthusiasm were duly recognised. When discussions about a prospective Youth League began, the youthful Mda was already on the ANC's Transvaal executive and a member of some standing in the party. Critical of the AAC for lacking inspirational leadership and being unduly influenced by Indians and coloureds, he argued persuasively for an African nationalism that was not dependent on alliances with non-African organisations.

In 1943, Mda had become room-mates with Lembede, striking up an intellectual and political partnership in which the pair would vigorously debate the merits and demerits of socialism, Marxism and other secular creeds. Together with Jordan Ngubane, who also admired him, and Lembede, Mda helped write the Youth League's combative draft manifesto.

Mda shared Lembede's concern about the need for vigilance against communists and other groups that 'seek to impose on our struggle cut-and-dried formulas which ... only serve to obscure the fundamental fact that we are oppressed not as a class but as a people'.[29] The two were as critical of white liberals, whose influence they regarded as negligible: Africans would be wasting their time and deflecting their forces if they looked to Europeans for inspiration or help, the pair asserted.[30]

By the time of Lembede's death, Mda had already moved to Roma, in Basutoland, to begin studying for a law degree at the Catholic University College (now the University of Lesotho). As the obvious successor, he agreed to become acting president of the CYL, but because of his distance from Johannesburg, he established a working committee, consisting of Nelson Mandela, Oliver Tambo and Walter Sisulu, to tend to the daily running of the League.

According to Jordan Ngubane, as new leader Mda set about hastening the overthrow of the old guard of the ANC, who 'believed in collaboration because of the voting rights enjoyed by the Africans in the Cape and the land rights the English extended to Africans in Natal'. Mda regarded a clash at some time in the future as inevitable, because the Congress's leadership reflected 'the dying order of pseudo-liberalism and conservatism, of appeasement and compromises'.[31]

Mda had been uncomfortable with some of Lembede's extreme stances,[32] and as his thinking matured he began also to move the League away from the purist idealism of its founder. When the CYL finally published its 'Basic Policy' in 1948, Mda was its moving spirit and author. Preferring the more moderate term 'African nationalism' to 'Africanism', he wrote that the Youth League now accepted that the different racial groups in South Africa had come to stay: 'But we insist that a condition for inter-racial peace and progress is the abandonment of white domination, and such a change in the basic structure of South African society that those relations which breed exploitation and human misery will disappear.'[33]

Two schools

By mid-1947, two rival schools of thought had developed within the ANC: a 'go it alone' school, typified by the Africanist faction within the CYL, most of whose members would later find a home in the Pan

Africanist Congress; and a nationalist school, represented by Xuma, the ANC old guard, and now the likes of Mda, prepared to adopt a more flexible approach to other groups. Mandela and his associates had been firmly in the Africanist camp, but were slowly shifting their allegiance to the nationalists. In the end, the two schools never satisfactorily resolved their philosophical differences, which led to much acrimony and infighting during the liberation struggle and which endure, in one form or another, in ANC-ruled South Africa.

Independent India

Both camps took great encouragement, however, from the formal independence of India in August 1947, an event that assumed 'monumental significance in the pages of African newspapers'.[34] Commentators speculated enthusiastically on the impact that an independent India – the 'jewel' of the British Empire – would have on the British Commonwealth and the colonial system in general, though some, particularly in Natal, worried that a sovereign India would strengthen the position of South African Indians to the detriment of Africans.[35] Enthusiasm began to wane slightly as the scale of the mass displacement and communal violence in the wake of partition 'outstripped anything that African leaders had previously contemplated'.[36]

To the youthful activists within the ANC, the handover by a ruling power to an indigenous population demonstrated exactly what could be achieved by unity of purpose and mass action.[37] For the rest of his life, Nelson Mandela felt a debt of gratitude to Nehru, who had involved himself in South Africa's liberation struggle since the 1920s and made India the first country to impose economic sanctions on South Africa. In his later years, Mandela would quote Nehru's sage advice on looking beyond narrow racial nationalism: 'Nationalism is good in its place, but it is an unreliable friend and an unsafe historian. It blinds us to many happenings, and sometimes distorts the truth, especially when it concerns us and our [own] country.'[38]

CHAPTER 25

Movers and Shakers

The Doctors' Pact helped to persuade some doubters within the ANC that Indian leaders were also committed to supporting the struggle of the African people to liberate themselves. The converts were outnumbered by the sceptics, however, who dismissed the Pact as mere 'window dressing' among politicians that would have little impact on the plight of the poor urban black.[1] As Parvathi Raman records, in general the country's Indians continued to be regarded with hostility by Africans.[2]

An immediate outcome of the Doctors' Pact was the launch of a nationwide 'Votes for All' campaign to demand the extension of the franchise to all South Africans. The campaign led to friction within the CYL, especially between Nelson Mandela, Oliver Tambo and Walter Sisulu. Mandela was among those who continued to insist on the necessity of African leadership of any campaign involving political organisations, as did Tambo.[3] The more practical Sisulu, by contrast, having helped to break up CPSA meetings in the past, had since come to appreciate that cooperation with other (but not white) organisations was essential if any national campaign were to succeed. The differences between the three friends burst into the open at a special meeting of the Transvaal ANC, called to discuss 'Votes for All', which broke up in disarray. 'Nelson and Oliver were so angry with me that instead of going to the station together to take the train home, as we usually did, we went separate ways,'[4] Sisulu recalled.

Mandela, in particular, was still deeply mistrustful of any organisation led by communists, especially if the leadership was white. As he recorded in *Long Walk to Freedom*:

> Even though I had befriended many white communists, I was wary of white influence in the ANC, and I opposed joint campaigns with the party. I was concerned that the communists were intent on taking over our movement under the guise of joint action. I believed that it was an undiluted African Nationalism, not Marxism or multiracialism, that would liberate us. With a few of my colleagues in the [Youth] League, I went so far as breaking up CP meetings by storming the stage, tearing up signs, and capturing the microphone.[5]

Mandela's misgivings about the CPSA's real intentions led also to a bitter clash with the president of the ANC's Transvaal region, Constantine Ramohanoe, a friend whom he admired for his 'integrity and devotion'.[6] As a supporter of the Doctors' Pact, Ramohanoe issued a statement calling on Africans to support 'Votes for All', in defiance of an executive-committee directive that the ANC should withdraw from the communist-led campaign.[7] Mandela had supported the Transvaal executive's decision because of his belief that the ANC should only be involved in campaigns in which it clearly took the lead. At this stage of his career, he explained, he was more concerned with who got the political credit than with the success of the campaign itself.[8]

At a meeting called to resolve the dispute, Mandela was asked to propose a motion of no confidence in Ramohanoe for his disobedience. Reluctant at first to condemn someone whose contribution to the liberation struggle had been so much greater than his, and knowing that Ramohanoe's attitude that Indians and Africans should cooperate was 'a noble one', Mandela decided nonetheless that the act of defiance was too serious to overlook: 'While an organisation like the ANC is made up of individuals, it is greater than any of its individual parts, and loyalty to the organisation takes precedence over loyalty to an individual. I agreed to lead the attack and proposed the motion condemning [Ramohanoe] that was seconded by Oliver Tambo.'[9] The Transvaal president walked out of the ANC in protest.

For the rest of his life, Mandela was to hold fast to his belief that loyalty to party trumped every other allegiance. Having sublimated his own will to the liberation movement, he was determined that others should do so too.[10] Whether or not this aspect of his legacy – an article of faith among his successors – has served the party or South Africa well in the democratic era is a matter for ongoing debate among political scientists.

Afrikaners cohere

With another election in the offing, HNP leader DF Malan knew he had no chance of defeating Smuts as long as Nationalist Afrikanerdom remained so splintered. His difficulty was uniting those Afrikaners who had clashed so violently during the course of the war.[11] For tactical reasons, Malan moderated the tone of his party's messaging, playing down the republican issue, stifling the anti-Semitism of some members, dropping his anti-British rhetoric and assuring war veterans they would be treated sympathetically by a Nationalist government. Besides Hofmeyr and the CPSA, the HNP's bogeymen were now the UN, India and the Soviet Union.[12]

Malan also began making overtures to Klasie Havenga's more temperate Afrikaner Party, which had broken away from the HNP in 1939 out of loyalty to Hertzog. Discussions went smoothly, and in early 1947 the two leaders issued a joint declaration in which they agreed to cooperate in order to bring an end to the 'Smuts-Hofmeyr regime'.[13]

This was not good enough for JG Strijdom, the fiery and combative Transvaal HNP leader, who sought more than an electoral alliance with Havenga. He wanted the Afrikaner Party to give up its identity and be absorbed into the HNP, and even threated resignation should he not get his way. His fear, apparently, was that the friendly relations between the Afrikaner Party and the Ossewabrandwag during the war might lead to the infiltration of the HNP by the Ossewabrandwag, whose fascist ideology even Strijdom detested. An obdurate Malan, who shared Strijdom's views on fascism but realised the need to bring Ossewabrandwag members back into the fold, stuck to his guns and overrode the Transvaler. Nothing was to be allowed to deflect the HNP leader from his chosen course – the road to Nationalist Afrikaner unity.[14]

In Parliament, the battle lines over South Africa's foreign policy became even clearer in May, when the HNP's FC Erasmus – seemingly impervious to international opinion – proposed to the House that the Ghetto Act, hitherto applicable to the Transvaal and Natal only, be extended to white areas in the Cape as well. With an eye on the forthcoming UN General Assembly session, Smuts refused to add further fuel to the flames by agreeing to the resolution, but declined also to make any concession to UN demands ahead of the 1948 election.[15]

Fort Hare

Following Anton Lembede's death, Nelson Mandela became secretary of the Congress Youth League, with responsibility for growing the organisation and setting up new branches. Helped by AP Mda, he persuaded Godfrey Pitje, a young anthropology lecturer at Fort Hare, to found a branch of the Youth League at the college. As Edgar and ka Msumza note, although inspired by mass action, the CYL at the time was not aiming to become an organisation of the masses. Fort Hare fitted Mda's vision of developing a cadre of intellectuals, committed to a nationalist outlook, who would be able to channel the grievances of grassroots African peasants.[16]

Though sceptical of the CYL's 'armchair intellectualism', Pitje's professor, ZK Matthews – the country's most distinguished black academic and an NRC member – allowed the group to operate on the campus. In time, as Sampson notes, Fort Hare became the Youth League's most valuable recruiting ground, attracting a militant generation of students whose ranks included Robert Sobukwe, Joe Matthews, Duma Nokwe and Ntatho Motlana.

The ANC's Fort Hare branch succeeded in keeping a number of budding African politicians out of the clutches of the AAC, as well as the NEUM movement in the Cape, dismissed by Mda as 'a narrow clique of intellectuals'.[17] The branch provided Mda with a strong base of support for the CYL campaign to develop a more radical programme not grounded upon *African Claims* and the Atlantic Charter.[18]

ZK Matthews

Born in Kimberley in 1901, Zachariah Keodirelang (ZK) Matthews was exposed to politics at a young age. His father was on the Cape voters' roll and his cousin, Sol Plaatje, was one of the founders of the ANC. Schooled at Lovedale College in the eastern Cape, where Tshekedi Khama was a fellow student, ZK became the first South African to graduate (with a BA degree) from Fort Hare, in 1924. A year later, he was appointed as head of Adams College in Natal, where Albert Luthuli was a staff member and Anton Lembede and Jordan Ngubane were among the students.

In his spare time, ZK studied law by correspondence through Unisa, and became the first African to obtain an LLB degree. He never practised law, because he wished first to improve his academic qualifications overseas. In 1932, Matthews won a scholarship to Yale University, where he gained an MA degree and thereafter took a course in social anthropology at the London School of Economics.

Returning to South Africa, he took up a teaching post at Fort Hare, and became deeply involved in African politics, protesting against the Hertzog Bills and helping DDT Jabavu and others to organise the first All African Convention in 1935. Although an executive member of the AAC, he also joined – and assumed a leading role in – the ANC, being elected to the national executive in 1943 and serving as chair of the Atlantic Charter Committee. The year before, he had become a member of the NRC.

In 1945, Matthews became a professor at Fort Hare, succeeding DDT

Left: Dr Zachariah K Matthews, distinguished ANC academic and politician, at a graduation ceremony at Fort Hare University.
CORY LIBRARY/AFRICA MEDIA ONLINE

Right: Margaret Ballinger, one of the three Native Representatives in Parliament. The Native Representative Council was finally abolished by the National Party government in 1951.
MUSEUM AFRICA/AFRICA MEDIA ONLINE

Jabavu as head of the department of African studies. Like Jabavu, Matthews was an exemplary Christian, and widely regarded as South Africa's leading academic and intellectual. Politically moderate, he served as a bridge between the ANC's old guard and the militants in the Congress Youth League, to whose boycott strategies he was instinctively opposed. In 1947, he was criticised by radicals for warmly welcoming King George VI and Queen Elizabeth to Fort Hare.

Alan Paton was a friend and admirer of Matthews, and judged his intellect to be the equal of JH Hofmeyr's. He described Matthews as a big, impressive man physically, but deliberate and gentle by nature, 'with none of the tricks of the demagogue'.[19] 'If the whites of South Africa had been willing to embark on a slow, steady pace of evolutionary change,' Paton wrote, 'they would have found no better man than Matthews to plan it with.'[20]

Despite strongly disapproving of his membership of the NRC, the CYL was almost unanimous in nominating Matthews to succeed AB Xuma as ANC president in 1949, but he was not prepared to stand, preferring to help draft the ANC's Programme of Action instead. After Malan's Nationalists came to power, ZK's moderation turned to militancy. Although studying in the US at the time, he helped from afar with preparations for the ANC's Defiance Campaign in 1952, and on returning home was the moving spirit behind the Congress of the People in June 1955, at which the Freedom Charter was approved.

Robert Sobukwe

The CYL's main rival at Fort Hare during the war was the Non-European Unity Movement, whose most notable representative was the uncompromising Cape activist, IB Tabata, an outspoken advocate of non-collaboration with segregated institutions such as the NRC. Intense arguments over tactics would rage between the two groups – in the classroom and in public.[21] AP Mda would also pay regular visits to the campus to address and recruit students. An unadmiring member of the NEUM described Mda as a 'little Hitler, a demagogue who stirred your emotions and who categorised anyone who disagreed with him as an enemy'.[22]

No new recruit was more prized than Robert Mangaliso Sobukwe, an early supporter of the NEUM for its non-collaborationist stance, but who was encouraged by Mda to switch allegiance to the ANC. Sobukwe's 'conversion' resulted in the majority of Fort Hare students signing up as members of the CYL. Unlike most of his peers, Sobukwe – a born linguist and brilliant public speaker – would address audiences in the vernacular of several African languages rather than in English.[23] He repudiated communism as a foreign ideology and dismissed the CPSA as a servant of the Soviet Union.

Sobukwe shared the belief of his political soulmate, Anton Lembede, that Africans were the only people whose material circumstances gave them an interest in the root-and-branch restructuring of South African society: 'We have admitted that there are Europeans who are intellectual converts to the African's cause, but because they benefit materially from the present set-up, they cannot completely identify themselves with that cause.'[24] Sobukwe's 'purist' outlook, more NEUM than ANC, was to lead many years later to an Africanist breakaway from the ANC and the birth of a new political organisation, the Pan Africanist Congress, of which he became the guiding light and founder-president.

OR Tambo

Nelson Mandela's new responsibilities in the CYL also brought him into closer contact with Oliver Tambo, the quiet man known to his friends as 'the Christian', with whom he was to launch the country's first black legal practice. In due course the two men were to form a political partnership that would influence the course of South African history even more profoundly than the Louis Botha-Jan Smuts alliance of a half-century earlier.

Like many of his contemporaries in the ANC, Oliver Reginald Tambo was a Transkeian, born in 1917 to an illiterate but 'fairly well-off' peasant farmer in the Bizana district of Pondoland. Educated, thanks to Anglican sponsorship, at St Peter's Secondary School in Johannesburg, where he was an outstanding student, the young Tambo was awarded a scholarship by the Bunga (the council of Transkei chiefs) to study at Fort Hare, from which he graduated with a BSc degree in 1941. It was there, as a fellow member of the Student Christian Association, that he met Nelson Mandela for the first time.

Staying on at Fort Hare to qualify for a teaching diploma, the young Tambo, by then secretary of the students' representative council (SRC), refused to sign a pledge of obedience to student rules promising good conduct and religious observance, whereupon he and 45 others were expelled from the college. Disregarding his expulsion, St Peter's hired Tambo as a science and mathematics teacher. Hoping to study eventually for the priesthood, he taught at the school until 1947, being popular with pupils for his gentle, interactive method of teaching.[25]

On his return to Johannesburg from Fort Hare, Tambo was drawn into the circle of young activists around Anton Lembede intent on radicalising the ANC. Responding to staff members at St Peter's who tried to persuade him it was wrong for teachers to be involved in politics, the normally mild-mannered Tambo retorted angrily that when men cannot help themselves, they must be helped by others who are able to: 'I want to help lead the struggle for African liberation. How can you claim that this is not the role of a teacher? I refuse to be diverted from it.'[26]

Along with Lembede, Mda, Mandela, Sisulu, Ngubane and others, Tambo was prominent in the founding of the CYL, becoming its national secretary and then Transvaal president and national president. Politically astute and widely respected for his Christian principles, he moved easily from a leading role in the CYL to the executive of the senior Transvaal ANC.

In the late 1940s, Tambo decided on a career change — from teaching to law. Articled to a firm of white attorneys in Johannesburg, he studied by correspondence through Unisa, working at night by candlelight. After qualifying in mid-1951, he was approached by Mandela, by this time a qualified lawyer himself, to go into partnership. The legal firm of Mandela & Tambo set up offices in Chancellor House, close to the law courts in downtown Johannesburg, where it rapidly became widely known. Clients came from far and wide to seek its services.

A difficult critic

From time to time, Mandela and his Youth League colleagues would find themselves the target of fierce criticism from African and coloured intellectuals within the rival AAC, a key constituent of the vocal, Cape-based NEUM. In his capacity as CYL secretary, Mandela visited Cape Town for the first time in the late 1940s, where he was confronted by a fellow Transkeian in the person of the formidable IB Tabata, the founder of the NEUM, who took the rather startled Youth Leaguer to task for even becoming a member of the ANC. Finding the NEUM leader more hostile to the ANC than to the white government, Mandela confessed later to Anthony Sampson that he had found it difficult to counter some of Tabata's strictures.[27]

Isaac Bangani (IB) Tabata was one of a small group of African Marxists from the Queenstown area who believed that any impetus for social revolution would have to come from the countryside. For much of the late 1940s and 1950s, Tabata travelled between Cape Town and the Transkei urging rural peasants to oppose the government's land rehabilitation programmes. Staunchly opposed to both the ANC and – as a Trotskyite – the Stalinist CPSA, he succeeded in establishing a significant NEUM network in rural Pondoland.

After his meeting with Mandela, Tabata wrote the younger man a long and remarkable letter in which he warned Mandela against the 'collaborationists' in the ANC. The letter reads in part:

> Can you give me any good reason why you joined the ANC – apart from the fact that your father and our father's father belonged to it and it was supposed to be an organisation for the African people? ... An organisation, if it is true to its principles, will seek to unite the oppressed people and will at the same time follow a course of non-collaboration with the government ... I am totally opposed to any organisation whose policy it is to collaborate with the government and disunite the people.[28]

'You and your fellow members of the Congress Youth League,' Tabata continued, 'are talking with two voices at one and the same time. As members of the Youth League, you speak the language of the modern intellectual – progressive, independent and rejecting inferiority. But as members of the ANC, your language is a negation of those things ... I think it of paramount importance that a man, and especially a young man like yourself entering politics, [should] establish the habit of basing his action on principles. He must be ready, if necessary, to swim against the stream. Thus armed, he is protected against the temptations of seeking popularity and ephemeral success.'[29]

Still convinced that the ANC was the only organisation capable of mobilising the people for mass action, Mandela persuaded himself that the NEUM's uncompromising principles were simply an excuse for inaction. However, as his own celebrated career in politics was to demonstrate, many of Tabata's exhortations must have registered with him subliminally.

Indian tensions

In late 1947, the South Africa-India contretemps surfaced again at the UN, where Mrs Pandit proposed a round-table conference of the two governments – as well as the new regime in Pakistan – to discuss implementation of the General Assembly's decision of 1946. Nothing had been done in the interim to patch up the quarrel between the two (now three, with Pakistan) members of the Commonwealth. Smuts wisely decided not to attend the Assembly this time, sending his justice minister, Harry Lawrence, in his stead. Supporting the Indian resolution, the leader of the Pakistani delegation, Sir Zafrullah Khan, said that while other countries also practised discrimination, 'two wrongs do not make a right'. He was in favour of negotiations between the three countries to resolve their differences.[30]

As Jeremy Lawrence records,[31] the four-day debate (and more than 50 speeches) in the General Assembly was less of a dispute between member countries than a testing ground for the human-rights provisions of the UN Charter. When the Indian resolution was put to the vote, it failed to win a two-thirds majority and was accordingly rejected. The unexpected outcome came as a severe setback to the Indian delegation and added to the disillusionment among Indians in South Africa, where it sharpened the political divisions between two warring factions.

The first was the militant 'new guard' led by Drs Dadoo and Naicker, whose members were drawn from both the NIC and the TIC, which favoured the continuation of passive resistance. The second was the 'old guard', opposed to passive resistance and in favour of negotiating with the government without outside interference, but fast losing influence. While Dadoo and Naicker were addressing mass meetings in India, a body of moderates, led by AI Kajee and PR Pather, were coming together in yet another body, the Natal Indian Organisation (NIO).[32]

Determined to bring about a resumption of diplomatic relations between South Africa and India, the NIO supported the UN's request for a round-table conference, but called for South African Indians to be included in the discussions as well. Smuts agreed, and embarked on a series of exploratory exchanges by cable with Jawaharlal Nehru, without being able to reach a compromise. With an election only months away, Smuts could offer no concessions to the Indian leader and prevaricated, trying simultaneously to placate his Nationalist opponents and reassure his own supporters without further provoking the hornets buzzing angrily about the heads of the South African delegation at the UN.

Earlier in the 1947 session, the dispute over the status of South West Africa had rumbled on in a General Assembly committee room for three long weeks, without conclusion. Dismissing South Africa's argument that the issue of South West Africa had nothing to do with India, the General Assembly adopted an Indian resolution noting that while South Africa had not proceeded to incorporate the mandated territory into the Union, it should come up with a trusteeship agreement for consideration at the 1948 session of the General Assembly. In a fighting speech before the final vote was taken, Lawrence described India's attitude towards South Africa as smacking of a 'vendetta'.[33]

CHAPTER 26

Smuts Defeated

It was Smuts's misfortune, and his opponents' good fortune, that the 1948 election should fall due at a time when internal opposition to segregation from Africans, Indians and coloureds began to coincide with criticism of the country from the international community.[1] With the British Empire in terminal decline, and mineral-rich Africa now open to competition from the world's two new superpowers, white-led South Africa found itself under regular attack for its racism from Afro-Asian countries as well as the Soviet Union and its satellites in Eastern Europe.

No one was more conscious of the country's growing isolation than Smuts, born into an age that took for granted the 'inevitability of gradualness' but now caught between competing nationalisms without any clear idea of how to navigate between them. Convinced that without his leadership, South Africa would fall prey to apartheid, he set out his dilemma succinctly in a letter to a friend:

> I am going to do whatever is politically possible and may even exceed the limits of political expediency. But I dare not do anything which will outpace public opinion too much on the eve of an election which may be the most important ever held in this country … I shall do as much of the right thing as possible, but always keep before me the paramount necessity of winning the election. What will it profit

this country if justice is done to the underdog and the whole caboodle then including that underdog, is handed over to the Wreckers?[2]

The Fagan Report

The 'right thing', in Smuts's mind, was a racial policy that recognised that blacks and whites had to live and work side by side, but that took account of similarities and differences between them.[3] The reforms he intended to introduce were based on the report of the Fagan Commission, which was released in February 1948. Fagan concluded that black urbanisation was inevitable, and rejected as 'a false policy' the notion that black workers in the cities were temporary visitors. If black labour were to be stabilised, workers had to be encouraged to bring their families with them from the reserves (as the NRC had been demanding all along).

As a possible alternative to influx control, Fagan proposed a nationwide system of labour bureaux. The report was ambivalent on the pass laws, however, recommending the replacement of passes with a new system of voluntarily applied-for identity cards linked to the provision of secure employment.[4] The whole tenor of the Fagan report was an unease with any kind of fixed blueprint for the future: what was needed, Fagan suggested, was a constant adaption to changing conditions and the smoothing out of difficulties between the races 'so that all may make their contribution and combine their energies for the progress of South Africa'.[5]

There was much in Fagan's proposals that moderate black opinion might have found acceptable had they appeared a few years earlier. The report would probably have altered black-white relations in the country for the better. But its release immediately before the 1948 election, allowing no time for its prescriptions to be tested in public debate, meant that the electorate was offered a 'liberal aspiration' rather than a clear policy choice.[6] And a large section of that electorate feared that accommodating urban blacks was a process that would bring the two races into confrontation with one another.[7]

Despite Fagan's acceptance of the permanence of urban workers and the economic interdependence of blacks and whites, his proposals were dismissed out of hand by the ANC. AB Xuma described the report as 'a typical South African political and legalistic document which recognises the facts of the situation, but avoids recommending the obvious remedy. It merely wants to palliate the system within the framework of existing policy.'[8] The Youth League's Jordan Ngubane described the stark choice before whites as lying between 'a greater South Africa of equal opportunity and a small white-dominated state of eventual tragedy'.[9]

Sauer Report

The report of the HNP's Sauer Commission, in contrast to Fagan, rejected both the 'exploitation and domination of blacks' and the equal rights of all races. Equality, it claimed, would result in the national suicide of whites. In accordance with the principle of 'Christian trusteeship', non-European groups should 'develop along their own character and calling'.[10] There should be wide-ranging segregation of the races and a ban on mixed marriages. The Indian population was unassimilable and should be repatriated.[11]

The ultimate aim, Sauer suggested, was complete separation of whites and blacks, to be implemented as far as practically possible without interfering with agriculture, industry and the economy generally. The African reserves should be consolidated and given their own political system based on traditional forms of government, while the NRC concept and the representation of other races in Parliament should be abolished. The aim of Sauer's recommendations was the elimination from white areas of 'surplus' black labour, and the channelling of a sufficient supply of workers from the reserves to the country's mines, farms and industries.[12]

As Hancock pithily observes, the Fagan Report set out to show how South Africans who differed from each other in race and colour might live together; the Sauer Report set out to explain how they could live apart. The 1948 election was to become a battle between these opposing conceptions of social reality in post-war South Africa.[13]

The election

When Parliament rose in March, ahead of the May election, Smuts's UP had good reason for confidence. The party had 89 seats in the House of Assembly, against the HNP's 49, with Labour (6), the Dominion Party (3), the white Native Representatives (3) and independents (3) making up the rest. The UP enjoyed an outright majority over all the opposition parties and on most issues could rely on the support of non-Nationalists in the House.

Despite the party's unanticipated reverse in the Hottentots-Holland by-election, Smuts felt confident of victory. With his own and South Africa's prestige after the war still relatively high, the economy growing steadily, business flourishing and no serious unemployment to speak of, the prime minister had little reason to believe the electorate had lost faith in him. Although most wartime governments lose favour in peacetime and there was general dissatisfaction at the ineffectiveness of the cabinet, the shortages of meat and white bread, and the high cost of living, the conventional wisdom – even among Nationalists – was that the UP would be returned to power with a reduced majority.

Smuts's lieutenants at party headquarters fed his overconfidence.[14] The recent death of Louis Esselen, his right-hand man in the party, had left Smuts without anyone brave enough to warn him of the extent of his alienation from Nationalist Afrikaners, not only in his own constituency of Standerton but also in the country at large. The experienced and tough-minded Esselen, says Paton, would also have realised the magnitude of the Hofmeyr/communism bogey and countered it aggressively.[15] Instead of which the UP – bereft of a formula that could satisfy both its conservative and liberal wings[16] – reacted defensively throughout the campaign, lamely arguing that Smuts's moderately liberal deputy Hofmeyr was not as extreme as the HNP made out. As Dan O'Meara succinctly records: 'Just as the war gave Smuts's UP its *raison d'être*, the end of the war left it with little political direction or purpose other than keeping out the Nationalists.'[17]

Esselen might also have persuaded Smuts to alter an outdated electoral system by which rural votes effectively counted for 15 per cent more than urban votes, and gave the HNP a decided advantage in the platteland. The 'wastage' of UP votes in highly populated urban constituencies was to cost Smuts the election.

The Nationalists, for their part, conducted their campaign with efficiency and thoroughness. Whereas the UP's organisation was centralised, lethargic and lacking a cadre of paid officials or even a youth wing, the National Party had an efficient branch structure, many more paid organisers, a core of dedicated activists who had not volunteered for war service and had been beavering away at grassroots, and a nationwide youth league.[18] It was, says Hancock, a case of professionalism against amateurism, youth against age, attack against defence. More than that, it was a holy crusade by the majority of the Afrikaner *volk* to capture and possess the South African state.[19]

Behind Malan's sombre exterior, wrote the UP MP Bernard Friedman, was an agile politician and extremely shrewd strategist, able to reduce political debate to a level where fear and prejudice rather than reason were the decisive factors. In a keynote speech in Paarl shortly before the vote, Malan asked whether the 'European' race would be able to maintain its purity and civilisation, or 'will it float along until it vanishes in the black sea of South Africa's non-European population?'[20] The UP's *niksdoen* (do-nothing) policies, he asserted, would not save white South Africa from the rising tide of colour. On the contrary, Smuts had already opened the floodgates by appointing Hofmeyr as his deputy. A Hofmeyr-led government, Malan asserted, was incompatible with white survival.[21]

Hofmeyr himself was forced to spend much of the campaign trying to prove he had never stood for racial equality. Nor did he expect to be Smuts's successor. His defenders reacted to the HNP's propaganda by distributing pamphlets quoting Hofmeyr's avowal at the UP conference in 1946 that he was not in favour of assimilation: 'The policy of Christian trusteeship I have in mind does not mean suppression, nor does it mean equality. It means the realisation of our responsibility not to ignore the interests of people of whom we are the guardians.'[22] This high-minded paternalism was no match for the *swart gevaar* drumbeat of the HNP. Whereas in Malan's camp there was unity, in Smuts's ranks there was disarray.[23]

The election result confounded every political pundit and dumbfounded the nation. Despite gaining 100 000 more votes than the Malan-Havenga alliance, Smuts's UP won only 65 seats against the National Party-Afrikaner Party's combined 79. Because fewer votes won more seats in rural areas, the Nationalists drove the UP out of almost every Afrikaans-speaking constituency in the country. Without the support of Labour, the Native Representatives and the independents, the National Party-Afrikaner Party alliance won a narrow majority of five in the House. To make matters worse, Smuts lost his own seat in Standerton. If every vote were to have had the same value, Smuts would have won 80 seats against Malan's 60, with ten going to the rest.[24] By allowing the country's most critical election since Union to be decided by a minority vote, Smuts had let power slip from his grasp.

NRC election

Shortly after the HNP's electoral victory, a second national poll of a different kind was held. Up for election after five years in office were the 12 members of the Native Representative Council and the three white representatives of blacks in Parliament. By now, the ANC had thought better of its earlier decision to boycott the poll and decided instead to recommend the re-election of all 12 sitting councillors to pursue the discussions with government about policy reforms. Some NRC members had foreseen that a boycott would play right into the hands of the Nationalists, who had already indicated a desire to abolish the council.

While the rival All African Convention, led by IB Tabata, continued to refuse on principle to participate in any segregated elections, the CPSA wavered, initially supporting the boycott call and then deciding not to miss the opportunity of putting up its own candidates. In spite of the boycott, the poll was as well supported by African voters as earlier polls had been.[25] Thanks to the publicity engendered by the NRC's adjournment resolution of 1946, 11 of the 12 incumbent councillors were re-elected, an indication of the support the council still enjoyed among the black electorate.

In the election for the three whites to represent the 'Natives', seeing as the HNP's majority in Parliament was so small, the party decided that it, too, should put up candidates. With no sense of irony, the new governing party's Transvaal party secretary approached AB Xuma to ask for the ANC's support for one JH (Kosie) van Rensburg, a Free State farmer, standing against Margaret Ballinger's husband, William. The party also circulated a pamphlet stating that if the voters put the HNP's candidates into Parliament, the party might revise its plans to abolish the council. Xuma responded by writing personally to every ANC election office, advising members to vote for Ballinger. Yet despite Xuma's efforts, no fewer than 25 ANC branches voted for Van Rensburg, including Alexandra township.[26] All five HNP candidates lost their deposits, however.

The most notable feature of the election was the comfortable victory of the CPSA's Sam Kahn over liberal and nationalist candidates for one of the three 'Native' seats. Kahn was the first communist to be elected by black Africans to represent their interests – though his tenure as an MP was brief, as the CPSA was banned in 1950. Significantly, whereas Africans chose a white CPSA member to represent them in Parliament, no communist ever won election to the Native Representative Council.

Soldiering on

While WWII may have added lustre to South Africa's international reputation, and to that of its defeated prime minister, it had split the Afrikaner people and galvanised opposition to Smuts's policies among the politically aware of all races. The 78-year-old general's immediate response to his defeat was that it was time to retire from politics, but he was quickly talked out of it by close colleagues. Smuts agreed instead to accept a safe seat at Pretoria East and soldier on as leader of the United Party. If he left politics, he rationalised to himself and others, the UP would split irretrievably between the supporters of Hofmeyr, who believed the party had to strike out in a new direction, and a much larger body of conservatives who blamed Hofmeyr's 'liberalism' for the party's shock defeat.

Though bewildered and astonished, then angered and saddened at his rejection by the electorate,[27] Smuts never tried to shift responsibility onto the shoulders of others. 'If there is a blame for the present failure, let it be mine ... I can take it,'[28] he declared. Buoyed by the knowledge that 20 per cent of the white electorate still preferred him to Malan, Smuts announced that he looked forward to the eventual completion of a task for which the preceding 50 years had been 'all too short a period': 'I hope to continue to take my part and do my duty as leader. We respect the constitutional verdict of the people, although in actual results, a minority of electors are now in charge of the government of the country.'[29] Three days after being talked out of retirement, the seemingly tireless ex-premier left South Africa briefly for the UK, to be installed as chancellor of Cambridge University.

Hand of Providence

The 74-year-old DF Malan, now prime minister at long last, and his ecstatic supporters found it difficult to believe their good fortune at having won the 1948 election. Against all the odds, power had fallen 'like a gift from heaven' into their lap.[30] Once again, as in great moments in Afrikaner history – notably Majuba and Blood River – devout believers were able to detect the hand of Providence in their unexpected victory. Now, a racially divided South Africa was theirs to reshape and rule according to their Calvinist prescriptions.

A day or two after the election results were announced, to the strains of '*Die Stem*' and the waving of the Vierkleur, a visibly emotional Malan – accompanied by his wife, Maria – boarded a train for Pretoria, where he was given a tumultuous welcome. Before leaving the Cape, the new prime minister issued the following statement: 'Today South Africa belongs to us once more. For the first time since Union, South Africa is our own and may God grant that it may always remain our own.'[31]

Sadly for Malan and his jubilant followers, his prayer to the deity would not be heeded.

Elsewhere in the World

In 1948

1 January	Britain's railways nationalised
30 January	Mahatma Gandhi assassinated in Delhi
25 February	Communist coup d'état in Czechoslovakia
5 April	World Health Organization established
14 May	State of Israel founded; first Arab-Israeli war begins on 15 May
24 June	Allied access to Berlin blocked by Soviets; Berlin airlift begins
29 June	Olympic Games open in London
5 July	National Health Service created in Britain
11 September	Death of Muhammad Ali Jinnah, founder of Pakistan
	Alan Paton's *Cry, the Beloved Country* published to international acclaim

PART FOUR

Aftermath

CHAPTER 27

The Screws Tighten

It was in 1948 that South Africa started to part company with the post-war world, to rejoin it almost half a century later. Malan's triumphant Nationalists came to power at a time when their determination to maintain white supremacy collided head-on with a revolution in attitudes towards race worldwide. As Allister Sparks observes, before WWII the kind of pragmatic separation enforced by successive South African governments was only slightly more stringent than racial practices throughout most of the colonial world. Even though Woodrow Wilson had declared, much earlier in the century, that every people had the right to self-determination, no one seriously had believed his views applied to non-white peoples.[1]

All that changed during the war and in the years that followed. Western imperialism, impoverished and debilitated, was forced to recognise the claims of millions of formerly colonised Asians and Africans, resulting in almost a hundred new nations being born – and becoming vocal members of the United Nations. Communism, with 'people's democracy' as its siren call, was rampant in Central and Eastern Europe and spreading its mostly malignant influence around the world. It was the new United Nations that provided the Soviet Union and its acolytes with a heaven-sent opportunity: anti-communist, capitalist and white-ruled South Africa offered a tempting target.

Heedless of international opinion, the HNP – now an alliance between the Afrikaner intelligentsia and the working class – wasted little time in setting about its two primary objectives: loosening South Africa's ties with Britain in order to further the ideal of an independent republic, and implementing the policy that had brought it to power – institutionalised segregation, or apartheid.

As Hermann Giliomee points out, the election of 1948 was not only about white domination but also about which whites would dominate.[2] In order to assert its authority right away, the new government immediately forced the retirement of the head of the UDF, General Sir Pierre van Ryneveld, replaced two of the country's most celebrated army chiefs, major-generals Evered Poole and Charles Powell, and confiscated a large cache of intelligence files relating to Afrikaner Broederbond and Ossewabrandwag activities during the war.[3] At the same time, it released from prison Robey Leibbrandt and other far-right figures jailed during the war.

The Nationalists also moved quickly to weaken ties with Britain by abolishing British citizenship and putting a stop to the recruitment of white immigrants from the UK and Europe, from which Smuts and the defeated United Party might benefit. The Smuts government had turned a blind eye to racial mixing during the war years; this was halted in 1950 by the passing of the Population Registration Act, which allocated every person to a specific racial group; by a law banning 'mixed' marriages between whites and other races; and by the Immorality Act, which made extramarital intercourse between whites and other races a serious offence.[4]

The public was unprepared for the lengths to which the new government was prepared to go to assert Nationalist Afrikaner control and bring about a pliant bureaucracy. Leading Broeders now directed or ran not only the government, the armed forces, the civil service and the public broadcaster, but began to make their presence felt in the economic sphere as well. According to Beinart, the apartheid edifice was constructed on seven pillars: a stricter definition of race; exclusive white control of political institutions (and the repression of opposition to them); spatial segregation in cities, towns and the countryside; separate territories and institutions for black Africans; control of African movement to urban areas; tighter division in the labour market (to protect Afrikaner workers); and the segregation of amenities and facilities – from educational institutions to park benches. The new regime's theorists insisted that whites had only two options: integration (and submersion) or much tighter segregation.[5]

Target CPSA

Another of the Nationalist government's early targets was the Communist Party, now entrenched in the African trade-union movement and growing closer to the ANC and Indian leadership by the year. Its new MP, Sam Kahn, was immediately banned from addressing public meetings and in 1950 a wide-ranging Suppression of Communism Act came into force. The Act empowered the minister of justice to prohibit the CPSA or any other organisation from advancing the aims of communism or encouraging hostility between blacks and whites, and to draw up a list of people suspected of being communists. Those on the list were barred from holding public office and had no right of appeal against the minister's decision. The draconian measure was one of several that the UP opposition – though equally fearful of communism – declined to support on the grounds that it infringed the principles of civil liberty on which the public law of the country was based.[6] In response to the Act, the CPSA went underground and formally changed its name to the South African Communist Party (SACP).

To further entrench racial separation in the political sphere, the government began dismantling the structures set up by its predecessor to provide for African, coloured and Indian representation. The token enfranchisement of Indians, proposed by Smuts in 1946 (and subsequently rejected), was reversed and the Native Representative Council abolished. An early attempt to remove coloured voters from the electoral roll in the Cape was temporarily (and surprisingly) resisted by Klasie Havenga, who queried its legality.

ANC upheaval

Among Africans, the unanticipated outcome of the 1948 election and the promulgation of apartheid laws such as the Population Registration Act and Group Areas Act provoked a strong counterreaction within the ranks of the ANC, whose leaders had failed to comprehend the power of the conviction that drove Afrikaner nationalism. 'South Africa has chosen the road to national suicide,' an angry AB Xuma declared after a year's experience of Nationalist rule. But Xuma's time as ANC leader was drawing to an end. For the angry young activists in the CYL, the days of talking about mass action but doing little were now over. When Xuma refused to back a Youth League-inspired Programme of Action because he was concerned about both the ANC's ability to implement it and the government's likely reaction, he was manoeuvred out of the presidency.

His replacement was Dr James S Moroka, a widely respected Free State medical practitioner and NRC member, born of a white father and black mother whose surname he took, who numbered many rural Afrikaners among his patients. Moroka had been active in the AAC since the 1930s and was a passionate advocate of multiracial political unity, but he was not yet an ANC member and his nomination was unconstitutional. As Mandela records, Moroka was 'not very knowledgeable about the ANC, neither was he an experienced activist, but he was respectable and amenable to our programme'.[7] The CYL's first choice for the ANC presidency was ZK Matthews, but he had declined the nomination. At a separate CYL meeting convened by AP Mda, Moroka accepted the nomination, promised the Youth Leaguers places on the ANC's national executive and agreed to implement their plan for civil disobedience and mass action. (According to Heidi Holland, Moroka was one of the wealthiest Africans in the country, with a number of large farms in the Thaba 'Nchu reserve in the Free State. He also had a history of cooperating with whites, helping

Dr James Moroka, who succeeded AB Xuma as ANC president.
DRUM SOCIAL HISTORIES/BAHA/AFRICA MEDIA ONLINE

to fund a school for poor Afrikaner children, and opening a medical practice for white patients.[8])

In the ANC presidential election, the old guard voted for Xuma and the Youth League for Moroka, who won a narrow victory. Walter Sisulu took over from the elderly James Calata as the Congress's secretary-general and the Programme of Action became official ANC policy. The Programme rejected any form of 'white trusteeship' and committed the Congress to a campaign of passive resistance against segregationist laws and structures. As Rich observes, the Programme's chief significance was to signal a change of consciousness among the African elite and to 'instil a new sense of mission among African nationalists'.[9]

With his control over the ANC having finally slipped away, an angry Xuma complained that the organisation been taken over by 'half-castes', alluding to Moroka, JB Marks and Sisulu, all men of mixed parentage.[10] As president, Moroka turned out to be a disappointment to his supporters, staying out of touch with the ANC and leaving much of the leadership and the day-to-day running of the organisation in the hands of the new secretary-general, Sisulu.[11]

Walter Sisulu

Like Mandela and Tambo, the ANC's new secretary-general, Walter Max Ulyate Sisulu, was born in the then Transkei. He was the son of a white foreman, who had come to the Engcobo district briefly to supervise road workers, and an African mother, a devout Anglican, who brought the young man up with the help of other members of her family. Walter never met his father and, embarrassed by the paleness of his skin, he grew up harbouring a bitter resentment of white people. Rebellious as a youngster, he left home for Johannesburg after a quarrel with his uncle, a tribal headman, and aunts over his rudeness to their occasional white visitors.[12]

Sisulu's antipathy to white authority intensified during a succession of menial jobs as a kitchen hand, labourer in a dairy, miner and packer in a bakery, during which time he became interested in the concept of collective bargaining and the activities of trade unions. Working in various factories, he lost one job after another because of his opposition to unfair labour practices. He overcame his frustration by studying English grammar and Xhosa history in order to improve his standard-four education. In 1940, he and some colleagues established an estate agency.

A spell in jail, following an altercation with a train conductor who had confiscated a black passenger's expensive season ticket, further embittered Sisulu, still searching for a form of political retaliation against white rule. When war was declared in 1939, he campaigned against the enlistment of Africans in the UDF and became a supporter of the Japanese, hoping they might 'liberate' South Africa. He was fortunate, at this time, to meet his future wife, Albertina Toriwe, who respected his opinions and gave him the self-confidence to overcome his mixed origins. 'I'm black enough for both of us,' Albertina would say of his pale skin.[13]

In 1940, Sisulu found his ideological home in the ANC, in the same year that AB Xuma, also from Engcobo, became the organisation's president-general. He also struck up a warm friendship with another lonely newcomer to Johannesburg, Nelson Mandela, whom he invited to move into the house his shared with his fiancé, Albertina, his mother and several relatives. Always sympathetic to black people out to better themselves, he offered Mandela a job in his estate agency – a gesture Mandela would always remember.

Sisulu was one of several recruits to the ANC who found the organisation insufficiently militant under Xuma and banded together to found the CYL, of which he became treasurer. Known among his colleagues as the most resistant to any form of contact or cooperation with whites, he was one of those most enthusiastic about promoting and putting into practice the ANC's new Programme of Action.[14]

Cato Manor

Earlier that year, a tragedy had occurred in Natal that almost brought an early end to the Doctors' Pact, and caused radical Indian leaders to seek closer ties with the ANC. An argument between an Indian shopkeeper and a young African near the Grey Street taxi rank in Durban had escalated into widespread racial violence directed by groups of armed Africans against Indians throughout the business district of the city and its surrounds, particularly Cato Manor.[15]

It took two days before the security forces began to suppress the rioting with heavy weapons fire, which caused many more casualties. During the bloody confrontation, 142 people were killed, Indian women were raped, and more than a thousand people were injured. The ANC alleged that the authorities had stood aside during the riots and had made little attempt to avert them.[16]

As Soske records, the Durban riots 'remain a charged part of Natal's living memory'.[17] The violence 'fractured local communities in ways that cut across race', split the leaderships of African and Indian political organisations, and 'resulted in the emergence of unprecedented relationships and alliances'.[18] The cause of the rioting was identified as the bitterness felt by impoverished Africans towards Indian traders and landowners.[19]

Whatever the reasons – which are still in dispute today – the violence exposed the serious tensions between two disadvantaged communities living cheek by jowl on the fringes of the city and led to renewed efforts on the part of radical Indian and African leaders to bring the two races closer together in order to coordinate the resistance to apartheid. In the Transvaal, however, a significant group within the Youth League – including Mandela and Tambo – continued to oppose Indian-African collaboration. The Newclare branch of the CYL called on the minister of the interior to impose residential segregation between Africans and Indians.[20] When Xuma publicly queried the decision, the Newclare branch wrote to him saying 'the committee feels that the president is working hand in glove with Indians in imposing these economic difficulties on Africans'.[21] This was grist to the mill of apartheid theorists, who claimed that the Durban rioting was proof of the mutual antagonism between South Africa's races and the need for separate residential and business areas.[22]

Programme of Action

In February 1950, a still resentful Xuma resigned his seat on the ANC's national executive, to be replaced – at Sisulu's suggestion – by Nelson Mandela, who viewed his appointment with mixed feelings as he had no real desire to become part of the ruling ANC hierarchy. It took until mid-1951 for Moroka eventually to convene a joint planning council of the ANC and the South African Indian Congress. By this time, events had overtaken the CYL, some of whose members (including Mandela) were still openly hostile to the involvement of other races, particularly communists, in the Programme of Action. It was Walter Sisulu who persuaded Mandela and his friends in the Africanist bloc to put aside their distrust of other organisations and participate in the first coordinated nationwide response to HNP policies.

Having eventually decided in favour of pragmatism, Mandela threw himself into the Programme of Action with enthusiasm, agreeing to become its volunteer-in-chief. Together with another devotee of passive resistance, Yusuf Cachalia, he traversed the country, holding hundreds of meetings at which Africans and Indians were encouraged to commit acts of non-violent civil disobedience to demonstrate their opposition to apartheid. In preparation for a nationwide campaign of defiance, Mandela travelled to Port Elizabeth for an ANC executive meeting at which a dinner was held in honour of ZK Matthews. Joe Matthews, son of ZK, recalls Mandela's saying that he (Mandela) would be the first black president of South Africa.[23]

On 26 June 1952, a date that would become a fixture on the resistance calendar for many years, a national Defiance Campaign was launched, during which Moroka, Mandela, Sisulu, JB Marks, Dadoo, Cachalia and Ahmed Kathrada were among many hundreds of people arrested. Over the next five months, some 8 000 people were imprisoned under the Suppression of Communism Act for periods of between one and three weeks. Mandela and Cachalia spent a couple of nights in jail themselves.

Unfortunately for the organisers, the campaign flared into violence at times, resulting in the further loss of black and white lives and prompting a strong response from the authorities, who raided the offices of the campaign's leaders and charged Mandela and 20 others with promoting communism. After a government ban made the holding of meetings virtually impossible, it did not take long before the Programme of Action lost its momentum. In a packed Johannesburg magistrates' courtroom, Mr Justice Rumpff found Mandela and the other defendants guilty of 'statutory communism', which, he acknowledged, was 'nothing like communism as it is commonly known', and sentenced the defendants to nine months' imprisonment with hard labour, suspended for two years.[24]

At the ANC's annual conference in December 1952, a politically inastute Dr Moroka lost his bid for re-election to the mild-mannered and deeply religious Zulu tribal leader and former teacher, Chief Albert Luthuli. Luthuli had been given the choice by the Nationalists of remaining in his state-paid tribal appointment or renouncing his membership of the ANC. He responded by saying, 'Who can deny that thirty years of my life have been spent knocking in vain, patiently, moderately and modestly, at a closed and barred door. What have been the fruits of moderation?'[25]

Despite often being banned and confined to his home in rural Natal, Luthuli remained president of the ANC for the next 15 years – the longest incumbency in its history.[26] It would win him the Nobel Prize for Peace in 1961.

Foreign affairs

On the international front, like Hertzog and Smuts before him, Prime Minister Malan decided to take personal responsibility for conducting South Africa's external (foreign) affairs. At the 1949 Commonwealth Conference in London, he made an initially favourable impression during the discussion of India's application to retain its membership of the Commonwealth. Conscious that South Africa was in need of friends, Malan announced to the conference that South Africa, like India, would remain in the Commonwealth as long as its sovereign rights – including the right to become a republic – were accepted. He also committed an SAAF squadron to assist United Nations forces in the Korean War.[27] These gestures, motivated by realpolitik, came as an unpleasant surprise to hardliners within the HNP caucus, led by the uncompromising Transvaler and future prime minister, JG Strijdom, who wished to sever all ties with the Commonwealth forthwith.[28]

Malan's attitude towards the United Nations was far less compromising. In the hope of persuading South Africa's new government to depart from the course set by its predecessor, Pakistan accepted an invitation from Malan for round-table talks, as had been ordered by the UN General Assembly. India also accepted South Africa's invitation, but when the Group Areas Act was promulgated, Mrs Pandit insisted that if any meeting were to take place, the Act had to be suspended. Malan ignored the demand and negotiations between the three countries were never to resume.

At The Hague, the International Court of Justice – at the request of the UN – ruled unanimously that South Africa's mandate over South West Africa still existed, but the Union could not change the status of the territory unilaterally nor could it be compelled to place South West Africa under UN trusteeship. South Africa was still obliged, however, to submit annual reports on its administration of the mandate. While taking no steps to incorporate South West Africa formally into the Union, Malan flatly refused to report to the UN each year as directed, on the grounds that his government, unlike the Smuts regime, did not recognise the UN as the successor to the League of Nations.

The International Court of Justice opinion brought South Africa little respite from scathing international opprobrium, which intensified when the Nationalists announced their intention of extending 'separate development' throughout South West Africa. Disregarding its critics, the government allocated the mandated territory six new seats in the South African Parliament, all of which were won by the HNP, at last giving it an outright majority over the other parties. With no need for Malan to depend on the support of Havenga's nine MPs any longer, the HNP and the Afrikaner Party merged in 1951 to become the National Party of South Africa (NP).

Smuts dies

The age of the generals – Botha, Hertzog and Smuts – came finally to its end on 11 September 1950, with the death of the 80-year-old Jan Smuts. His passing, following that of his right hand and potential successor, JH Hofmeyr, more than a year earlier left the United Party in disarray, its caucus deeply divided between liberals and conservatives. The party's prospects were strengthened for a brief period by the emergence of the Torch Commando, an ex-servicemen's organisation led by the renowned ex-RAF fighter pilot, AG (Sailor) Malan. The Torch Commando was formed in 1951 to defend the constitution against attempts by the Nationalists to remove coloured people in the Cape from the voters' roll. At its height, the Torch Commando had 250 000 signed-up members, almost one-tenth of the white population. It derived its name from the mass protest meetings in the major cities, which often drew crowds in the tens of thousands and were preceded by torchlight parades.

Supported by the new leader of the opposition, Advocate JGN Strauss, the 'Torch', the Labour Party and the UP temporarily joined forces to form a United Democratic Front (UDF) to contest the 1953 general election. Unfortunately for apartheid's opponents, a combination of the Malan regime's fury, the application of anti-communist measures, the fear of job losses in the public service and armed forces, as well as dissension within the ranks of the UP over the involvement of coloured ex-servicemen, prevented the UDF from making any impact in the 1953 election, and enthusiasm for the 'Torch' soon petered out. Yet the Torch Commando had brought home to the Nationalists the fact that thousands of South Africans who had fought fascism in WWII had not lost their determination to stand up for freedom and civil liberties in post-war South Africa.

Epilogue

Nationalism flows from the dignity that a vibrant national consciousness bestows on a nation's members.
– G John Ikenberry

The narrowness of the parliamentary vote of 1939 invites speculation about what might have happened had South Africa not chosen to fight in WWII and opted instead for neutrality. How would Hertzog have met his constitutional obligations to the Commonwealth, while resisting overtures from the German Reich? And where might a neutral South Africa have found itself in the aftermath of Hitler's defeat? What would the future of the United Party have been if Smuts had retired at the end of the war, and who might have succeeded him? Would white politics have turned out differently had Hofmeyr, an Afrikaner second only to Smuts in intellect, not died prematurely from overwork a few months after the war? What might have happened had the Smuts regime taken proper notice of the popular and once-respected Native Representative Council? And, most importantly, what would South Africa look like today had the war not produced the demographic upheaval and economic stimulus that galvanised both Afrikaner and African nationalisms? Might apartheid have been accelerated, postponed or even averted had the Union not gone to war for the second time?

As the distinguished historian CW de Kiewiet explained to a Canadian audience in the 1950s, the gateway to understanding most political issues in South Africa is the Anglo-Boer War.[1] More than any other single event, that war 'intensified, complicated and embittered the already ensnarled relationship of Boer and Britain, Bantu and Indian, white and non-white ... It is the bitter paradox of modern South African history that the war which united the country politically, divided it racially.'[2]

The Anglo-Boer War's aftermath may have brought together the four provinces in South Africa administratively and geographically, but it failed to bridge the cultural divide between Englishmen and Afrikaners. That was the price that both had to pay 'to mend the errors of almost a century and in order to cement the unity without which neither peace nor prosperity were possible'.[3]

It was the Boer generals Botha and Smuts, who – unlike a third general, Hertzog – recognised that no country could stand aside from the great tide of world history. 'They were willing to trade a century of wrong for a new century of hope,' wrote De Kiewiet.[4] In their view, a reconciled and united white community was the essential preliminary to confronting all the other great economic, social and racial issues facing the new Union. Unfortunately, as De Kiewiet explained, 'the pain of war left [in many Afrikaners] a hunger for a compensating victory, for a retroactive declaration of independence, for some symbolic act of rebellion and defiance that would purge the memory of defeat and wrong. A war and not a peaceful constitution became the seedbed of nationalist feeling and racial passion.'[5] The compensating victory to which De Kiewiet refers was to come eventually in two stages: the triumph of Afrikaner nationalism in the election of 1948 and the birth of a white-led republic in 1961.

★ ★ ★

No re-examination of South Africa in the 1940s is possible without weighing up the motivations of Jan Smuts, the dominant – and dominating – figure of that time. Were it not for his accurate reading of Hitler's intentions, and determination that the Union should, in its own interests as much as Britain's, uphold its constitutional obligations to the Commonwealth,

EPILOGUE

South Africa would have remained on the sidelines, isolated and ostracised by the Dominions alongside which it had fought in WWI. Since that war, South Africa's prime minister had become an international celebrity, prominent on the councils of Europe and the Commonwealth, a key participant in the founding of the League of Nations and a self-appointed seeker after world peace.

Yet, if truth be told, there were two Smutses: there was the philosopher, international moralist and defender of the Rights of Man; and then there was the political pragmatist, intellectually liberal but instinctively conservative, prepared to temper his idealism in order to remain at the centre of South Africa's affairs. As Willem Gravett explains, 'Smuts lived on several planes. On the world stage his vision was universal, his analysis acute. He displayed statesmanship of the highest character marked by vision and courage. On the South African plane, however, he was a politician fighting for his party, seeking immediate objectives and using whatever means came to hand.'[6]

Aloof in manner and set apart from the common herd by his powerful intellect, Smuts's cold-eyed realism won him not only the support and loyalty of thousands of his countrymen who shared his outward-looking vision, but also the distrust and enmity of many who did not. His ultimate failure lay in not being able to apply his holistic vision in international affairs to the issue of racial equality at home. Yet, as the liberal academic Edgar Brookes wrote, 'he was a great human, gifted in everything outside South African party politics with insight, profound knowledge and living hope ... a far greater figure than many of his critics will admit.'[7] On hearing of Smuts's death, the ANC's president-general, James Moroka, said of him: 'In the heat of the bitterest political battles that Africans had ceaselessly waged against him, they had been irresistibly and continually conscious of the giant nature of his mind and soul.'[8]

From a constitutional and strategic perspective, Smuts was right to take South Africa into the war. His understanding of world affairs made him appreciate, as Hertzog did not, that without Commonwealth solidarity,

South Africa and much of Africa might easily fall prey to the revived colonial ambitions of the German Reich. The prize to be gained if the war was won was for South Africa's borders to remain intact and the country to be recognised as an honoured member of the Western alliance. The price Smuts would have to pay personally was having to abandon – he hoped only temporarily – his lifelong efforts to heal the rift between Englishmen and Afrikaners and, more importantly, any attempt to address timeously the question of how to accommodate the aspirations and demands of South Africa's black majority.

Hertzog's argument for remaining neutral in 1939 showed his lack of understanding of the threat posed by Hitler's Germany. After the signs became obvious in Czechoslovakia, the clearer-sighted Smuts, by contrast, had to remind audiences in speech after speech that the world was a dangerous place for small nations. Letting his reluctance to side with Britain over Germany override his judgement of where South Africa's true interests lay, Hertzog disregarded Hitler's declared intention to demand the return of South West Africa. He used the unfairness of the Treaty of Versailles to rationalise the Führer's behaviour, and to justify why, notwithstanding the Simonstown Agreement to protect the Cape sea route, South Africa should stay out of the war. Yet, as Hancock notes, the 'wild rush' of events in Europe would soon have shaken Hertzog's formula for a modified neutrality.[9]

On several occasions early in the war – when it looked like Hitler was invincible – both Hertzog and Malan brought motions before Parliament urging Smuts to make a separate peace with Germany. Had Hertzog been prime minister when France was overrun in 1940, such were Nationalist pressures on him at the time that he might easily have abandoned neutrality and forged such a peace. The consequences for the country's international reputation would have been devastating. Thanks to Smuts, it is to South Africa's everlasting credit that its men and women made an honourable contribution to the defeat of Nazi Germany and the preservation of the remains of Western democracy.

EPILOGUE

As for Hertzog's complaint that by taking South Africa to war again, Smuts had brought an end to the great experiment of Fusion, Smuts might well have pointed out that had South Africa remained neutral, Hitler's advances in Europe and subsequent argument over an appropriate South African response would inevitably have driven the two wings of the United Party apart, later if not sooner. In retrospect, this country has reason to be thankful that it was Smuts rather than Hertzog at the helm during the greatest challenge of the 20th century.

★ ★ ★

Going to war in 1939 brought many material benefits to South Africa. It stimulated industry, both primary and secondary, as foreign capital poured in to buy gold. The ports of Cape Town and Durban, in particular, were filled with ships and flooded with troops, opening new opportunities for shopkeepers, traders, and men and women in service industries,[10] while the demand for wartime armaments raised the wages of skilled and semi-skilled workers of all races, with white unemployment falling to a record low. As the economist Nicoli Nattrass points out, involvement in the war brought about a significant redistribution of assets to (and within) South Africa. The spurt in manufacturing led to a rapid expansion of work opportunities for black labour, especially after almost a quarter of the white workforce left their jobs to volunteer for military service. 'Paternalistic' Wage Board determinations ensured that non-white wages went up faster than those of whites, leading to a decrease in the racial wage gap during the war years.[11]

By the war's end, the economy was in much better shape than ever before, enabling finance minister Hofmeyr to set aside additional financing for African education and school feeding, and to provide funding for African pensioners and the disabled for the first time. In his 1946/47 budget speech, Hofmeyr reminded Parliament that the country's ability 'to buy from the world the goods which we do not produce at home is not limited, as is the case with so many war-torn countries, by a lack of internationally acceptable money'.[12] To many in rationed and ravaged Europe, post-war South Africa beckoned as a land of opportunity, beckoning and attracting thousands of skilled immigrants as soon as the conflict was over.

On the debit side of the ledger, Smuts's preoccupation with events outside South Africa and his failure to entertain any suggestion of delimitation ahead of the 1948 election undoubtedly advanced the advent of apartheid. Given that it took until 1958 for the Nationalists to win a majority of white votes, the policy of 'separate development' might conceivably have been delayed for at most a decade, but its coming was almost inevitable. Fear is always the most powerful driver in politics, and among the numerically outnumbered whites, the dread of African nationalism, black retribution, Soviet-style communism, African *uhuru* (freedom) and pressure from the UN would more than likely have brought the Nationalists to power at some time in the early 1950s.

In Arthur Keppel-Jones's classic, deeply pessimistic exercise in futurology, *When Smuts Goes*, written in 1947, he predicted a Nationalist victory in 1953. To those who consoled themselves at the prospect by taking refuge in bromides such as '*Môre is nog 'n dag*' (tomorrow is another day), '*Alles sal regkom*' (everything will be all right) or 'It can't happen here', he suggested the next half century would be shaped for the worse by the forces of Afrikaner nationalism.[13] The purpose of his prescient book was to warn whites that salvation lay 'only in a reversal of historic tendencies, a reversal so thorough as to constitute a revolution'.[14] This was easier said than done, for, as De Kiewiet observed, among racial minorities tolerance does not flourish easily in an atmosphere of fear and insecurity.[15]

By the end of WWII, attitudes had hardened in all racial groups – white, African, coloured and Indian – and the middle ground in politics had been substantially weakened. Despite an improved economy, the rapid pace of urbanisation, steadily growing slums and the lawlessness in overcrowded locations had given rise to new social problems that an out-of-touch government and hard-pressed bureaucracy had little hope of solving. More ominously, the Smuts government's failure to enact meaningful political reforms had caused patience and hope among non-whites to give way to the policies and tactics of resistance and mass action.

★ ★ ★

It was the South African-born foreign minister of Israel, Abba Eban, who once famously accused the Palestinians of never missing an opportunity to miss an opportunity. The same might be said of successive South African governments since 1912 for failing to take advantage of the moderation and goodwill of many, although not all, black African leaders. It was particularly true of the wartime United Party leadership, which turned a deaf ear to the pleadings – and warnings – of men of moderation such as Dr John L Dube, Selope Thema, RH Godlo, ZK Matthews, Paul Mosaka, AB Xuma and Albert Luthuli. As Gail Gerhart has reflected, throughout the 1940s and beyond, the great majority of educated, mission-trained Africans rejected the materialistic outlook of communism and continued to adhere to a basically liberal set of social and political goals, as well as to an evolutionary view of change. What most Africans wanted – and whites were at pains to deny them – 'was the fulfilment of paternalistic promises of "trusteeship", unfettered opportunity to assimilate European culture and learn modern skills, the opportunity to demonstrate African competence, and to be accepted, however gradually, as equals in a common, competitive society'.[16]

Smuts's former UP colleague, Bernard Friedman, claimed that as an institution, the Native Representative Council could have been vital in establishing 'a cooperative relationship between the regime and the Native peoples, between government and governed'.[17] If the NRC had been allowed to function effectively, Friedman wrote, it could have given an immense impetus to the evolution of a common society in South Africa. The members of the NRC had a better understanding of Western civilisation, a deeper appreciation of the Western values that Smuts, in particular, claimed to hold so dear, and a greater passion for advancing the growth of democracy than the majority of the black community. Their wisdom and eloquence, Friedman argued, would have graced the proceedings of the highest forum of the land.[18]

Instead of which, the Smuts regime, fearful of being dubbed *kafferboeties* by the opposition, deliberately kept its distance from the NRC, lest voters think the Council was exerting an influence over policy-making. And the more the NRC's representations were ignored, the less moderate and more resentful the councillors became. It was especially unfortunate for Smuts that he failed to heed the council's plea, made shortly before the 1948 election, for seven more representatives in Parliament. An additional seven seats for him rather than Malan would have kept his United Party in power.

★ ★ ★

It is tempting, too, to speculate on what might have happened had premature death not robbed South Africa of the talents of two remarkable figures of the 1940s – JH Hofmeyr and Anton Lembede. The former, whose intellect and experience put him head and shoulders above his colleagues in a lacklustre UP cabinet, was widely regarded as Smuts's heir apparent. (Hofmeyr's sudden death came a day after the passing of Dr HJ van der Bijl, founder of Iscor and the wartime director of war supplies, from cancer at the age of 61. In a letter to Margaret Gillett in Oxford, Smuts expressed 'our surprise and shock' at the loss within 24 hours 'of our greatest industrialist' and 'our most distinguished parliamentarian'.[19])

It is unlikely, however, that Hofmeyr would have succeeded Smuts or led the United Party, whose right wing was closer to the Nationalists than to their deputy leader. It was Hofmeyr's cautious liberalism, the UP diehards believed, that had brought about their party's defeat. Amid the repercussions of the UP's election loss, attempts were already under way to sideline Hofmeyr and make overtures to the Afrikaner Party leader,

Havenga, as a possible replacement. In retrospect, it seems far more likely that had he lived, Hofmeyr would have left the UP and led the small group of 'progressives' who broke away from the party in the late 1950s.

The other significant loss, to black politics of the time, was the tragically early demise of Anton Lembede, whose Africanist philosophy lived on in the Congress Youth League of AP Mda, Nelson Mandela, Oliver Tambo and Walter Sisulu. Lembede's religious and anti-communist convictions might well have led him to side eventually with Robert Sobukwe, whose Pan Africanist version of nationalism and non-racialism (in contrast to the ANC's multiracialism) was to become a forerunner of the influential Black Consciousness movement of Steve Biko and others in the 1970s.[20]

★ ★ ★

It was WWII, Winston Churchill observed, that shattered the colonial calm of Africa, and nowhere was this more true than in South Africa. In hindsight, the most lasting outcome of Smuts's determination to take South Africa into the war on the Allied side was the powerful boost it gave to Afrikaner and African nationalisms. It enabled Malan to unite and heal the breach in Afrikanerdom, split asunder since the time of Fusion in 1933, and to channel the outrage of the *volk* at having to subordinate itself again to what were perceived as Britain's interests. The war vote of September 1939 was the catalyst for drawing diverse strands of Afrikanerdom together into a powerful alliance between cultural purists, farmers seeking cheap labour, businessmen seeking capital, religious leaders seeking followers, and workers seeking training. All came together to bring about and sustain Nationalist Afrikaner supremacy for more than the next four decades.[21]

In response, African nationalists – submissive and disorganised since the 1930s – began to mobilise actively for the first time. A new generation of leaders sprang up, prepared to forge alliances with other races in an effort to rid the country of apartheid. The Defiance Campaign they launched in the early 1950s led to the founding of the multiracial Congress Alliance, and in 1955 to the Freedom Charter, the ANC's programmatic blueprint for the next four decades.

The victims of these unintended consequences were Smuts and his followers, who had taken South Africa to war only to find themselves trying, with ever-increasing desperation, to hold on to the centre ground and avoid being overrun by the demands of white politicians on one side and black activists on the other. Instead of being acclaimed for the sacrifices that so many people of all races had made in the war, the Union found itself isolated and pilloried for its racism.

Such were the bitter fruits of the war that changed South Africa forever.

Acknowledgements

The seed for this book was planted some 30 years ago when I reviewed for my newspaper the book *Vyf Dae*, written by the late Dr At van Wyk, the Afrikaner political journalist and historian. It described in fascinating detail the intrigues leading up to the climactic war vote in September 1939, but, for reasons best known to its publisher, the book appeared in Afrikaans only. I thought it a pity that such an account had not been published in English as well, and tucked away in my mind the idea of writing my own version one day, although from a slightly different perspective. In Part One of this book, I have leant heavily on *Vyf Dae*, and readily acknowledge my debt to At van Wyk, whom I never had the pleasure of meeting.

My second thank-you is to Professor Bill Nasson, esteemed historian, author and major contributor to the influential *Cambridge History of South Africa*. Bill read the manuscript chapter by chapter, made many helpful suggestions and has saved me (I hope) from egregious error. I was also fortunate in having the top brass of Jonathan Ball Publishers, in the person of Jonathan himself, Eugene Ashton and Jeremy Boraine – history buffs all three – read the manuscript and offer criticisms and suggestions. I am also indebted to academics Charles van Onselen and Anne Samson for helpful advice, comments and directions as to sources at various times.

I have been singularly fortunate in having two excellent libraries close at hand. Being made a Research Associate of the Wits Institute for Social and Economic Research (WISER), through the kind offices of Professors Sarah Nuttall and Keith Breckenridge, and their assistant Najibha Deshmukh, has enabled me to spend many productive hours in the Cullen Library at Wits. I should also like to thank the staff of the Brenthurst Library, and in particular Jennifer Kimble, for their invaluable assistance and the use of their incomparable facilities. I must also acknowledge my debt to the British Library in London, whose services and facilities are the most remarkable I've encountered anywhere. Here, I must also record my sincere thanks to Gary and Marie-France Ralfe who, not for the first time, made their apartment available to me during my researches in London.

Once again, it has been a pleasure to submit my manuscript to the judgement and editorial guidance of Alfred LeMaitre, to whom I extend sincere thanks. Alfred made many helpful suggestions, almost all of which have been implemented. Such errors that remain in the text are of my own making.

Once again, the book's design has been in the capable hands of Kevin Shenton and Danel van Jaarsveld, while Ceri Prenter and Caren van Houwelingen steered it through production. My thanks go to all of them.

Notes

Preface
1. Thompson, *A History of South Africa*, p 182.
2. Giliomee and Mbenga (eds), *New History of South Africa*, p 296.
3. Dubow and Jeeves (eds), *South Africa's 1940s*, p 2.

PART ONE: SEVEN VOTES

Chapter 1 The Principals
1. Van den Heever, *General JBM Hertzog*, p 14.
2. Giliomee, *The Afrikaners*, p 301.
3. Fisher, *The Afrikaners*, p 216.
4. Ibid, p 217.
5. Hancock, *Smuts: The Fields of Force 1919–1950*, p 242.
6. Ibid, p 241.
7. Fisher, p 218.
8. Ibid, p 220.
9. Giliomee, p 358.
10. Hancock, p 243.
11. Giliomee, p 300.
12. Fisher, p 220.
13. Ibid, p 215.
14. Hancock, p 356.
15. Ibid, p 357.
16. Ibid, p 358.
17. Fisher, p 229.
18. Crafford, *Jan Smuts*, p 107.
19. Krüger, *The Making of a Nation*, p 203.
20. Koorts, *DF Malan*, p 18.
21. Ibid.
22. Ibid, p 131.
23. Fisher, p 238.

Chapter 2 Overture
1. Blackwell, *Farewell to Parliament*, pp 64–65.
2. Hancock, *Smuts: The Sanguine Years 1870–1919*, p 232.
3. Ibid, p 243.
4. Giliomee and Mbenga (eds), *New History of South Africa*, p 247.
5. Kruger, *The Age of the Generals*, p 125.
6. Hancock, *Smuts: The Fields of Force 1919–1950*, p 251.
7. Wilson and Thompson (eds), *The Oxford History of South Africa, Vol II*, p 381.
8. Crowder (ed), *Cambridge History of Africa, Vol 8*, p 278.
9. Cameron and Spies (eds), *An Illustrated History of South Africa*, p 258.
10. Blake, *Wit Terroriste*, pp 18–19.
11. Ibid.
12. Giliomee, *The Afrikaners*, p 423.
13. Krüger, *The Making of a Nation*, p 168.
14. Solomon, *Time Remembered*, p 123.
15. Ibid.
16. Krüger, *The Making of a Nation*, p 189.
17. Van Wyk, *Vyf Dae*, p 11.

Chapter 3 Friday and Saturday
1. Blackwell, *Farewell to Parliament*, p 56.
2. Van Wyk, *Vyf Dae*, p 16.
3. Smuts, *Jan Christian Smuts*, p 372.
4. Ibid.

5   Van Wyk, *Vyf Dae*, p 23.
6   Ibid.
7   Ibid, p 27.
8   Ibid, p 37.
9   Reitz, *Adrift on the Open Veld*, p 516.
10 Ibid.
11 Hancock, *Smuts: The Fields of Force 1919–1950*, p 319.
12 Lawrence, *Harry Lawrence*, p 105.
13 Ibid.
14 Van Wyk, *Vyf Dae*, p 47.
15 Pirow, *James Barry Munnik Hertzog*, p 246.
16 Van Wyk, *Vyf Dae*, p 52.
17 Ibid, p 54.

Chapter 4 Sunday
1   Van Wyk, *Vyf Dae*, p 63.
2   Lawrence, *Harry Lawrence*, p 106.
3   Reitz, *Adrift on the Open Veld*, pp 516–517.
4   Ibid, p 516.
5   Nasson, *South Africa at War, 1939–1945*, p 55.
6   Van Wyk, *Vyf Dae*, p 79.
7   Ibid, p 80.

Chapter 5 Monday
1   Van Wyk, *Vyf Dae*, p 96.
2   Ibid, p 99.
3   Ibid, p 100.
4   Lawrence, *Harry Lawrence*, p 105.
5   Reitz, *Adrift on the Open Veld*, p 517.
6   Ibid.
7   Hancock, *Smuts: The Fields of Force 1919–1950*, p 321.
8   Ibid.
9   Smuts, *Jan Christian Smuts*, p 375.
10 Van Wyk, *Vyf Dae*, p 102.
11 Ibid, p 104.
12 Solomon, *Time Remembered*, p 136.
13 Van Wyk, *Vyf Dae*, pp 104–105.
14 Ibid, p 103.
15 Crafford, *Jan Smuts*, p 282.
16 Van Wyk, *Vyf Dae*, p 105.
17 Ibid.
18 Hancock, *Smuts: The Fields of Force 1919–1950*, pp 321–322.
19 Long, *In Smuts's Camp*, pp 44–45.
20 Hancock, *Smuts: The Fields of Force 1919–1950*, p 323.
21 Van Wyk, *Vyf Dae*, p 109.
22 Solomon, *Time Remembered*, p 138.
23 Van Wyk, *Vyf Dae*, p 114.

24 Wilson, *Gone Down the Years*, p 212.
25 Reitz, *Adrift on the Open Veld*, p 518.
26 Ibid.
27 Hancock, *Smuts: The Fields of Force 1919–1950*, p 323.
28 Van Wyk, *Vyf Dae*, p 119.

Chapter 6 Tuesday and Wednesday
1   Van Wyk, *Vyf Dae*, p 114.
2   Ibid, p 122.
3   Ibid, p 123.
4   J Simpson, in De Villiers (ed), *Better Than They Knew*, p 20.
5   Ibid.
6   Van Wyk, *Vyf Dae*, p 14.
7   Barlow, *Almost in Confidence*, p 150.
8   Blackwell, *Farewell to Parliament*, p 182.
9   Simpson, in De Villiers, p 22.
10 Blackwell, *Farewell to Parliament*, p 184.
11 Van Wyk, *Vyf Dae*, p 95.
12 Ibid, p 129.
13 Ibid, p 132.
14 Ibid, p 133.
15 Paton, *Hofmeyr*, p 324.
16 Van der Poel (ed), *Selections from the Smuts Papers*, Vol VI, p 189.
17 Hancock, *Smuts: The Fields of Force 1919–1950*, p 333.
18 Van Wyk, *Vyf Dae*, p 120.
19 Ibid, p 137.
20 Wilson, *Gone Down the Years*, p 212.
21 Simpson, in De Villiers (ed), p 38.
22 Pirow, *James Barry Munnik Hertzog*, p 250.
23 'Round Table', *Commonwealth Journal of International Affairs*, Vol 30, 1939, p 202.
24 Nasson, *South Africa At War, 1939–1945*, p 15.
25 Van den Heever, *General JBM Hertzog*, p 283.
26 Hancock, *Smuts: The Fields of Force 1919–1950*, p 331.
27 Ibid, p 325.
28 Ibid, p 331.
29 Van der Poel (ed), *Selections from the Smuts Papers*, Vol VI, p 101.

PART TWO: A DIVIDED NATION

Chapter 7 Two Streams
1   Hancock, *Smuts: The Fields of Force 1919–1950*, p 329.
2   Van der Waag, *A Military History of Modern South Africa*, p 185.

NOTES

3   Krüger, *The Age of the Generals*, p 197.
4   Bruton, 'The vision that gave SA power'.
5   P Kapp, in *They Shaped Our Century*, p 333.
6   Van der Waag, *A Military History of Modern South Africa*, p 175.
7   Krüger, *The Age of the Generals*, p 196.
8   Crwys-Williams, *A Country at War, 1939–1945*, p 51.
9   Crafford, *Jan Smuts*, p 306.
10 Nasson, *South Africa at War, 1939–1945*, p 52.
11 Davenport and Saunders, *South Africa: A Modern History*, p 346.
12 Krüger, *The Age of the Generals*, p 197.
13 Furlong, *Between Crown and Swastika*, p 134.
14 De Villiers, 'African nationalism in South Africa, 1910–1964', in Wilson and Thompson (eds), *The Oxford History of South Africa, Vol II*, p 383.
15 Davenport and Saunders, *South Africa: A Modern History*, p 347.
16 Krüger, *The Age of the Generals*, p 195.
17 Pirow, *James Barry Munnik Hertzog*, p 252.
18 Davenport and Saunders, *South Africa: A Modern History*, p 351.
19 Meiring, *Tien Politieke Leiers*, p 75.
20 Ibid.
21 Ibid, p 80.
22 Long, *In Smuts's Camp*, pp 66–67.
23 Nasson, *South Africa at War, 1939–1945*, pp 38–39.
24 McCormack, 'Man with a Mission', pp 543–557.
25 Meiring, *Tien Politieke Leiers*, p 86.
26 Pirow, *James Barry Munnik Hertzog*, pp 230–231.
27 McCormack, 'Man with a Mission', pp 543–557.
28 Meiring, *Tien Politieke Leiers*, p 83.
29 Van der Waag, *A Military History of Modern South Africa*, p 170.
30 Koorts, *DF Malan and the Rise of Afrikaner Nationalism*, p 357.
31 Pirow, *James Barry Munnik Hertzog*, p 257.
32 Ibid, p 260.
33 Ibid, p 259.
34 Krüger, *The Age of the Generals*, p 199.

Chapter 8 'By Their Fruits …'

1   Furlong, *Between Crown and Swastika*, p 139.
2   Davenport and Saunders, *South Africa: A Modern History*, p 349.
3   Blake, *Wit Terroriste*, p 29.
4   Ibid, p 35.
5   Ibid, p 78.
6   Shear, 'Colonel Coetzee's War'.
7   Malherbe, *Never a Dull Moment*, p 245.
8   Ibid.
9   Blake, *Wit Terroriste*, p 73.
10 Ibid.
11 Ibid, p 111.
12 Ibid, p 115.
13 Marx, *Oxwagon Sentinel*, p 241.
14 Furlong, *Between Crown and Swastika*, p 41.
15 Marx, *Oxwagon Sentinel*, p 243.
16 Munger (ed), *The Afrikaners*, p 62.
17 Furlong, *Between Crown and Swastika*, p 37.
18 Ibid, p 39.
19 De Villiers, 'African nationalism in South Africa, 1910–1964', in Wilson and Thompson (eds), *The Oxford History of South Africa, Vol II*, p 387.
20 Visser, *OB: Traitors or Patriots?*, p 15.
21 Crowder (ed), *The Cambridge History of Africa, Vol 8*, p 287.
22 Krüger, *The Making of A Nation*, p 212.
23 Ibid, p 213.
24 Furlong, *Between Crown and Swastika*, p 145.
25 Ibid, p 146; Strydom, *For Volk and Fuhrer*, p 2; and Wikipedia.
26 Blake, *Wit Terroriste*, p 181.
27 Strydom, *For Volk and Fuhrer*, p 2.
28 Wikipedia.
29 Blake, *Wit Terroriste*, p 185.
30 Strydom, *For Volk and Fuhrer*, p 147.
31 Blake, *Wit Terroriste*, p 188.
32 Furlong, *Between Crown and Swastika*, p 147.
33 Shear, 'Colonel Coetzee's War'.
34 Blake, *Wit Terroriste*, pp 60–61.
35 Hancock, *Smuts: The Fields of Force 1919–1950*, p 370.
36 Marx, *Oxwagon Sentinel*, p 519.

Chapter 9 Fights and Strikes

1   Katz, *South Africans versus Rommel*, p 21.
2   Nasson, *South Africa at War, 1939–1945*, pp 70–71.
3   Katz, *South Africans versus Rommel*, p 35.
4   Ibid
5   Giliomee, *Historian: An Autobiography*, p 240.
6   Blake, *Wit Terroriste*, p 47.

7   Nattrass, 'Economic growth in the 1940s', in Dubow and Jeeves (eds), *South Africa's 1940s*, p 33.
8   Ibid, p 34.
9   Ibid; and Van der Waag, *A Military History of Modern South Africa*, p 195.
10 Van der Waag, *A Military History of Modern South Africa*, p 195.
11 'Council of Non-European Trade Unions', South African History Online.
12 Lodge, *Black Politics in South Africa since 1945*, pp 18–19.
13 Van der Waag, *A Military History of Modern South Africa*, p 190.
14 Crwys-Williams, *A Country at War, 1939–1945*, p 129.
15 Ibid.
16 Blackwell, *Blackwell Remembers*, p 92.
17 Paton, *Hofmeyr*, pp 200–201.
18 Murray and Stadler, in Cameron and Spies (eds), *An Illustrated History of South Africa*, p 25.
19 Paton, *Hofmeyr*, p 174.
20 Ibid, p 221.
21 Ibid, p 228.
22 Ibid, pp 228–229.
23 Blackwell, *Blackwell Remembers*, pp 55–56.
24 Murray & Stadler, in Cameron and Spies (eds), *An Illustrated History of South Africa*, p 256.
25 Ibid.
26 Paton, *Hofmeyr*, p 333.
27 Nattrass, 'Economic growth in the 1940s', in Dubow and Jeeves (eds), *South Africa's 1940s*, p 21.

Chapter 10 The ANC Awakens
1   Walshe, *The Rise of African Nationalism in South Africa*, p 262.
2   Ibid.
3   Barber, *South Africa in the Twentieth Century*, p 125.
4   Gerhart, *Black Power in South Africa*, p 25.
5   Ibid, p 26.
6   Ibid, p 27.
7   Lodge, *Black Politics in South Africa since 1945*, p 11.
8   Gerhart, *Black Power in South Africa*, p 34.
9   Walshe, *The Rise of African Nationalism in South Africa*, p 263.
10 Munger, *Afrikaner and African Nationalism*, p 86.
11 Crowder (ed), *The Cambridge History of South Africa, Vol 8*, p 278.
12 Lodge, *Black Politics in South Africa since 1945*, p 11.
13 Karis and Gerhart, *From Protest to Challenge, Vol 4*, pp 39–40.
14 Giliomee and Mbenga (eds), *New History of South Africa*, p 297.
15 Barber, *South Africa in the Twentieth Century*, pp 126–127.
16 Ibid.
17 'Dr Alfred Xuma', South African History Online.
18 Holland, *100 Years of Struggle*, p 37.
19 'Dr Alfred Xuma', South African History Online.
20 Giliomee and Mbenga (eds), *New History of South Africa*, p 297.
21 'Dr Alfred Xuma', South African History Online.
22 Giliomee and Mbenga (eds), *New History of South Africa*, p 297.
23 Walshe, *The Rise of African Nationalism in South Africa*, p 269.
24 Roth, 'Elections under the Representation of Natives Act', in Lodge (ed), *Resistance and Ideology in Settler Societies*, p 144.
25 Davenport and Saunders, *South Africa: A Modern History*, p 354.
26 Walshe, *The Rise of African Nationalism in South Africa*, p 317.
27 Ibid, p 270.
28 Giliomee and Mbenga (eds), *New History of South Africa*, p 297.
29 Ibid.
30 Walshe, *The Rise of African Nationalism in South Africa*, p 269.
31 Barber, *South Africa in the Twentieth Century*, p 126.
32 Walshe, *The Rise of African Nationalism in South Africa*, p 320.
33 Ibid.
34 Hancock, *Smuts: The Fields of Force 1919–1950*, p 476.
35 Ibid.
36 Ibid.
37 Morris, *Farewell the Trumpets: An Imperial Retreat*, p 397.

Chapter 11 Seismic Shifts
1   Ross, Mager and Nasson (eds), *The Cambridge History of South Africa, Vol 2*, p 314.

NOTES

2 Dubow and Jeeves (eds), *South Africa's 1940s*, pp 2–3.
3 Krüger, *The Making of A Nation*, p 208.
4 Liebenberg in Muller (ed), *Five Hundred Years*, p 423.
5 Giliomee and Mbenga (eds), *New History of South Africa*, p 295.
6 Crwys-Williams, *A Country at War, 1939–1945*, p 295.
7 Wessels, 'South Africa and the War against Japan 1941–1945'.
8 Kleynhans, '"Good Hunting": German Submarine Offensives and South African Countermeasures off the South African Coast during the Second World War, 1942–1945', p 171.
9 Van der Waag, *A Military History of Modern South Africa*, p 202.
10 Ibid, p 201.
11 Wessels, 'South Africa and the War against Japan 1941–1945'.
12 Kleynhans, '"Good Hunting"', p 184.
13 www.zonderwater.com/en
14 Ibid.
15 Malherbe, *Never a Dull Moment*, p 215.
16 Ibid.
17 Cardo, '"Fighting A Worse Imperialism": White South African Loyalism and the Army Education Services (AES) during the Second World War', p 141.
18 Crowder (ed), *The Cambridge History of South Africa, Vol 8*, p 285.
19 Paton, *Hofmeyr*, p 345.
20 Ibid.
21 Ibid.
22 Walshe, *The Rise of African Nationalism in South Africa*, p 307.
23 Ibid.
24 Giliomee and Mbenga (eds), *New History of South Africa*, p 298.
25 Katz, *South Africans versus Rommel*, p 212.
26 Roberts, *Churchill*, p 738.
27 Ibid, p 740.
28 Ibid, p 744.
29 Crwys-Williams, *A Country at War, 1939–1945*, p 206.
30 Hancock, *Smuts: The Fields of Force 1919–1950*, p 375.
31 Krüger, *The Age of the Generals*, p 212.
32 Ibid, p 203.
33 Hancock, *Smuts: The Fields of Force 1919–1950*, p 375.
34 Churchill, *The Second World War, Vol V*, pp 112–115.
35 Krüger, *The Age of the Generals*, p 206.
36 Ibid.

Chapter 12 Opposed to Racism

1 Lodge, *Black Politics in South Africa since 1945*, p 7.
2 Ellis and Sechaba, *Comrades Against Apartheid*, p 18.
3 Andrew and Mitrokhin, *The Mitrokhin Archive II*, p 504.
4 Karis and Gerhart, *From Protest to Challenge, Vol 5*, p 426.
5 Ellis and Sechaba, *Comrades Against Apartheid*, pp 20–21.
6 Ibid.
7 Lodge, *Black Politics in South Africa since 1945*, p 9.
8 Bonner, 'South African Society and Culture, 1910–1948', in Ross, Mager and Nasson (eds), *The Cambridge History of South Africa, Vol 2*, p 315.
9 Giliomee and Mbenga (eds), *New History of South Africa*, p 298.
10 Drew (ed), *South Africa's Radical Tradition: A Documentary History, Vol 2*, p 320.
11 Filatova, 'Communism in South Africa'.
12 Reader's Digest, *Illustrated History of South Africa*, p 361.
13 'A History of the Springbok Legion', South African History Online.
14 Simons, *Class and Colour in South Africa 1850–1950*, p 540.
15 Reader's Digest, *Illustrated History of South Africa*, p 362.
16 Long, *In Smuts's Camp*, p 120.
17 Reader's Digest, *Illustrated History of South Africa*, p 362.
18 Walshe, *The Rise of African Nationalism in South Africa*, p 270.
19 Koorts, *DF Malan and the Rise of Afrikaner Nationalism*, pp 361–362.
20 Walshe, *The Rise of African Nationalism in South Africa*, p 270.
21 Hancock, *Smuts: The Fields of Force 1919–1950*, p 477.
22 Wollheim, 'Margaret Ballinger: A Tribute', pp 4–5.
23 Walshe, *The Rise of African Nationalism in South Africa*, p 270.
24 Ibid.
25 Hancock, *Smuts: The Fields of Force 1919–1950*, p 480.
26 Lodge, *Black Politics in South Africa since 1945*, p 15.

27 Ibid, p 16
28 'James "Sofasonke" Mpanza', South African History Online.
29 Lodge, *Black Politics in South Africa since 1945*, p 16.
30 Ibid.

Chapter 13 Year of Tumult
1 Drew (ed), *South Africa's Radical Tradition*, p 16.
2 Karis, *From Protest to Challenge, Vol 2*, p 112.
3 Walshe, *The Rise of African Nationalism in South Africa*, p 280.
4 Karis, *From Protest to Challenge, Vol 2*, p 112.
5 Gerhart, *Black Power in South Africa*, p 50.
6 Ibid, p 51.
7 Holland, *100 Years of Struggle*, p 41.
8 Lodge, *Black Politics in South Africa since 1945*, p 21.
9 Gerhart, *Black Power in South Africa*, p 53.
10 Karis and Gerhart, *From Protest to Challenge, Vol 4*, pp 55–56.
11 Holland, *100 Years of Struggle*, p 42.
12 Gerhart, *Black Power in South Africa*, p 58.
13 Ibid, p 59.
14 Ibid, p 55.
15 Karis and Gerhart, *From Protest to Challenge, Vol 4*, p 56.
16 Reader's Digest, *Illustrated History of South Africa*, p 363.
17 Gerhart, *Black Power in South Africa*, p 54
18 Ibid, p 55.
19 Meredith, *Nelson Mandela*, p 42.
20 Ibid.
21 Holland, *100 Years of Struggle*, pp 44–45.
22 Ibid.
23 Sampson, *Mandela*, p 40.
24 Lodge, *Black Politics in South Africa since 1945*, p 25.
25 Walshe, *The Rise of African Nationalism in South Africa*, p 351.
26 Karis and Gerhart, *From Protest to Challenge, Vol 4*, p 72.
27 Ross, Mager and Nasson (eds), *The Cambridge History of South Africa, Vol 2*, p 53.
28 Giliomee and Mbenga (eds), *New History of South Africa*, p 269.
29 'Dr Alfred Xuma', South African History Online.
30 Davenport and Saunders, *South Africa: A Modern History*, p 363.
31 Sampson, *Mandela*, p 42.
32 Lodge, *Black Politics in South Africa since 1945*, p 13.
33 Rich, *State Power and Black Politics in South Africa 1912–51*, p 111.
34 Ibid.
35 Walshe, *The Rise of African Nationalism in South Africa*, p 272.
36 Rich, *State Power and Black Politics in South Africa 1912–51*, p 113.
37 Walshe, *The Rise of African Nationalism in South Africa*, p 273.

Chapter 14 Indian Winter
1 Hancock, *Smuts: The Fields of Force 1919–1950*, p 473.
2 Paton, *Hofmeyr*, p 222.
3 Hancock, *Smuts: The Fields of Force 1919–1950*, p 451.
4 Bhana, *Gandhi's Legacy*, p 37.
5 Giliomee and Mbenga (eds), *New History of South Africa*, p 269.
6 Hancock, *Smuts: The Fields of Force 1919–1950*, p 459.
7 Ibid.
8 Ibid, p 457.
9 Pachai, *The International Aspects of the South African Indian Question 1860–1971*, p 153.
10 Bhana, *Gandhi's Legacy*, p 47.
11 Pachai, *The International Aspects of the South African Indian Question*, p 152.
12 Ibid, p 160.
13 Ibid, p 161.
14 Ibid.
15 Paton, *Hofmeyr*, pp 367–368.
16 Hancock, *Smuts: The Fields of Force 1919–1950*, p 459.
17 Pachai, *The International Aspects of the South African Indian Question*, p 163.
18 Davenport and Saunders, *South Africa: A Modern History*, p 367.
19 Hancock, *Smuts: The Fields of Force 1919–1950*, p 460.
20 Ibid.
21 Lawrence, *Harry Lawrence*, p 150.
22 Bhana, *Gandhi's Legacy*, p 36.
23 Pachai, *The International Aspects of the South African Indian Question*, pp 154–155.
24 Ibid.
25 Ibid, p 170.
26 Ibid, p 174.

27 Hancock, *Smuts: The Fields of Force 1919–1950*, p 460.
28 Pachai, *The International Aspects of the South African Indian Question*, p 175.
29 Ibid.

Chapter 15 In the Middle
1 Davenport and Saunders, *South Africa: A Modern History*, p 343.
2 Thompson, *A History of South Africa*, p 171.
3 Reader's Digest, *Illustrated History of South Africa*, p 396.
4 Thompson, *A History of South Africa*, p 171.
5 Reader's Digest, *Illustrated History of South Africa*, p 396.
6 Goldin, *Making Race*, p 56.
7 Ibid.
8 Van der Ross, *The Rise and Decline of Apartheid*, p 155.
9 Gleeson, *The Unknown Force*, p 106.
10 Field, *Alex La Guma*, p 41.
11 Ibid.
12 Lewis, *Between the Wire and the Wall*, p 207.
13 Lawrence, *Harry Lawrence*, p 152.
14 Ibid.
15 Giliomee and Mbenga (eds), *New History of South Africa*, p 266.
16 Lewis, *Between the Wire and the Wall*, p 198.
17 Ibid, pp 198–199.
18 Ibid, p 200.
19 Adhikari, in *They Shaped Our Century*, p 439.
20 Lewis, *Between the Wire and the Wall*, p 198.
21 Adhikari, in *They Shaped Our Century*, p 441.
22 Goldin, *Making Race*, p 54.
23 Lewis, *Between the Wire and the Wall*, p 212.
24 Ibid.
25 Ibid, pp 214–215.
26 Goldin, *Making Race*, p 57.
27 Lewis, *Between the Wire and the Wall*, p 214.
28 Ibid, p 215.
29 Ibid.
30 Ibid, p 216.
31 Ibid.
32 Ibid.
33 Ibid, p 218.
34 Goldin, *Making Race*, p 57.
35 Ibid, p 58.
36 Simons and Simons, *Class and Colour in South Africa 1850–1950*, p 546.

Chapter 16 Smuts Wins
1 Krüger, *The Making of A Nation*, p 214.
2 Van der Waag, *A Military History of Modern South Africa*, p 105.
3 Cameron, *Jan Smuts*, p 152.
4 Hancock, *Smuts: The Fields of Force 1919–1950*, p 381.
5 Barber, *South Africa in the Twentieth Century*, p 121.
6 Paton, *Hofmeyr*, p 372.
7 Ibid, p 370.
8 Hancock, *Smuts: The Fields of Force 1919–1950*, p 384.
9 Giliomee, *The Afrikaners*, p 445.
10 Barber, *South Africa in the Twentieth Century*, p 121.
11 Hancock, *Smuts: The Fields of Force 1919–1950*, p 412.
12 Ibid, p 409.
13 Paton, *Hofmeyr*, p 375.
14 Ibid, p 377.
15 Rich, *State Power and Black Politics in South Africa*, p 115.
16 Walshe, *The Rise of African Nationalism in South Africa*, p 312.
17 Rich, *State Power and Black Politics in South Africa*, p 115.
18 Bhana, *Gandhi's Legacy*, p 48.
19 Ibid.
20 Ibid, p 51.
21 Pachai, *The International Aspects of the South African Indian Question*, p 176.
22 Bhana, *Gandhi's Legacy*, p 52.
23 Hancock, *Smuts: The Fields of Force 1919–1950*, p 465.
24 Ibid.
25 Ibid, p 466.

Chapter 17 Congress Youth League
1 Grobler, *A Decisive Clash?*, p 88.
2 Holland, *100 Years of Struggle*, p 46.
3 Ibid.
4 Lodge, *Black Politics in South Africa since 1945*, p 20.
5 Walshe, *The Rise of African Nationalism in South Africa*, p 353.
6 Ibid, pp 353–354.
7 Ibid, p 280.
8 Grobler, *A Decisive Clash?*, pp 89–90.

9   Walshe, *The Rise of African Nationalism in South Africa*, p 353.
10 Ibid, p 355.
11 Lodge, *Black Politics in South Africa since 1945*, p 37.
12 Walshe, *The Rise of African Nationalism in South Africa*, p 356.
13 Munger, *Afrikaner and African Nationalism*, p xvii.
14 Karis and Gerhart, *From Protest to Challenge*, Vol 5, p 115.
15 Ibid.
16 Munger, *Afrikaner and African Nationalism*, p xvii.
17 Ibid.
18 Hancock, *Smuts: The Fields of Force 1919–1950*, p 467.
19 Smuts, *Jan Christian Smuts*, p 453.
20 Krüger, *The Making of A Nation*, p 225.
21 Paton, *Hofmeyr*, p 384.
22 Ibid.
23 Ibid.
24 Ibid, p 351.
25 Ibid, p 263.
26 Ibid, p 264.
27 Ibid, p 263.
28 Macdonald, *Jan Hofmeyr*, p 129.
29 Paton, *Hofmeyr*, p 353.
30 Nattrass, in Dubow and Jeeves (eds), *South Africa's 1940s*, p 38.
31 Ibid.
32 Ibid, p 39.
33 Ibid.
34 Paton, *Hofmeyr*, p 382.
35 Ibid.
36 Ibid, p 380.
37 Ibid, p 381.
38 Ibid, pp 381–382.
39 Lodge, *Black Politics in South Africa since 1945*, p 26.
40 Ibid.
41 Rich, *State Power and Black Politics in South Africa*, p 115.
42 Walshe, *The Rise of African Nationalism in South Africa*, p 366.
43 Rich, *State Power and Black Politics in South Africa*, p 117.
44 Lawrence, *Harry Lawrence*, pp 159–160.

Chapter 18 Victory

1   Hancock, *Smuts: The Fields of Force 1919–1950*, p 443.
2   Ibid, p 445.
3   Van der Poel (ed), *Selections from the Smuts Papers, Vol VI*, p 534.
4   Paton, *Hofmeyr*, p 389.
5   Cameron, *Jan Smuts*, p 158.
6   Van der Poel (ed), *Selections from the Smuts Papers, Vol VI*, p 534.
7   Krüger, *The Making of A Nation*, pp 218–219.
8   Lawrence, *Harry Lawrence*, p 164.
9   Van der Waag, *A Military History of Modern South Africa*, p 218.
10 Ibid.
11 Lawrence, *Harry Lawrence*, p 157.
12 Ibid, p 162.
13 Ibid, p 165.
14 Koorts, *DF Malan and the Rise of Afrikaner Nationalism*, p 364.
15 Ibid, p 369.
16 Ibid, p 366.
17 Ibid, p 367.
18 Ibid.
19 Ibid, p 368.
20 Ibid.
21 Hancock, *Smuts: The Fields of Force 1919–1950*, p 467.
22 Smuts, *Jan Christian Smuts*, p 482.
23 Reader's Digest, *South Africa's Yesterdays*, p 318.
24 Ibid, p 308.
25 Paton, *Hofmeyr*, p 403.
26 Ibid.
27 Ibid, p 404.
28 Reader's Digest, *South Africa's Yesterdays*, p 319.
29 Paton, *Hofmeyr*, p 405.
30 Ibid.

PART THREE: POST WAR

Chapter 19 Taking Stock

1   Freund, *Twentieth-Century South Africa*, p 64.
2   Lumby, 'The Development of Secondary Industry: The Second World War and After', in Coleman (ed), *Economic History of South Africa*, p 220.
3   Nattrass, 'Economic Growth in the 1940s', in Dubow and Jeeves (eds), *South Africa's 1940s*, p 21.
4   Seekings, 'Welfare Reform', in Dubow and Jeeves (eds), *South Africa's 1940s*, p 45.
5   Ibid.
6   Ibid, p 48.

NOTES

7. Paton, *Hofmeyr*, p 406.
8. Ibid, p 407.
9. Muller (ed), *Five Hundred Years*, p 424.
10. Koorts, *DF Malan and the Rise of Afrikaner Nationalism*, p 369.
11. Ibid, p 370.
12. Ibid.
13. Barber, *South Africa in the Twentieth Century*, p 131.
14. Ibid, p 132.
15. Wikipedia.
16. Rich, *State Power and Black Politics in South Africa*, p 117.
17. Grobler, *A Decisive Clash?*, p 82.
18. Bloomberg, *Christian Nationalism and the Rise of the Afrikaner Broederbond*, p 190.
19. Ibid.
20. Ibid, p 193.
21. Ibid.
22. Pachai, *The International Aspects of the South African Indian Question*, p 186.
23. Ibid.
24. Paton, *Hofmeyr*, p 420.
25. Ibid.
26. Hancock, *Smuts: The Fields of Force 1919–1950*, p 466.
27. Pachai, *The International Aspects of the South African Indian Question*, p 190.
28. Krüger, *The Making of a Nation*, p 228.
29. Ibid, p 229.
30. Pachai, *The International Aspects of the South African Indian Question*, p 192.
31. Ibid.
32. Kathrada, *Memoirs*, p 52.
33. Furlong, *Between Crown and Swastika*, p 176.
34. Koorts, *DF Malan and the Rise of Afrikaner Nationalism*, p 351.
35. Lawrence, *Harry Lawrence*, p 181.
36. Ibid, p 182.
37. Ibid, p 181.
38. Koorts, *DF Malan and the Rise of Afrikaner Nationalism*, p 351.

Chapter 20 Miners' Strike

1. Crush, Jeeves and Yudelman, *South Africa's Labour Empire*, p 58.
2. Rich, *State Power and Black Politics in South Africa*, p 144.
3. Davenport and Saunders, *South Africa: A Modern History*, p 358.
4. James, 'Grounds for a Strike', p 15.
5. Crush Jeeves and Yudelman, *South Africa's Labour Empire*, p 58.
6. Wilson, *Labour in the South African Gold Mines*, p 79.
7. Reader's Digest, *Illustrated History of South Africa*, p 365.
8. Lodge, *Black Politics in South Africa since 1945*, p 20.
9. Reader's Digest, *Illustrated History of South Africa*, p 365.
10. James, 'Grounds for a Strike', p 15.
11. Lodge, *Black Politics in South Africa since 1945*, p 20.
12. Rich, *State Power and Black Politics in South Africa*, p 108.
13. James, 'Grounds for a Strike', p 18.
14. Paton, *Hofmeyr*, p 433.
15. Ibid.
16. Ibid.
17. Ibid, p 434.
18. Rich, *State Power and Black Politics in South Africa*, p 144.
19. Ibid.
20. Paton, *Hofmeyr*, p 434.
21. Ibid, p 435.
22. Davenport and Saunders, *South Africa: A Modern History*, p 359.
23. Ibid.
24. Ibid.
25. Paton, *Hofmeyr*, p 440.
26. Ibid.
27. Ibid.
28. Ibid.
29. Sampson, *Mandela*, p 44.
30. Roth, 'Elections under the Representation of Natives Act', in Lodge (ed), *Resistance and Ideology in Settler Societies*, p 155.
31. Ibid, p 156.
32. Ibid.
33. Ibid, p 157.
34. Paton, *Hofmeyr*, p 439.
35. Walshe, *The Rise of African Nationalism in South Africa*, p 285.
36. Bonner, 'South African Society and Culture, 1910–1948', in Ross, Mager and Nasson (eds), *The Cambridge History of South Africa, Vol 2*, p 315.
37. Meredith, *Nelson Mandela*, p 61.

Chapter 21 Prejudices Rearranged

1. Sampson, *Mandela*, p 45.
2. Mandela, *Long Walk to Freedom*, p 98.
3. Ibid, p 97.
4. Meredith, *Nelson Mandela*, p 62.

5. Meredith, *Nelson Mandela*, p 63.
6. Ibid, p 64.
7. Kathrada, *Memoirs*, p 30.
8. Ibid.
9. Ibid.
10. Ibid, p 31.
11. 'Dr Yusuf Mohamed Dadoo', South African History Online.
12. Ibid.
13. Ibid.
14. Ibid.
15. Bonner, 'South African Society and Culture, 1910–1948', in Ross, Mager and Nasson (eds), *The Cambridge History of South Africa*, Vol 2, p 309.
16. Ibid.
17. Reader's Digest, *Illustrated History of South Africa*, p 371.
18. Giliomee, *The Afrikaners*, pp 476–477.
19. Ibid.

Chapter 22 Pandit Attacks

1. Pandit, *The Scope of Happiness*, p 206.
2. Lloyd, '"A Most Auspicious Beginning"', p 131.
3. Friedman, *Smuts*, p 175.
4. Ibid.
5. Ibid, p 179.
6. Thakur, *Jan Smuts and the Indian Question*, p 58.
7. Hancock, *Smuts: The Fields of Force 1919–1950*, p 468.
8. Thakur, *Jan Smuts and the Indian Question*, p 66.
9. Ibid, p 68.
10. Hancock, *Smuts: The Fields of Force 1919–1950*, p 469.
11. Smuts, *Jan Christian Smuts*, p 497.
12. Hancock, *Smuts: The Fields of Force 1919–1950*, p 469.
13. Lloyd, '"A Most Auspicious Beginning"', p 131.
14. Pachai, *The International Aspects of the South African Indian Question*, p 202.
15. Hancock, *Smuts: The Fields of Force 1919–1950*, p 470.
16. Ibid.
17. Lloyd, '"A Most Auspicious Beginning"', p 141.
18. Lawrence, *Harry Lawrence*, pp 208–209.
19. Lloyd, '"A Most Auspicious Beginning"', p 142.
20. Ibid.
21. Friedman, *Smuts*, p 178.
22. Pachai, *The International Aspects of the South African Indian Question*, p 204.
23. Thakur, *Jan Smuts and the Indian Question*, pp 73–74.
24. Ibid, p 74.
25. Ibid, p 75.
26. Ibid, p 76.
27. Ibid, p 77.
28. Lloyd, '"A Most Auspicious Beginning"', p 143.
29. Ibid, p 148.
30. Ibid, p 149.
31. Pachai, *The International Aspects of the South African Indian Question*, p 207.
32. Soske, *Internal Frontiers*, p 239.
33. Lloyd, '"A Most Auspicious Beginning"', p 132.
34. Pachai, *The International Aspects of the South African Indian Question*, p 206.
35. Hancock, *Smuts: The Fields of Force 1919–1950*, p 467.
36. Krüger, *The Age of the Generals*, p 231.
37. Ibid.
38. Hancock, *Smuts: The Fields of Force 1919–1950*, p 468.
39. Ibid, p 450.
40. Gish, *Alfred B Xuma*, p 144.
41. Rich, *State Power and Black Politics in South Africa*, p 118.
42. Gish, *Alfred B Xuma*, p 144.
43. Ibid.
44. Ibid, p 149.
45. Crowder, 'Tshekedi Khama, Smuts, and South West Africa', p 40.
46. Ibid, p 28.
47. Benson, *The Struggle for a Birthright*, pp 139–140.

Chapter 23 Out of Step

1. Van der Poel (ed), *Selections from the Smuts Papers*, Vol VII, p 113.
2. Thakur, *Jan Smuts and the Indian Question*, p 87.
3. Pachai, *The International Aspects of the South African Indian Question*, p 207.
4. Thakur, *Jan Smuts and the Indian Question*, pp 87–88.
5. Ibid, p 88.
6. Paton, *Hofmeyr*, p 442.
7. Hancock, *Smuts: The Fields of Force 1919–1950*, p 455.
8. Ibid.

NOTES

9. Pachai, *The International Aspects of the South African Indian Question*, p 207.
10. Paton, *Hofmeyr*, pp 443–444.
11. Smuts, *Jan Christian Smuts*, p 500.
12. Paton, *Hofmeyr*, p 444.
13. Koorts, *DF Malan and the Rise of Afrikaner Nationalism*, pp 372–373.
14. Henkes, 'Shifting Identifications in Dutch-South African Migration Policies (1910–1961)'.
15. Smuts, *Jan Christian Smuts*, p 500.
16. Lawrence, *Harry Lawrence*, p 185.
17. Henkes, 'Shifting Identifications in Dutch-South African Migration Policies'.
18. Davenport and Saunders, *South Africa: A Modern History*, p 370.
19. Krüger, *The Making of a Nation*, p 233.
20. Hancock, *Smuts: The Fields of Force 1919–1950*, p 497.
21. Paton, *Hofmeyr*, p 443.
22. Krüger, *The Making of a Nation*, p 233.
23. Sapire, 'African Loyalism and Its Discontents'.
24. Ibid.
25. Ibid.
26. Pimlott, *The Queen*, p 117.
27. Sapire, 'African Loyalism and Its Discontents'.
28. *Cape Times*, 18 February 1947.
29. Smuts, *Jan Christian Smuts*, p 501.
30. Paton, *Hofmeyr*, p 450.
31. Viney, *The Last Hurrah*, p 304.
32. Ibid, p 167.
33. Ibid, p 139.
34. Sampson, *Mandela*, p 51.
35. Sapire, 'African Loyalism and Its Discontents'.
36. Ibid.
37. Viney, *The Last Hurrah*, p 297.
38. Ibid, p 301.
39. Ibid, p 304.
40. Ibid, p 270.
41. Wilks, *The Biography of Douglas Mitchell*, p 5.

Chapter 24 The Doctors' Pact
1. Gish, *Alfred B Xuma*, p 125.
2. Ibid, p 136.
3. Soske, *Internal Frontiers*, p 88.
4. Rich, *State Power and Black Politics in South Africa*, p 119.
5. Soske, *Internal Frontiers*, p 78.
6. Ibid.
7. Ibid, p 79.
8. Ibid.
9. Edgar and ka Msumza, *Freedom In Our Lifetime*, p 44.
10. Soske, *Internal Frontiers*, p 93.
11. Ibid, p 91.
12. Hancock, *Smuts: The Fields of Force 1919–1950*, p 489.
13. Friedman, *Smuts*, p 201.
14. Paton, *Hofmeyr*, p 454.
15. Ibid.
16. Ibid.
17. Friedman, *Smuts*, p 202.
18. Ibid.
19. Ibid, p 203.
20. Hancock, *Smuts: The Fields of Force 1919–1950*, p 489.
21. Benson, *The African Patriots*, p 103.
22. Benson, *The Struggle for a Birthright*, p 114.
23. Holland, *100 Years of Struggle*, p 50.
24. Benson, *The Struggle for a Birthright*, p 114.
25. Gerhart, *Black Power in South Africa*, p 125.
26. Mandela, *Long Walk to Freedom*, p 91.
27. Ibid, p 101.
28. Gerhart, *Black Power in South Africa*, p 126.
29. Meredith, *Nelson Mandela*, pp 65–66.
30. Ibid.
31. Ngubane, *An African Explains Apartheid*, p 244.
32. Mandela, *Long Walk to Freedom*, p 52.
33. Meredith, *Nelson Mandela*, p 65.
34. Soske, *Internal Frontiers*, p 107.
35. Ibid.
36. Ibid, p 109.
37. Sampson, *Mandela*, pp 47–48.
38. Ibid.

Chapter 25 Movers and Shakers
1. Raman, 'Yusuf Dadoo: A Son of Africa', in Dubow and Jeeves (eds), *South Africa's 1940s*, p 238.
2. Ibid.
3. Meredith, *Nelson Mandela*, p 64.
4. Ibid, p 65.
5. Mandela, *Long Walk to Freedom*, p 101.
6. Ibid, p 103.
7. Ibid.
8. Ibid.
9. Ibid.
10. Sampson, *Mandela*, p 49.
11. Muller (ed), *Five Hundred Years*, p 461.
12. Troup, *South Africa*, p 284.
13. Muller (ed), *Five Hundred Years*, p 461.

14 Ibid, p 462.
15 Pachai, *The International Aspects of the South African Indian Question*, p 211.
16 Edgar and ka Msumza, *Africa's Cause Must Triumph*, p 160.
17 Rich, *State Power and Black Politics in South Africa*, pp 150–151.
18 Ibid.
19 Paton, *Hofmeyr*, p 438.
20 Ibid.
21 Edgar and ka Msumza, *Africa's Cause Must Triumph*, p 161.
22 Ibid.
23 Holland, *100 Years of Struggle*, p 97.
24 Ibid, p 98.
25 Ibid, p 44.
26 Ibid.
27 Sampson, *Mandela*, p 50.
28 Giliomee and Mbenga (eds), *New History of South Africa*, p 299.
29 Ibid.
30 Pachai, *The International Aspects of the South African Indian Question*, p 214.
31 Lawrence, *Harry Lawrence*, p 210.
32 Pachai, *The International Aspects of the South African Indian Question*, p 212.
33 Lawrence, *Harry Lawrence*, p 205.

Chapter 26 Smuts Defeated
1 Davenport and Saunders, *South Africa: A Modern History*, p 369.
2 Hancock, *Smuts: The Fields of Force 1919–1950*, p 488.
3 Giliomee and Mbenga (eds), *New History of South Africa*, p 309.
4 Davenport and Saunders, *South Africa: A Modern History*, p 361.
5 Giliomee and Mbenga (eds), *New History of South Africa*, p 309.
6 Davenport and Saunders, *South Africa: A Modern History*, p 361.
7 Giliomee and Mbenga (eds), *New History of South Africa*, p 310.
8 Walshe, *The Rise of African Nationalism in South Africa*, p 286.
9 Ibid.
10 Giliomee and Mbenga (eds), *New History of South Africa*, p 309.
11 Ibid.
12 Ibid.
13 Hancock, *Smuts: The Fields of Force 1919–1950*, p 491.
14 Ibid, p 496.

15 Paton, *Hofmeyr*, p 480.
16 Krüger, *The Making of a Nation*, p 237.
17 Quoted in Dubow, 'Introduction: South Africa's 1940s', in Dubow and Jeeves (eds), *South Africa's 1940s*, p 12.
18 Hancock, *Smuts: The Fields of Force 1919–1950*, p 498.
19 Ibid.
20 Friedman, *Smuts*, p 205.
21 Hancock, *Smuts: The Fields of Force 1919–1950*, p 500.
22 Paton, *Hofmeyr*, p 478.
23 Hancock, *Smuts: The Fields of Force 1919–1950*, p 504.
24 Ibid, p 505.
25 Roth, in Lodge (ed), *Resistance and Ideology in Settler Societies*, p 158.
26 Ibid, pp 158–159.
27 Krüger, *The Making of a Nation*, p 236.
28 Smuts, *Jan Christian Smuts*, p 512.
29 Ibid.
30 Friedman, *Smuts*, p 212.
31 Ibid.

PART FOUR: AFTERMATH

Chapter 27 The Screws Tighten
1 Sparks, *The Mind of South Africa*, pp 183–184.
2 Giliomee, *The Afrikaners*, p 487.
3 Reader's Digest, *Illustrated History of South Africa*, p 374.
4 Davenport and Saunders, *South Africa: A Modern History*, p 178.
5 Beinart, *Twentieth-Century South Africa*, p142.
6 Davenport and Saunders, *South Africa: A Modern History*, pp 384–385.
7 Mandela, *Long Walk to Freedom*, p 108.
8 Holland, *100 Years of Struggle*, p 53.
9 Rich, *State Power and Black Politics in South Africa*, p 151.
10 Holland, *100 Years of Struggle*, p 53.
11 Karis and Gerhart (eds), *From Protest to Challenge*, Vol 4, p 144.
12 Holland, *100 Years of Struggle*, p 20.
13 Ibid, p 22.
14 Karis and Gerhart (eds), *From Protest to Challenge*, Vol 4, p 144.
15 Soske, *Internal Frontiers*, p 103.
16 Meli, *A History of the ANC*, p 99.
17 Soske, *Internal Frontiers*, p 104.
18 Ibid, p 105.

19 Reader's Digest, *Illustrated History of South Africa*, p 384.
20 Soske, *Internal Frontiers*, p 98.
21 Ibid.
22 Benson, *The African Patriots*, p 155.
23 Sampson, *Mandela*, p 68.
24 Meredith, *Nelson Mandela*, p 92.
25 Ibid, p 109.
26 Sampson, *Mandela*, p 74.
27 Koorts, *DF Malan and the Rise of Afrikaner Nationalism*, p 383.
28 Ibid, p 384.

Epilogue
1 De Kiewiet, *The Anatomy of South African Misery*, pp 8–9.
2 Ibid.
3 Ibid.
4 Ibid, p 18.
5 Ibid, p 16.
6 Gravett, 'Jan Christian Smuts (1870–1950) in Context', p 7.
7 Brookes, in Z Friedlander (ed), *Jan Smuts Remembered*, pp 20–21.
8 Benson, *The African Patriots*, p 170.
9 Hancock, *Smuts: The Fields of Force 1919–1950*, p 324.
10 Van der Waag, *A Military History of Modern South Africa*, p 217.
11 Nattrass, 'Economic growth in the 1940s', in Dubow and Jeeves (eds), *South Africa's 1940s*, p 21.
12 Ibid, p 20.
13 Keppel-Jones, *When Smuts Goes*, p xi.
14 Ibid, p xii.
15 De Kiewiet, *The Anatomy of South African Misery*, p 45.
16 Gerhart, *Black Power in South Africa*, p 38.
17 Friedman, *Smuts*, p 181.
18 Ibid, p 182.
19 Van der Poel (ed), *Selections from the Smuts Papers, Vol VII*, p 269.
20 Giliomee and Mbenga (eds), *New History of South Africa*, p 331.
21 Ibid, p 303.

Sources

Books and book chapters
Andrew, C and V Mitrokhin. *The Mitrokhin Archive II: The KGB in the World*. Allen Lane, 2005.
Barber, J. *South Africa in the Twentieth Century*. Blackwell, 1999.
Barlow, A. *Almost in Confidence*. Juta & Co, 1952.
Beinart, W. *Twentieth-Century South Africa*. Oxford University Press, 1994.
Benson, M. *The African Patriots*. Faber & Faber, 1963.
Benson, M. *The Struggle for a Birthright*. Penguin, 1966.
Bhana, S. *Gandhi's Legacy: The Natal Indian Congress, 1894–1994*. University of Natal Press, 1997.
Blackwell, L. *Farewell to Parliament*. Shuter & Shooter, 1946.
Blackwell, L. *Blackwell Remembers*. Howard Timmins, 1971.
Blake, A. *Wit Terroriste: Afrikaner-Saboteurs in Die Ossewabrandwagjare*. Tafelberg, 2018.
Bloomberg, C. *Christian Nationalism and the Rise of the Afrikaner Broederbond*. Macmillan, 1990.
Bonner, P. 'South African Society and Culture, 1910–1948'. In R Ross, A Mager and B Nasson (eds), *The Cambridge History of South Africa, Vol 2: 1885–1994*. Cambridge University Press, 2016.
Cameron, T. *Jan Smuts: An Illustrated Biography*. Human & Rousseau, 1994.
Cameron, T and SB Spies (eds). *An Illustrated History of South Africa*. Human & Rousseau, 1988.
Cartwright, AP. *South Africa's Hall of Fame*. Central News Agency, undated.
Churchill, WS. *The Second World War, Vol V: Closing the Ring*. Cassell, 1952.
Coleman, F (ed). *Economic History of South Africa*. HAUM, 1983.
Crafford, FS. *Jan Smuts: A Biography*. George Allen & Unwin, 1946.
Crowder, M (ed). *The Cambridge History of Africa, Vol 8: c 1940–c 1975*. Cambridge University Press, 1985.
Crush, J, A Jeeves and D Yudelman. *South Africa's Labour Empire: A History of Black Migrancy to the Gold Mines*. David Philip, 1991.
Crwys-Williams, J. *A Country at War, 1939–1945: The Mood of a Nation*. Ashanti, 1992.

SOURCES

Davenport R and C Saunders. *South Africa: A Modern History*. Fifth edition. Macmillan, 2000.
De Kiewiet, CW. *The Anatomy of South African Misery*. Oxford University Press, 1956.
De Villiers, R. 'African nationalism in South Africa, 1910–1964'. In M Wilson and L Thompson (eds), *The Oxford History of South Africa, Vol II: 1870–1966*. Clarendon Press, 1971.
De Villiers, RM (ed). *Better Than They Knew*. Purnell, 1972.
D'Oliveira, J. *Vorster – The Man*. Ernest Stanton, 1977.
Drew, A (ed). *South Africa's Radical Tradition: A Documentary History, Vol 2: 1943–1964*. UCT Press, 1997.
Dubow, S. 'Introduction: South Africa's 1940s'. In S Dubow and A Jeeves (eds), *South Africa's 1940s: Worlds of Possibilities*. Double Storey, 2005.
Dubow, S and A Jeeves (eds). *South Africa's 1940s: Worlds of Possibilities*. Double Storey, 2005.
Edgar, RR and L ka Msumza. *Freedom In Our Lifetime: The Collected Writings of Anton Muziwakhe Lembede*. Ohio University Press, 1996.
Ellis, S and T Sechaba. *Comrades Against Apartheid: The ANC and the South African Communist Party in Exile*. James Currey, 1992.
Field, R. *Alex La Guma: A Literary and Political Biography*. James Currey, 2010.
Fisher, JF. *The Afrikaners*. Cassell, 1969.
Friedlander, Z (ed). *Jan Smuts Remembered: A Centennial Tribute*. Howard Timmins, 1970.
Friedman, B. *Smuts: A Reappraisal*. Hugh Keartland, 1975.
Freund, W. *Twentieth-Century South Africa: A Developmental History*. Cambridge University Press, 2018.
Furlong, P. *Between Crown and Swastika: The Impact of the Radical Right on the Afrikaner Nationalist Movement in the Fascist Era*. Wits University Press, 1991.
Gerhart, G. *Black Power in South Africa: The Evolution of an Ideology*. University of California Press, 1979.
Giliomee, H. *The Afrikaners: Biography of a People*. Tafelberg, 2003.
Giliomee, H. *Historian: An Autobiography*. Tafelberg, 2016.
Giliomee, H and B Mbenga (eds). *New History of South Africa*. Tafelberg, 2007.
Gish, S. *Alfred B Xuma: African, American, South African*. New York University Press, 2000.
Gleeson, I. *The Unknown Force: Black, Indian and Coloured Soldiers Through Two World Wars*. Ashanti, 1994.
Goldin, I. *Making Race: The Politics and Economics of Coloured Identity in South Africa*. Maskew Miller Longman, 1987.
Grobler, J. *A Decisive Clash? A Short History of Black Protest Politics in South Africa, 1875–1976*. Acacia, 1988.
Hancock, WK. *Smuts: The Fields of Force 1919–1950*. Cambridge University Press, 1968.
Hancock, WK. *Smuts: The Sanguine Years 1870–1919*. Cambridge University Press, 1968.
Heale, J. *They Made this Land*. Ad Donker, 1981.
Holland, H. *100 Years of Struggle: Mandela's ANC*. Penguin Books, 2012.
Johnson, RW. *The First Man, The Last Nation*. Phoenix, 2006.
Karis, T and G Carter. *From Protest to Challenge: A Documentary History of African Politics in South Africa 1882–1964, Vol 2: Hope and Challenge, 1935–1952*. Hoover Institution Press, 1973.
Karis, T and G Gerhart. *From Protest to Challenge: A Documentary History of African Politics in South Africa 1882–1884, Vol 4: Political Profiles 1882–1964*. Indiana University Press, 2010.
Karis, T and G Gerhart. *From Protest to Challenge: A Documentary History of African Politics in*

South Africa 1882–1884, Vol 5: Nadir and Resurgence 1964–1979. Unisa Press, 1997.
Kathrada, AM. *Memoirs.* Zebra Press, 2004.
Katz, DB. *South Africans Versus Rommel: The Untold Story of the Desert War in World War II.* Delta, 2019.
Keppel-Jones, A. *When Smuts Goes.* Shuter & Shooter, 1949.
Koorts, L. *DF Malan and the Rise of Afrikaner Nationalism.* Tafelberg, 2014.
Krüger, DW. *The Age of the Generals.* Dagbreek, 1958.
Krüger, DW. *The Making of a Nation.* Macmillan, 1969.
Lawrence, J. *Harry Lawrence.* David Philip, 1978.
Lewis, G. *Between the Wire and the Wall: A History of South African 'Coloured' Politics.* David Philip, 1987.
Lodge, T. *Black Politics in South Africa since 1945.* Ravan Press, 1985.
Lodge, T (ed). *Resistance and Ideology in Settler Societies: South Africa Studies, Vol 4.* Ravan Press, 1986.
Long, BK. *In Smuts's Camp.* Oxford University Press, 1945.
Lumby, AB. 'The Development of Secondary Industry: The Second World War and After'. In F Coleman (ed), *Economic History of South Africa.* HAUM, 1983.
Macdonald, T. *Jan Hofmeyr: Heir to Smuts.* Hurst & Blackett, 1948.
Malherbe, EG. *Never a Dull Moment.* Timmins Publishers, 1981.
Mandela, NR. *Long Walk to Freedom.* Little, Brown, 1994.
Marx, C. *Oxwagon Sentinel: Radical Afrikaner Nationalism and the History of the Ossewabrandwag.* Unisa Press, 2008.
Matthews, ZK and M Wilson. *Freedom for My People.* David Philip, 1981.
Meiring, P. *Tien Politieke Leiers.* Tafelberg, 1973.
Meli, F. *A History of the ANC: South Africa Belongs to Us.* Zimbabwe Publishing House, 1989.
Meredith, M. *Nelson Mandela: A Biography.* Simon & Schuster, 2014.
Millin, SG. *The South Africans.* Constable, 1937.
Morris, J. *Farewell the Trumpets: An Imperial Retreat.* Penguin Books, 1979.
Muller, CFJ (ed). *Five Hundred Years: A History of South Africa.* Academica, 1973.
Munger, ES. *Afrikaner and African Nationalism.* Oxford University Press, 1967.
Munger, ES (ed). *The Afrikaners.* Tafelberg, 1979.
Nasson, B. *South Africa at War, 1939–1945.* Jacana, 2012.
Nattrass, N. 'Economic Growth in the 1940s'. In S Dubow and A Jeeves (eds). *South Africa's 1940s: Worlds of Possibilities.* Double Storey, 2005.
Ngubane, J. *An African Explains Apartheid.* Pall Mall, 1963.
Pachai, B. *The International Aspects of the South African Indian Question 1860–1971.* Struik, 1971.
Pandit, VL. *The Scope of Happiness: A Personal Memoir.* Crown Publishers, 1979.
Paton, A. *Hofmeyr.* Oxford University Press, 1964.
Pimlott, B. *The Queen: Elizabeth II and the Monarchy.* Harper Press, 2012.
Pirow, O. *James Barry Munnik Hertzog.* Howard Timmins, no date.
Raman, P. 'Yusuf Dadoo: A Son of Africa'. In S Dubow and A Jeeves (eds), *South Africa's 1940s: Worlds of Possibilities*, Double Storey, 2005.
Reader's Digest. *South Africa's Yesterdays.* Reader's Digest Association South Africa, 1981.
Reader's Digest. *Illustrated History of South Africa: The Real Story.* Reader's Digest Association South Africa, 1994.
Reitz, D. *Adrift on the Open Veld: The Anglo-Boer War and Its Aftermath, 1899–1943.* Stormberg, 1999.

SOURCES

Rich, PB. *State Power and Black Politics in South Africa 1912–51*. St Martin's Press, 1996.
Roberts, AA. *Churchill: Walking with Destiny*. Penguin, 2019.
Robins, E. *This Man Malan*. SA Scientific Publishing Co, 1953.
Ross, R, A Mager and B Nasson (eds). *The Cambridge History of South Africa, Vol 2: 1885–1994*. Cambridge University Press, 2016.
Roth, M. 'Elections under the Representation of Natives Act, 1937–1948'. In T Lodge (ed), *Resistance and Ideology in Settler Societies: South Africa Studies, Vol 4*. Ravan Press, 1986.
Sampson, A. *Mandela: The Authorised Biography*. HarperCollins, 1999.
Seekings, J. 'Welfare reform'. In S Dubow and A Jeeves (eds), *South Africa's 1940s: Worlds of Possibilities*. Double Storey, 2005.
Simons, J and R Simons. *Class and Colour in South Africa 1850–1950*. International Defence and Aid Fund, 1983.
Smuts, JC. *Jan Christian Smuts: By His Son*. Cassell, 1952.
Solomon, B. *Time Remembered*. Howard Timmins, 1968.
Soske, J. *Internal Frontiers: African Nationalism and the Indian Diaspora in Twentieth-Century South Africa*. Wits University Press, 2018.
Sparks, A. *The Mind of South Africa*. Alfred A Knopf, 1990.
Strydom, H. *For Volk and Fuhrer: Robey Leibbrandt and Operation Weissdorn*. Jonathan Ball Publishers, 1984.
Thakur, V. *Jan Smuts and the Indian Question*. University of KwaZulu-Natal Press, 2018.
Thompson, L. *A History of South Africa*. Radix, 1990.
Troup, F. *South Africa: An Historical Introduction*. Eyre Methuen, 1972.
Van den Heever, CM. *General JBM Hertzog*. APB Bookstore, 1946.
Van der Poel, J (ed). *Selections from the Smuts Papers, Vol VI: December 1934–August 1945*. Cambridge University Press, 1973.
Van der Poel, J (ed), *Selections from the Smuts Papers, Vol VII: August 1945–October 1950*. Cambridge University Press, 1973.
Van der Ross, RE. *The Rise and Decline of Apartheid: A Study of Political Movements Among the Coloured People of South Africa 1880–1985*. Tafelberg, 1986.
Van der Waag, IJ. *A Military History of Modern South Africa*. Jonathan Ball Publishers, 2015.
Van Wyk, A. *Vyf Dae: Oorlogskrisis van 1939: 'n Spanningsverhaal Uit SA Se Geskiedenis*. Tafelberg, 1985.
Various authors. *They Shaped Our Century: The Most Influential South Africans of the Twentieth Century*. Human & Rousseau, 1999.
Viney, G. *The Last Hurrah: South Africa and the Royal Tour of 1947*. Jonathan Ball Publishers, 2018.
Visser, GB. *OB: Traitors or Patriots?* Macmillan, 1977.
Walshe, P. *The Rise of African Nationalism in South Africa*. Ad Donker, 1987.
Wilks, T. *The Biography of Douglas Mitchell*. King & Wilks, 1980.
Wilson, F. *Labour in the South African Gold Mines 1911–1969*. Cambridge University Press, 1972.
Wilson, GH. *Gone Down the Years*. Howard Timmins, 1947.
Wilson, M and L Thompson (eds). *The Oxford History of South Africa, Vol II: South Africa 1870–1966*. Clarendon Press, 1971.

Journal articles
Cardo, M. '"Fighting A Worse Imperialism": White South African Loyalism and the Army

Education Services (AES) during the Second World War'. *South African Historical Journal*, vol 46 (2002), pp 141–174.

Crowder, M. 'Tshekedi Khama, Smuts, and South West Africa'. *The Journal of Modern Africa Studies*, vol 25, no 1 (1987), pp 25–42.

Fokkens, AM. 'Afrikaner Unrest Within South Africa During the Second World War and the Measures Taken to Suppress it'. *Journal for Contemporary History*, vol 37, no 2 (December 2012), pp 123–142.

Gravett, W. 'Jan Christian Smuts (1870–1950) in Context: An Answer to Mazower and Morefield'. *The Round Table*, vol 106, no 3 (2017), pp 261–277.

Henkes, B. 'Shifting Identifications in Dutch-South African Migration Policies (1910–1961)'. *South African Historical Journal*, vol 68, no 4 (2016), pp 641–649.

James, WG. 'Grounds for a Strike: South African Gold Mining in the 1940s'. *African Economic History*, no 16 (1987), pp 1–22.

Kleynhans, E. '"Good Hunting": German Submarine Offensives and South African Countermeasures off the South African Coast during the Second World War, 1942–1945'. *Scientia Militaria*, vol 44, no 1 (1996), pp 168–189.

Lloyd, L. '"A Most Auspicious Beginning": The 1946 United Nations General Assembly and the Question of the Treatment of Indians in South Africa'. *Review of International Studies*, vol 16, no 2 (April 1990), pp 131–153.

McCormack, R. 'Man with a Mission: Oswald Pirow and South African Airways, 1933–1939'. *Journal of African History*, vol 20, no 4 (October 1979), pp 543–557.

'Round Table'. *Commonwealth Journal of International Affairs*, vol 30 (1939).

Sapire, H. 'African Loyalism and Its Discontents: The Royal Tour of South Africa, 1947'. *The Historical Journal*, vol 54, no 1 (March 2011), pp 215–240.

Shear, K. 'Colonel Coetzee's War: Loyalty, Subversion and the South African Police 1939–1945'. *South African Historical Journal*, vol 65, no 2 (2013), pp 222–248.

Wessels, A. 'South Africa and the War against Japan 1941–1945'. *SA Military History Journal*, vol 10, no 3 (June 1996).

Wollheim, OD. 'Margaret Ballinger: A Tribute'. *Reality*, vol 12, no 3 (1980).

Online sources

'A History of the Springbok Legion'. South African History Online, 27 August 2019.

Bruton, M. 'The vision that gave SA power'. IOL, 10 February 2012.

'Council of Non-European Trade Unions'. South African History Online, 27 August 2019.

'Dr Alfred Xuma'. South African History Online, 3 September 2019.

'Dr Yusuf Mohamed Dadoo'. South African History Online, 10 December 2019.

Filatova, I. 'Communism in South Africa'. Oxford Research Encyclopedia of African History, February 2017.

'James Sofasonke Mpanza'. South African History Online, 23 August 2019.

'Zonderwater POW camp'. www.zonderwater.com/en, no date.

Index

Page numbers in *italics* indicate photographs.

1st South African Infantry Brigade 82, 84, 115, 154
6th South African Armoured Division 125, 166, 173, 183

AAC *see* All African Convention
Abdurahman, Abdullah 148–150
Abrahams, Peter 190
Active Citizen Force (ACF) 9, 59, 62
Adams College 127, 164
Adhikari, Mohamed 149
ADP *see* African Democratic Party
AES *see* Army Education Service
African Claims in South Africa 104, 134
African Democratic Party (ADP) 126–127
'Africanism' 128–132, 164, 246, 291
African Metals Corporation (Amcor) 61
African Mine Workers' Union (AMWU) 87–88, 118, 198–201, 210
African National Congress (ANC)
   African Claims in South Africa 104, 134
   Africanism 246–247
   All African Convention and 97–98
   anti-pass campaign 158–159, 170–171
   apartheid 274
   Atlantic Charter 103–104, 189–190
   Congress Youth League and 104, 126–127, 129–132, 162–164, 210–211
   CPSA and 116–118, 132–133, 210
   Doctors' Pact 248
   Durban riots 277
   Fagan Commission 262
   'Ghetto Act' 193
   housing 124
   Indian-African collaboration 239–242, 278
   leadership of 101, 126, 128, 165, 245, 252–254, 256, 274–277, 279–280
   loyalty to 249–250
   miners' strike of 1946 201–202
   nationalism 246–247
   Native Trust and Land Act 107
   NEUM and 132–133
   NRC and 101–102, 205–206, 265–266
   Pan African Congress, 5th 190
   Programme of Action 275, 278–279
   royal tour in 1947 235–236
   Smuts and 121
   support for 95–96, 98–99, 118, 189–190
   at United Nations General Assembly 219, 227–229
   Unity Conference 153
   'Votes for All' campaign 248–250
   wage demands 112

Women's League 100
World War Two xii, 96, 180
see also Congress Youth League
African nationalism xiv, 95–96, 132–133, 164, 210, 246–247, 288, 291–292
African People's Organisation (APO) 149–150, 193
Africans
    Indian-African collaboration 195, 209, 277–278
    mining industry 15
    moderate leaders 289
    Native Trust and Land Act 107
    NEAS 62
    political rights of xi, 95–105
    trade unions 87–88
    unity 153
    urbanisation 19
    World War One 63
    World War Two 55, 62–63, 187
Afrikaans- and English-speakers, divisions between xi, 5–8, 14, 16, 18, 20, 39, 69–70, 111, 284, 286
see also Afrikaners
Afrikaans language 6, 7, 13, 66, 157
Afrika Korps 84, 113
Afrikaner Broederbond 18, 21, 22, 64, 76, 191–192, 272
Afrikaner nationalism xiv, 14, 21–22, 127–128, 274, 284, 288, 291
Afrikaner Party 66, 70, 155, 250–251, 265, 281
Afrikaner rebellion of 1914–1915 77
Afrikaners
    divisions in xi, 11, 13–14, 18, 250–251
    Great Trek centenary 21–22, 64
    urbanisation 15, 20–21, 107–108
    World War One 8–9
    World War Two 56, 63, 72, 115
agent-general, role of 141–142
agriculture 86, 108, 195
Alexandra bus boycotts 127, 133–134, 215
Ali, Sir Syed Raza 141
All African Convention (AAC)
    ANC and 98, 252, 256

Anti-CAD movement 153
    divisions in 126
    launched 96–97
    Mda and 245
    Native Bills of 1936 92, 98
    NEUM and 132, 252
    NRC and 265
    support for 97–98, 101–102, 118
    World War Two 214
Amcor *see* African Metals Corporation
America *see* United States
AMWU *see* African Mine Workers' Union
ANC *see* African National Congress
Andrews, WH (Bill) 119, 201
Anglo-Boer War 5–6, 8, 28, 75, 110, 283–284
Anti-CAD movement 150–153
anti-pass campaign 158–159, 170–171, 206, 215
Anti-Segregation Council (ASC) 160
anti-Semitism 21, 64, 74, 78, 86, 250
apartheid xiii, 142, 177–178, 189, 232, 260–261, 272–274, 288
APO *see* African People's Organisation
armaments industry 62, 84, 104, 287
Army Education Service (AES) 111
ASC *see* Anti-Segregation Council
Asiatic (Transvaal) Land and Trading Act 137
Asiatic Land Tenure and Indian Representation Bill *see* 'Ghetto Act'
Asvat, Ebrahim 213
Athenia (passenger liner) 42
Atlantic Charter 94, 95, 103–105, 122, 160, 190
atomic bombs 106, 182, 183
Back, Vera 89
Balfour Declaration of 1926 17
Ballinger, Margaret 99, 102, 121–123, 242, 253
Ballinger, William 121, 266
Banda, Hastings Kamuzu 190
Bantu World 165
Barber, J 105, 190
Barlow, Arthur 50
Barry, James 4

INDEX

Basner, Hyman 126, 219, 228
'Battle of Andringa Street' 85
BBC 31
beer sales 108
Beinart, W 272–273
Beyers, CF 9
Bhana, Surendra 139
bilingualism 6, 157
black people *see* Africans
black peril (*swart gevaar*) 17, 265
Blackshirts 77
Blackwell, Leslie 13, 23, 50, 91
Blake, Albert 20, 76–77
'Boer rebellion' of 1914–1915 9
Bonner, Philip 118, 206–207
Botha, Louis 5–9, 12, 14, 284
boycotts 127, 130, 133–134, 151, 195, 205–206, 215, 235–236
bread 108
Bremer, Karl 196
Brink, George 94, 157
Britain
  gold standard 17
  South Africa and xii, 7, 16–17, 19, 63, 250, 272
  United Nations 224
  World War Two 31, 82–84, 94, 106, 113, 115, 173
British titles for South Africans abolished 17, 50
Broederbond *see* Afrikaner Broederbond
Brookes, Edgar 99, 102, 121, 203, 285
Broome Commissions 137–141, 143, 160
Bulletin, The 151
bureaucracy 176, 233
Burger, Die 11, 24, 27, 50–51, 53
bus boycotts *see* Alexandra bus boycotts
'bushcarts' 68

CAC *see* Coloured Advisory Council
Cachalia, Yusuf 278–279
Calata, James 98, 101, 239
Cambridge University 4, 121, 267
Cape Argus 27

Cape Corps 62, 146
Cape sea route xii, 62–63, 76, 88, 109–110, 155–156, 287
Cape Times 24, 27, 53, 197
Cape Town Agreement 141–142, 159
capitalism 177
Cardo, Michael 111
Cartwright, AP 182
Cato Manor, conflict in 277–278
Chagla, MC 225
Chamberlain, Neville 3, 30, 31, 38–39, 68
Chamber of Mines 15, 88, 198–201
Champion, AWG 102, 165, 241
Christian Nationalism 76
'Christian trusteeship' 262, 264–265
Christopher, Albert 219
Churchill, Winston
  Atlantic Charter 94, 95, 103
  as prime minister 82, 183
  Smuts and 56, 156, 166
  World War Two 113–115, 125, 179, 181, 207, 291
Clark, Sir William 38–39
Clarkson, CF 52, 143
CNETU *see* Council of Non-European Trade Unions
Collins, WR 43, 52, 172
colour bar xiii, 15, 103, 149
Coloured Advisory Council (CAC) 147–148, 150–153
coloured people
  'Battle of Andringa Street' 84–85
  CAC 147–148, 150–153
  Congress Youth League 163
  elections 144–145, 152
  franchise 150–152, 154, 177–178, 273–274, 281–282
  NEUM 132
  trade unions 87
  World War Two 55, 62, 63, 145–146
Comintern 116–117
Commonwealth 56, 189, 280
Commonwealth Conferences 159–160, 165–166, 280

315

communism
  HNP 119–120, 155, 172, 174–175, 176–178, 189, 279, 288
  Pirow on 67
  United Nations 271
Communist Party of South Africa (CPSA)
  All African Convention and 97
  ANC and 116–118, 132–133, 205, 210, 245, 254, 289
  anti-pass campaign 158–159, 170–171
  banned 266, 273
  Chamber of Mines and 15
  Congress Youth League and 164–165
  Dadoo and 212, 214–215
  founded 116–117
  HNP and 119–120
  housing 124
  La Guma and 146
  Lembede and 129, 240
  miners' strike of 1946 199–201, 207
  Native Trust and Land Act 107
  NRC and 265–266
  support for 116–118, 120, 207
  'Votes for All' campaign 249
  World War Two 63, 87, 116, 118, 180, 214–215
  see also South African Communist Party
Congress of the People 254
Congress Youth League (CYL)
  Alexandra bus boycotts 134
  ANC and 104, 126–127, 129–132, 162–164, 210–211
  communism and 133
  established 127, 162–165
  Fagan Commission 262
  Fort Hare and 251–252
  Indian-African collaboration 209–210, 240–241, 278
  leadership of 239, 244, 245–246, 253–254, 256, 274–275, 277
  NEUM and 254, 256–258
  NRC and 205
  royal tour in 1947 235
  'Votes for All' campaign 248–249

Conradie, JH 176
Conroy, EA 44, 52
conscription 60
constitution of Union of South Africa 6, 19
Council of Non-European Trade Unions (CNETU) 87, 118, 200, 201, 206–207
Council on African Affairs 228
coup d'état, planned 79
Coward, Noël 172–173
CPSA see Communist Party of South Africa
Cradock Agreement 72
Crafford, FS 9
CYL see Congress Youth League

Dadoo, Yusuf 138–139, 158–159, 171, 180, 207, 211–216, *213*, 240, *241*, 258–259, 279
defence expenditure 68, 168
'Defend South Africa' campaign 214–215
Defiance Campaign 171, 254, 279, 291–292
De Kiewiet, CW 283–284, 288
demobilisation 157, 175–176
Denk, Hans 195–197
  wife of 195–196
detention camps for Italian POWs 110
detention-without-trial laws 76
developmental state, South Africa as 187
Dhlomo, HIE 235–236
Directorate of Demobilisation 157, 176
District Six 149
Doctors' Pact 240–242, *241*, 248–250, 277
Dominion Party 18, 41, 54, 137, 139, 154, 156–157, 160–161, 263
Dönitz, Karl 109, 179
'Draft Declaration of Unity' 134–135
droughts 15, 17, 200
Dube, John L 102, 289
Dubow, Saul xiii, 107–108
Duncan, Sir Patrick 3, 15, 27, *34*, 35–37, 47–54, 125
Durban July horse race 114
Durban riots 277–278
Dutch Reformed Church 10, 20, 78, 119, 217

INDEX

East Africa, WWII in 83–84
Eban, Abba 289
economic issues 15–20, 63, 94, 108, 117–118, 122, 168–170, 175–176, 187–188, 287–288
economic sanctions against South Africa 143, 193, 247
Economist, The (London) 237–238
Edgar, Robert 251
education 6, 65, 152, 157, 170, 188
Eighth Army 84, 94, 106, 113, 115
elections
    1915 9–10
    1920 14–15
    1921 15
    1923 16
    1929 17
    1933 18
    1938 21
    1943 120–121, 136, 140, 144–145, 152, 154–155, 157
    1944 172
    1945 188
    1947 232
    1948 76, 216–217, 238, 250–251, 260–265, 272, 284, 290
    1953 282
    expected after war vote 48, 51–52, 54–55
    NRC 265–266
electoral system 97, 264
Electricity Supply Commission (Escom) 61, 168, 187
Elizabeth, Princess 234, 238
Elizabeth, Queen 233–235, 253
'elsewhere in the world' summaries 71, 82, 94, 106, 125, 173, 182–183, 207–208, 238, 268
English- and Afrikaans-speakers, divisions between xi, 5–8, 14, 16, 18, 20, 39, 69–70, 111, 284, 286
English language 66, 69–70, 157
'Equality Now' slogan 160
Erasmus, FC 77, 251
Escom *see* Electricity Supply Commission

Esselen, Louis 24, 28, 30, 37, 46, 263–264

Fagan Commission 216–217, 261–262
Farewell to Parliament 50
farming *see* agriculture
far-right 'Shirt' movements 77–78, 118–119
fear, in politics 288
fifth column 75, 75, 114
firearms, confiscation of 74
First, Ruth 164
First World War *see* World War One
Fischer, Bram 134, 207
flag, national 17
food 82, 86, 108, 120, 175, 195, 200
Fort Hare *see* University College of Fort Hare
Fourie, AP 93
Fourie, Jopie 77
France 31, 82–83, 208
franchise
    Africans 120–121
    coloured people 150–152, 154, 177–178, 273–274, 281–282
    election of 1929 17
    HNP 273
    as human right 224
    Indians in South Africa 192, 224
    Native Bills of 1936 19–20, 92, 95–98, 144, 245, 252
    qualified 100
    reform 188
    'Votes for All' campaign 248–250
    World War Two 167
Franco, Francisco 68, 71
Frederica, Princess of Greece 172
Freedom Charter 254, 292
Freund, Bill 187
Friedman, Bernard 220, 264, 289–290
Friends of the Soviet Union (FSU) 119
'Fusion' government ix–xi, 18–22, 25, 33, 44, 53, 91, 118, 287

gambling 89
Gandhi, Mohandas K 136–138, 195, 209, 214,

218, 225, 268
George VI, King 233–234, 237, 253
Gerdener, GBA 217
Gerhart, Gail 244, 289
German South West Africa 9–10
  see also South West Africa
German war orphans 196
Germany
  Molotov-Ribbentrop Pact 24, 71, 119
  South Africa and 63, 79, 115, 195–197, 286
  World War One 22
  World War Two 31, 71, 82–83, 94, 106, 109–110, 114–115, 125, 179–183
Gesuiwerde Nasionale Party (GNP) 18, 26, 36, 41, 54, 64
'Ghetto Act' 192–195, *194*, 205–206, 209, 211, 219, 251
Gibson, Perla Siedle 180
Gifts and Comforts Fund 172–173
Giliomee, Hermann 6, 85, 272
Gish, Steven 227, 239
GNP *see* Gesuiwerde Nasionale Party
Godlo, RH 102, 289
gold mining 19–20, 94, 108, 112, 168–169, 199–200, 287
gold standard 17–18
Gool, Goolam 145, 151, 153
Gool, Zainunissa (Cissie) 145, 151
Gow, FH 150
Graaff, Sir De Villiers 232
Gravett, Willem 285
Great Trek centenary 21–22, 64
Greyshirts 77–78
Group Areas Act 280
Gumede, Josiah 116

Hall, Madie 100
Hancock, Sir Keith 46–47, 52–53, 55, 141, 156, 222, 243, 262, 264, 286
Havenga, NC (Klasie) 26–31, 36, 46, 66, 274, 291
Herenigde Nasionale Party (HNP)
  Afrikaner Broederbond 191–192
  apartheid 177–178, 189, 272–273

communism 119–120, 174–175, 273
divisions in 66, 69–70
Dominion Party and 188–189
education 157
elections 120, 152, 154–155, 172, 188, 216–217, 232, 250–251, 263–265, 281, 288
established 64–65
Hofmeyr and 167–168, 170
immigrants from Britain and Europe 232
Indians in South Africa 161, 231–232
New Order and 69
NRC and 242, 266
Ossewabrandwag and 72, 78, 81
pass laws 158
royal tour in 1947 234–235
Sauer Commission 178, 262
South West Africa 231–232, 281
swart gevaar (black peril) 265
United Nations 231–232, 281
World War Two 74, 113–114, 154, 156, 171–172, 181, 196
Hertzog, James Barry Munnik 34
  background of 3–4
  Botha and 6–8
  death of 71
  defence expenditure 59
  HNP 54, 65–66, 69–70
  Hofmeyr and 91–92
  language 6, 69–70
  Native Bills of 1936 19–20, 92, 95–98, 144, 245, 252
  NP 8
  as prime minister 16–18
  resignations of 51–54, 69–71, 95
  SAA 68
  Smuts and 5–6, 13–14, 15, 17–18, 70
  war vote ix–x, 22–42, 46–48, 50–56
  World War One 9
  World War Two 11–12, 65–66, 286–287
high commissioners, role of 141–142
Hitler, Adolf
  comes to power 3
  death of 179
  last public speech 182

INDEX

Leibbrandt and 79, 81
Ossewabrandwag 73
Pirow and 67–68
on South West Africa 22, 47, 286
war vote 41–43, 46–47
World War Two 22, 71, 83, 94
Hlubi, Mark 190
HNP *see* Herenigde Nasionale Party
Hodgson, John 121
Hofmeyr, Jan Hendrik *90*
    as acting prime minister 52–53, 90, 156, 167, 202–204
    background of 90–94
    death of 281, 290–291
    elections 189, 232, 238, 263–265, 267
    'Jan Tax' 168
    Native Bills of 1936 19
    'Pegging Act' 141
    World War Two 166–168, 169–171, 180–181, 188, 287–288
Hofmeyr, Steve 74
'Holism' 13
Holland, Heidi 100, 274
Holm, Eric 64
horse racing 89, 114
housing xii, 108, 123–124, 176, 233, 288–289
Hoy, Charles 146
human rights 189, 222, 224, 258

idealism 111–112
Ikenberry, G John 283
Ilanga lase Natal 165
immigrants from Britain and Europe 15, 232–233, 272, 288
Immorality Act 272
Imperial Airways 68
Imperial Conferences 15, 137
imperialism 177
Imperial War Cabinet 11
India 142–143, 149, 178–179, 192–195, 218–227, 230, 247, 250, 258–259
Indian & Malay Corps 62, 146
Indians in South Africa
    Broome Commissions 137–141, 143, 160
    divisions in 212–214, 258–259
    Doctors' Pact 240–242, *241*, 248–250, 277
    franchise 161
    'Ghetto Act' 192–195, *194*, 205–206, 209, 211, 219, 251
    history of 136–138
    Indian-African collaboration 132, 195, 209–211, 239–242, 247, 277–278
    NEAS 62
    'Pegging Act' 140–141, 142–143, 159–161, 178–179, 192
    Pretoria Agreement 159–161
    repatriation of 141, 262
    United Nations 190, 218–226
    World War Two xi, 55, 63, 139
Industrial and Commercial Workers' Union 121, 129
industrial development xii, 108, 187
inequality 187
inflation 86, 120, 168, 175–176
influx controls 102–103, 123
    see also pass laws
Inkundla ya Bantu 165
Inter-Asian Conference 240
international community, criticism of South Africa 260, 271
International Court of Justice 221, 223, 226, 280–281
internment camps 75–76
Iron and Steel Corporation (Iscor) 60, 61, 168, 187
Italian prisoners of war (POWs) 84, *85*, 110
Italy 66, 71, 82–84, 125

Jabavu, Davidson Don Tengo (DDT) 97–98, 134, 153, 214, 236, 252–253
Jabavu, Tengo 97
Jagger, JW 15
James, Wilmot 201
Jameson Raid 5
Jansen, EG 41, 53
Japan 83, 88, 94, 101, 106, 109, 114–115, 125, 173, 182–183, 194, 276
Jinnah, Muhammad Ali 218, 268

319

Johannesburg Stock Exchange 25
Joint Declaration of Cooperation *see*
  Doctors' Pact
Joint Passive Resistance Council
  (JPRC) 219
Jones, JD Rheinallt 99–100
JPRC *see* Joint Passive Resistance Council
Junkers aircraft 60, 68
jute 195

Kadalie, Clements 129
Kahn, Sam 266, 273
Kajee, AI 138, 143, 159–160, 192–193, 259
Karis, Tom 129
Kathrada, Ahmed (Kathy) 195, 211, 213, 279
Kathrada, Solly 211
Kemp, Jan 29, 36, 234–235
Kenyatta, Jomo 117, 190
Keppel-Jones, Arthur 288
Khama, Tshekedi 228–229, 252
Khan, Sir Shafa'at Ahmad 143
Khan, Sir Zafrullah 258
Kies, Ben 151–152
Kimberley 4
Kleynhans, E 109–110
Klopper, HB 113
Klopper, Henning 21
Koorts, Lindie 10, 177, 197
Korean War 280
Kotane, Moses 98–99, 118, 158–159, 171, 201, 205, 210–211
Krüger, DW 62, 64, 71, 108, 114, 115, 194, 233
Kruger, Paul 5

Laas, JC 73
labour, cost of 15, 88, 112, 200
labour, shortage of 199–200
Labour Party 14–16, 41, 54, 154, 156, 161, 263, 282
labour policies 18
La Guma, James (Jimmy) 145, 146–147
land ownership 19, 93, 192–195, 205–206, 209, 211, 212–214, 219, 251
Lansdown Commission 199–200

Lawrence, Harry 29–32, 40, 52–53, 81, 138, 147–148, 150, 176, 196–197, 258–259
Lawrence, Jeremy 172, 258
Leader, The 142, 225
Leibbrandt, Meider 81
Leibbrandt, Robey 79–81, 272
Lembede, Anton Muziwakhe *131*
  background of 127–129
  Congress Youth League 129–130, 162, 164–165, 205, 210–211
  death of 243–244, 290–291
  Doctors' Pact 240–241
  Matthews and 252
  Mda and 245–246
  royal tour in 1947 236
  Sobukwe and 254–255
  Tambo and 256
Leuchars, Sir George 8
Lewis, Gavin 148–149, 152
liberalism 189, 246
Liberal Party 165
Lie, Trygve 228
Lloyd, Lorna 218–219, 222, 225
Lloyd George, David 12
Lodge, Tom 87–88, 96
Long, BK 43–44, 67
Long Walk to Freedom 209, 249
Louw, Eric 32, 46, 197
loyalty to ANC 249–250
Lusitania (ship) 42
Luthuli, Albert 127, 165, 236, 252, 279–280, 289

MacArthur, Douglas 182
Madagascar 114–115
Madeley, Walter 52, 148, 161, 188–189
Malan, AG (Sailor) 281
Malan, Daniel Francois (DF) *34*
  Afrikaner Broederbond 191–192
  apartheid 177–178, 189, 232
  background of 10–11
  communism 176–177
  elections 120, 154, 250–251, 264–265
  'Fusion' government 18

INDEX

GNP 18
HNP 54, 64–65, 69–70
Indians in South Africa 161, 231–232
New Order for South Africa 69
Ossewabrandwag 72, 78
    as prime minister 267–268, 280–281
    royal tour in 1947 237–238
    South West Africa 231, 281
    United Nations 231–232, 280–281
    war vote 25–28, 31–32, 36, 44
    World War One 12
    World War Two 3, 174–175, 180–181, 195–197, 286, 291
Malherbe, EG 111
Mampuru, Self 126
Mandela, Nelson R 131
    Alexandra bus boycotts 133–134
    ANC 247, 278
    communism 133, 210
    Congress Youth League 129–130, 162, 164, 211, 246, 251, 274
    Defiance Campaign 279
    Indian-African collaboration 210–211, 247, 278
    Lembede and 243–244
    miners' strike of 1946 209
    as president 150
    Programme of Action 278–279
    royal tour in 1947 236
    Sisulu and 276–277
    Tabata and 256–258
    Tambo and 255–256
    'Votes for All' campaign 248–250
manufacturing sector xii, 187, 287
Marks, JB 87, 98–99, 118, 158, 171, 180, 201, 210–211, 275, 279
Marquard, Leo 111
marriages, 'mixed' 262, 272
Marxism 129, 152, 153, 158, 164, 166, 179, 249, 257
Masakeng camp 124
mass action 130, 132
Matthews, Joe 252, 279
Matthews, Zachariah Keodirelang (ZK) 102, 104, 203–204, 236, 242, 251–254, *253*, 274, 289
Mda, Ashby Peter Solomzi (AP) 128–130, 162, 164–165, 239, 244–247, 251–252, 254, 274
Mda, Zakes 244
Mears, WG 202, 227
Medical Aid for Russia 119
Meer, Ismail 210, 240
Meiring, Piet 67, 68
Meredith, M 130
middle class 96, 104
migrant labour system 21, 87–88, 96, 107–108, 112, 121, 206–207, 216–217
Miles Cadman, Rev. CF 175
militancy 87–88, 134
Milner, Sir Alfred 5, 49
mineral resources xii, 15, 76
miners' strike of 1946 198–207, *199*, 209, 211, 215–216
mining industry xii, 20–21, 87–88, 107–108, 112, 170, 187
mission schools 96
Mitchell, Douglas 238
'mixed' marriages 262, 272
Mofutsanyana, Edwin 87
Molotov-Ribbentrop Pact 24, 71, 119
Molteno, Donald 99, 102, 121, 170, 242
Moroka, James S 182, 202, 204, 236, 274–275, *275*, 278–279, 285
Moroka housing scheme 124
Mosaka, Paul 102, 126, 171, 205–206, 236, 242, 289
Motlana, Ntatho 252
Mpanza, James 123–124
Msimang, Selby 241
Munger, ES 77–78, 165
Munich Agreement 3
Mussolini, Benito 66, 68, 83

Naicker, GM (Monty) 160, 193–194, 212, 215–216, 240, *241*, 258–259
Naidoo, SR 143
Nasson, Bill 35, 55, 63

Natal Indian Association (NIA) 138–139, 142–143
Natal Indian Congress (NIC) 138–139, 142–143, 159–161, 192–193, 215, 240, 258
Natal Indian Organisation (NIO) 259
Natal Mercury 230
Natal Municipal Association 139
Natal Provincial Council 160, 192
Natal Witness, The 230
national flag 17
nationalisation 104
nationalism 283
  see also African nationalism; Afrikaner nationalism; Christian Nationalism
Nationalist Socialist Rebels (NSR) 80–81
National Liberation League (NLL) 145
National Party (NP) 8, 9, 10–11, 14–16, 18, 21, 36, 281
National Socialism 70–72, 74, 79
National Supplies Board 63
National War Fund 88–89
Native (Urban Areas) Consolidation Act 182
Native Bills of 1936 19–20, 92, 95–98, 144, 245, 252
Native Military Corps (NMC) 62
Native Representative Council (NRC)
  abolished 262, 273
  anti-pass campaign 159
  elections 265–266
  importance of 102, 289–290
  miners' strike of 1946 202–206
  Native Bills of 1936 97
  Smuts and 182, 242–243
Native Representatives in Parliament 41, 54, 99, 121, 155, 263, 265–266
Natives Land Act 8
Native Trust and Land Act 107, 204
Nattrass, Nicoli 168, 187, 287
Naude, Tom 24, 42
Nehru, Jawaharlal 195, 208, 212, 218, 220, 240, 247, 259
Netherlands 65, 82, 183
NEUF *see* Non-European Forum

NEUM *see* Non-European Unity Movement
New Order for South Africa 66, 69, 155, 172
newsreels 85–86
Ngubane, Jordan 128–130, 162, 164–165, 245–246, 252, 262
NIA *see* Natal Indian Association
NIC *see* Natal Indian Congress
Nicholls, George Heaton 43, 219, 223–224
Nimitz, Chester 182
NIO *see* Natal Indian Organisation
Nkomo, William 162, 164
Nkrumah, Kwame 190
NLL *see* National Liberation League
NMC *see* Native Military Corps
Nobel Prize for Peace 280
Nokwe, Duma 252
Non-European Forum (NEUF) 145
Non-European United Front 132, 212
Non-European Unity Movement (NEUM) 97–98, 126, 132–135, 153, 252, 254, 256–258
noon-day gun, Cape Town 84–85
NP *see* National Party
NRC *see* Native Representative Council
NSR *see* Nationalist Socialist Rebels
Nzula, Albert 117

OB *see* Ossewabrandwag
Official Secrets Act 76
Olympic Games 66, 67, 79, 268
O'Meara, Dan 263
Operation Barbarossa 119
Operation Eisbär (Polar Bear) 109
Operation Overlord 166
Operation Weissdorn (Hawthorn) 79–81
Oppenheimer, Sir Ernest 79
Oranjehemde (Orange shirts) 77
Order for Meritorious Service (gold) 150
Order of Merit 234
Orlando township 123–124
orphans 196
Ossewabrandwag (OB) xiii, 72–74, 73, 76–81, 118–119, 155, 172, 191, 251, 272

'Pact' government 16–17
Pakistan 238, 258
Pan African Congress, 5th 190
Pan Africanist Congress 255
Pandit, Vijaya Lakshmi 218–219, 221–226, 258, 280
'passive resistance' 137–138, 193, 205–206
Passive Resistance Council (PRC) 215, 235
pass laws
   anti-pass campaign 158–159, 170–171, 206, 215
   arrests 120, 158
   Fagan Commission 261
   for Indians 137, 209
   influx controls 102–103, 123
   NRC 203–204
   World War Two xiii
Pather, PR 159–160, 219, 259
Paton, Alan
   on communism 175
   Cry, the Beloved Country 268
   on education 157
   elections 155, 263
   'Ghetto Act' 193
   Great Trek centenary 22
   on idealism 111
   on Matthews 253
   miners' strike of 1946 202
   Native Bills of 1936 93
   NRC 204, 242
'Pegging Act' 140–141, 142–143, 159–161, 178–179, 192
Permanent Force 59
petrol, shortage of 108, 120
Pienaar, Dan 82, 84, 94, 115
Pirow, Oswald 24, 27–28, 30, 35–36, 46, 54, 59, 66–71, 118
Pitje, Godfrey 251
Plaatje, Sol 252
Poland 23, 71, 238
Policy and Platform of the African National Congress, The 101
poll taxes 137, 209

Poole, WH Evered 173, 272
Population Registration Act 272
posters 75, *89*, *194*
Powell, Charles 272
PRC *see* Passive Resistance Council
press opinion 27, 230–231, 237
Pretoria Agreement 159–161
price controls 86, 175
Prinsloo, Hendrik F 110
prisoners of war (POWs), Italian 84, *85*, 110
Programme of Action 275, 277, 278–279
Progressive Youth Council 164
propaganda 75, 85–86, *89*
Purified National Party *see* Gesuiwerde Nasionale Party

race classification 178
race relations 19, 111, 122–123, 168–170, 194, 210–211, 239–242
racism 116, 142, 168–170, 260
Radebe, Gaur 87
radio stations 64, 142
RAF *see* Royal Air Force
Raman, Parvathi 248
Ramohanoe, Constantine 249–250
Rand Daily Mail 215, 230
Rand Revolt of 1922 15–16, 116
Reciprocity Act 143
Red Cross 110
'red peril' 119–120, 174–175
red tape *see* bureaucracy
Reichskolonialbund 43
Reitz, Deneys 28, 30, 33, 35, 46, 52, 101, 123, 173
repatriation of Indian population 141, 262
Representation of Natives Act 205–206
republicanism 12, 14, 19, 64–65, 154, 191, 250, 284
reserves 17, 19–21, 96, 169, 262
Reunited National Party *see* Herenigde Nasionale Party
Rhodes, Cecil John 5
Rich, Paul 134, 201, 275
Richter, Maurice 117

Richter, Paul 117
Riebeek West 4, 10
Robeson, Paul 228
Rodseth, Fred 202
Rommel, Erwin 84, 106, 113
Roos, Tielman 17, 67
Roosevelt, Franklin D 82, 94–95, 125, 173, 182–183
Rose-Innes, Sir James 92
Roth, M 102, 206
Round Table 54–55
Royal Air Force (RAF) 109, 173
Royal Navy 59, 109
royal tour of South Africa in 1947 233–238, 253
Rumpff, Justice 279
Russia *see* Soviet Union
Rustomjee, Sorabjee 192, 219

SAA *see* South African Airways
SAAF *see* South African Air Force
SABC *see* South African Broadcasting Corporation
sabotage 76–77, 80
SACP *see* South African Communist Party
SAIC *see* South African Indian Congress
Salazar, António 68
Saldanha Bay 88
Sampson, Anthony 130, 251, 257
sanctions against South Africa 143, 193, 247
SAP *see* South African Party; South African Police
Sapire, Hilary 233, 236
satyagraha see 'passive resistance'
Sauer, Paul 24, 26–27, 32, 46
Sauer Commission 178, 217, 262
Schiller, Friedrich ix
sea route *see* Cape sea route
Second World War *see* World War Two
Seekings, J 168, 188
segregation xii–xiii, 17, 103, 105, 120–121, 123, 144–145, 152–153
Seme, Pixley ka Isaka 98, 117, 128
Senate Bill x–xi, 23–24, 26–27, 40–41, 51

SEPC *see* Social and Economic Planning Council
Shawcross, Sir Hartley 223
Shear, Keith 74–75
Shepstone, DG 219
'Shirt' movements, far-right 77–78, 118–119
Sierra Leone 109
Simons, Jack 153
Simons, Ray 153
Singh, Jaydew 210
Sisulu, Albertina (née Toriwe) 162, 276
Sisulu, Walter Max Ulyate 129–130, *131*, 162, 164, 211, 244, 246, 248–249, 275–279
Smartt, Sir Thomas 14–15
Smit, Douglas 103, 122, 203
Smuts, Isie 14, 172–173
Smuts, Jan Christiaan *34*
  Afrikaner Broederbond 191–192
  background of 4–5, 10, 13–14, 284
  Churchill and 56, 156, 166
  death of 281
  economic policy 187–188
  elections 14–16, 120–121, 154–155, 260, 263–265
  Hertzog and 5–7, 13–14, 17–18, 70
  Hofmeyr and 91–93, 141
  immigrants from Britain and Europe 232
  Indians in South Africa 136–138, 140, 143, 159–160, 165, 178–179, 192–195, 214, 251, 259
  as leader of opposition 266–267
  NRC 102, 122, 242–243, 290
  as prime minister 12, 52–53, 59–60
  Rand Revolt 16
  royal tour in 1947 234, 237–238
  segregation xiii, 260–261
  social welfare 102–103, 105
  South West Africa 165–166, 179
  United Nations 160, 174, 178–179, 218–227, 231, 242, 258
  war vote ix–xi, 3, 22–38, 42–43, 46–47, 50, 52–53, 55–56, 66, 284–288, 292
World War One 9, 11
World War Two xii–xiii, 62, 74–77, 79–81,

INDEX

83–84, 88–90, 101, 104–105, 111, 113–114, 142, 155–156, 166–167, 171–176, 181, 196
Xuma and 229
Sobukwe, Robert Mangaliso 252, 254–255
Social and Economic Planning Council (SEPC) 103, 168–170
social welfare 93, 102–103, 105, 121, 168–170, 188, 287
Sofasonke (political party) 124
Solomon, Bertha 21, 42, 44
Sophiatown 99
Soske, J 277
'South Africa First' policy 7, 67
South African Air Force (SAAF) 59, 68, 84, 106, 109, 114, 173, 280
South African Airways (SAA) 60, 68
South African Broadcasting Corporation (SABC) 25, 52, 119
South African College 90, 148
South African Communist Party (SACP) 117, 273
  see also Communist Party of South Africa
South African Fascists 77
South African Indian Congress (SAIC) 138, 143, 153, 159–160, 192, 213, 218–220, 278
South African Institute of Race Relations 99
South African Navy 60, 109
South African Party (SAP) 6, 10, 14–16, 18
South African Police (SAP) 75, 200–201
South African War *see* Anglo-Boer War
South West Africa
  International Court of Justice 280–281
  United Nations xii, 179, 190, 206, 219, 226–229, 231, 259
  World War One 9–10
  World War Two 22, 25–26, 43, 47, 165–166, 286
'South West Africa: Annexation or United Nations Trusteeship' (pamphlet) 228
Soviet Union
  HNP on 172, 177, 250
  Molotov-Ribbentrop Pact 24, 71, 119
  United Nations 271

World War Two 63, 71, 82–83, 87, 94, 115, 118–119, 166, 268
Spanish Civil War 71, 146
Sparks, Allister 271
Special Reserve Battalion 59
'special type of colonialism' 117
spies 117
sport 163–164
Springbok Legion 119
squatting 123–124
  see also housing
Stadler, AW 123
Stalin, Joseph 117, 182
Stallard, CP 52, 161, 188–189
Star, The 45, 52, 180, 215
Status of Union Act 17, 19, 44, 149
Statute of Westminster x–xi, 17–19, 44
Stellenbosch University 84–85
Steyn, Colin 52–53, 119, 219
Steyn, MT 5
Stormjaers 74, 76–77, 79–81
St Peter's Secondary School 255–256
Strauss, JGN 175, 282
Strijdom, Hans 79
Strijdom, JG 26, 46, 65, 69, 167, 170, 189, 197, 250–251, 280
strikes 88, 107, 112
submarines 109–110
subsidies 86, 108
Sullivan, JR 170
Sunday Times (London) 67
Suppression of Communism Act 273, 279
Swart, CR 65
swart gevaar (black peril) 17, 265

Tabata, Isaac Bangani (IB) 254, 256–258, 265
Taillard, Jan 80–81
Taj Mahal Hotel 160
Tambo, Oliver Reginald 129–130, *131*, 162, 164, 211, 246, 248–250, 255–256, 278
taxation 169–170, 188
Teachers' League of South Africa (TLSA) 151, 152
Thakur, Vineet 223

325

Theal, George McCall 10
Thema, Selope 102, 165, 182, 242, 289
TIC *see* Transvaal Indian Congress
Tloome, Dan 118, 210–211
TLSA *see* Teachers' League of South Africa
Tobruk, fall of 112–114
Torch Commando 112, 281–282
Toriwe, Albertina *see* Sisulu, Albertina
trade unions 16, 20, 87–88, 95, 104, 107, 118, 198–204, 207, 242
Trading and Land Bill *see* 'Pegging Act'
Transvaal Indian Congress (TIC) 138, 139, 192, 212–214, 240, 258
Transvaler, Die 21, 235
Treasury 63
Treaty of Versailles 46, 286
'trusteeship' 91–92, 104–105, 134, 174, 187, 262, 264–265, 275, 289

U-boats 109–110
UDF *see* Union Defence Force; United Democratic Front
UN *see* United Nations
unemployment 15, 170, 188, 263, 287
uniforms of ACF volunteers 62
Union Defence Force (UDF)
  1st South African Infantry Brigade 82, 84, 115, 154
  6th South African Armoured Division 125, 166, 173, 183
  ANC and 96
  coloured people 62, 145–146
  CPSA and 119
  demobilisation 157, 175–176
  election of 1943 154
  HNP and 272
  Indians in South Africa 62, 139
  World War One 8–9
  World War Two 56, 59–60, 62–63, 72–74, 83–84, 85, 94, 106, 113–115, 173
Unionist Party 14–15
unions *see* trade unions
Unisa *see* University of South Africa
United Democratic Front (UDF) 282

United Nations (UN)
  founding conference 160, 174, 178–179
  'Ghetto Act' 192, 195
  HNP and 189, 250–251, 280–281, 288
  Indians in South Africa 190, 218–226, 258–259
  South West Africa xii, 179, 190, 206, 219, 226–229, 231, 259
  Soviet Union and 271
  UN General Assembly of 1946 218–231
United Nations Organisation (UNO) *see* United Nations
United Party (UP)
  Africans and 289
  communism 273
  criticism of 156–157, 188–189, 233
  deaths of Smuts and Hofmeyr 281
  elections 21, 136, 152, 154–155, 157, 188, 216, 263–265, 282, 290
  established 18
  Native Bills of 1936 19–20
  pass laws 158
  World War Two 41, 187
United States (US)
  economic depression in 17
  South Africa and xii, 60–61
  World War Two 81, 88, 94, 103, 106, 115, 125, 172–174, 177, 182–183
Unity Conference 153
University College of Fort Hare 97–98, 251–255
University of South Africa (Unisa) 128, 252, 256
UNO (United Nations Organisation) *see* United Nations
UP *see* United Party
urbanisation xii, 19, 20–21, 107–108, 112, 123, 216–217, 261, 288–289
US *see* United States

Vaderland, Die 180
Van Aarde, HJ 232
Van den Bergh, Hendrik 76
Van der Bijl, Hendrik J 60–61, 168, 169, 290

INDEX

Van der Bijl Engineering Works Corporation (Vecor) 61
Van der Byl, Piet 123
Van der Merwe, NJ 50, 65
Van der Ross, RE 146
Van der Waag, Ian 68, 176
Van Eck, Hendrik 168
Vanguard, HMS 234
Van Niekerk, PW le Roux 181
Van Rensburg, JFJ (Hans) 67, 73–74, 73, 78, 80–81
Van Rensburg, JH (Kosie) 266
Van Ryneveld, Sir Pierre 272
Van Wyk, At 28, 29, 38, 42, 46
Vecor *see* Van der Bijl Engineering Works Corporation
VE Day *see* Victory in Europe (VE) Day
Verwoerd, HF xiii, 65, 192
Vichy France 83, 114–115
Victoria College 4, 10, 60
Victory in Europe (VE) Day 179–181
Volunteer Reserve 59
Von Moltke, Johannes Strauss 77
Voortrekker Monument 22, 64
Vorster, BJ (John) 76
Vorster, Koot 76
'Votes for All' campaign 248–250

wages 88, 103, 112, 121, 170, 198–200, 287
Walshe, P 104
war materials 60, 61–63
War Measure 1425 200
War Measures Act 112, 139
Wavell, Lord 143, 192
Weichardt, Louis 77
welfare system *see* social welfare
Wessels, Manie 77
When Smuts Goes 288
white population, divisions in xi–xiii, 24, 52, 55, 63–64, 76–77, 84–86
see also English- and Afrikaans-speakers, divisions between
white supremacy (*baasskap*) 189
'white trusteeship' *see* 'trusteeship'
Wilson, GH 53
Wilson, Woodrow 12, 271
Wit Terroriste 77
Wollheim, Oscar 121–122
Women's League, ANC 100
World War One (WWI) x, 8–10, 11–12, 63
World War Two (WWII)
  start of 3, 23, 31, 52, 59–60
  war vote 38–47, 283, 291–292
  end of 179–181

Xuma, Alfred Bitini 100
  ANC xii, 95–96, 98–99, 104, 121, 126–127, 134, 247, 274–275, 289
  anti-pass campaign 158–159, 171
  background of 99–101
  Congress Youth League 130–132
  Doctors' Pact 240–242, *241*
  Durban riots 278
  Fagan Commission 262
  miners' strike of 1946 201–202
  Native Representative Council 102, 205–206, 243
  royal tour in 1947 236
  Smuts and 229
  at United Nations General Assembly xiii, 219, 227–229, 239–240

Young Communists 164
Youth League, ANC *see* Congress Youth League

Zeesen radio 64
Zonderwater detention camp 110

www.ingramcontent.com/pod-product-compliance
Lightning Source LLC
Chambersburg PA
CBHW070527090426
42735CB00013B/2886